S0-DTD-502

THE BEST OF
Inc.
GUIDE TO
MARKETING
AND
SELLING

THE BEST OF

GUIDE TO

MARKETING AND SELLING

BY

THE EDITORS OF
Inc. MAGAZINE

PRENTICE HALL PRESS

NEW YORK • LONDON • TORONTO • SYDNEY • TOKYO

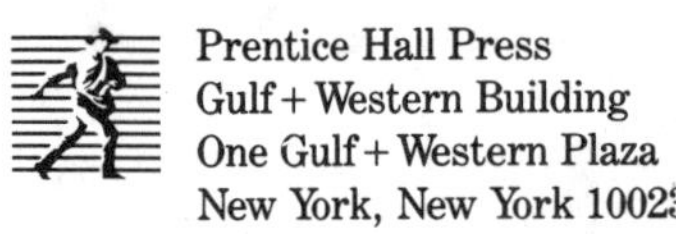
Prentice Hall Press
Gulf + Western Building
One Gulf + Western Plaza
New York, New York 10023

Copyright © 1988 by Inc. Publishing Corporation

All rights reserved
including the right of reproduction
in whole or in part in any form.

Published by the Prentice Hall Trade Division

PRENTICE HALL PRESS and colophon are registered
trademarks of Simon & Schuster, Inc.

Library of Congress Cataloging-in-Publication Data

Inc. guide to marketing and selling

(The Best of Inc.)
Includes index.
ISBN 0-13-454018-2
1. Marketing—United States. 2. Marketing—United States–
Management. 3. Sales management—United States.
HF5415.1.I53 1988 658.8—dc19 88-9854

Designed by Stanley S. Drate, Folio Graphics Company

Produced by Rapid Transcript, a division of March Tenth, Inc.

Manufactured in the United States of America

CONTENTS

PART
I

PART II

SALES MANAGEMENT *119*

PART III

PRODUCT MARKETING *175*

PART I

MARKETING STRATEGY

A product without a market is like an airplane without wings. It won't fly. So the ability to match products and services with the appropriate markets is crucial to business success, and that's where a good marketing strategy comes in. With it, you and your product or service can go out and attack the market. Without it, the market attacks you.

In this collection of *Inc.* articles, we see how companies gain customers and increase sales by using well-focused marketing strategies. Finding the proper market and getting a product or service to that market may seem procedural, and in some respects it is. Before entrepreneurs can go to market they've got to figure out who wants their product and how to reach those consumers. Some marketing skills can help out here—charts of targeted areas, an objective view of the marketplace, maybe a graph or two—but there's more to a successful marketing strategy than textbook skills. It also takes a healthy dose of intuition and the foresight and flexibility to change ideas and plans when they fail to reach their potential. Spunk has a lot to do with it, too.

In this section, we present stories that focus on some of the basic issues involved in formulating a good strategy for marketing your product or service. We hope this collection will leave you not only with ideas but also with questions: What is your market? What is its potential? And what effective strategies can you develop to reach new customers, retain the old ones, or—ideally—do both?

We'll look at how two brothers parlayed a no-frills commodity—a rubber-soled boot—into a fashionable, top-selling brand. We'll also show you how a group of manufacturers who make ice cubes—that's right, ice cubes—joined forces to give their product a new status. It's not designer ice, but it's close.

Can a company increase sales just by sprucing up its corporate image? Three companies did just that by creating bold new logos and packaging to project upscale images. The third article in this section explains how they did it. But what if your product is, well, kind of dull? How can you get consumers interested in giving it a whirl? "They Made a $25-Million Name for Themselves" looks at how a product originally called Thixo-tex, a combination of chemicals for rust-proofing automobiles, got a name change and a fictitious character to sell this now million-dollar product.

We also see how two companies learned to retain control by relying on their sales forces to demonstrate the uniqueness of their products in the marketplace.

Markets change, and in "The Baby Boom" and "Selling to the New America" we look at some of these changes and how businesses may have to reposition themselves to continue reaching the market.

Down in Virginia there's a man by the name of Colonel S. Stone Gregory, Jr., who sells just about everything that comes out of his land—from White Hickory Smoke Bits and Sassafras Root Bits to Virgin Spring Water and Hog Crap. He's got some tobacco, too. His family has been on the rich Virginia farmland for six generations, but the Colonel was the first to make a point of looking for new market needs and finding a way to fill them. His miscellaneous products bring in seven-figure sales annually and he's always on the lookout for new ideas. "Just a Poor, Dumb Dirt Farmer" looks at some of the Colonel's innovations and his own brand of marketing: do-it-yourself promotion; MBAs be damned.

Rob Mancuso is probably the type of hotshot the Colonel would not take a shine to. His father, grandfather, and great-grandfather all sold cars. So does the young Mancuso, but he does it with the benefit of a Princeton education, a three-piece suit, and a Macintosh computer. There are two things, though, that Mancuso has done that the Colonel would likely applaud—he's taken big risks and he has made nice money. What Mancuso has done is look at a traditional market with a fresh eye. Customer service was a long-forgotten ideal in the average car dealership. Mancuso brought it into vogue and, in the process, brought increased revenues and repeat customers to his dealership. "Putting the Customer in the Driver's Seat" looks at how this fourth-generation car salesman has turned his once ailing business into a success—and inspired a whole new generation of car dealers.

When one thinks of things English, one tends to dream up images of fog, tweed, and tea—lots of tea. Think again. These days Londoners—by the thousands—are gorging themselves on deep-dish pizza and barbecued spareribs served in authentic American cuisine with fifties and sixties rock 'n' roll blaring in the background. The food and the atmosphere are brought to them by American ad-man-turned-restaurateur Bob Payton, who owns two pizza joints and two ribs "shacks" in London. Don't some Londoners chafe at Payton's imported cuisine? You bet, but enough of their countrymen crave the Yankee delicacies to earn Payton's establishments a cool $9 million annually. In "Payton's Place," *Inc.* investigates how this man—a rather loud, déclassé sort of fellow—has managed, singlehandedly, to cultivate a fickle sociological trend. The English, he claims, have a love-hate relationship with things American. His strategy, then, is simplicity itself: Give the English American food with American service in an American environment and let them have an American fantasy—all for about $12.00.

In the world of business everything, it seems, must be done ASAP. And, FYI, there are no ifs, ands, or buts. At least that's the way it is when it comes to air freight delivery. Or is it? Two California entrepreneurs—both with experience in the air freight industry—found out that the near instantaneous delivery is, in many businesses, of secondary importance to accuracy and accountability. But how could they turn that observation into a profitable business? "Pressure-Point Marketing" looks at just that—the buttons an observant entrepreneur can push to squeeze a share of business out of a competitive market. With their industry observations in mind, the two entrepreneurs pushed here, pulled there, and built an effective alternative to fast, competitive—and expensive—air freight.

What if your product is in a field that is increasingly competitive? You look out on the horizon and all you see are mergers and acquisitions or the sad relics of the unfortunate outfits that bit the dust. Such was the case of a small beer concern called Hudepohl Brewing Company, in Cincinnati. When you've got to compete with the likes of Miller Lite, life can look grim. But the management at Hudepohl took a gamble—they took their whole marketing budget and spent it on one night of fireworks just to see if people would notice. "Special Effects" scrutinizes this high-risk, no guarantee investment and how it can do wonders to update tired or forgotten company images.

Mineral waters, like domestic beers, are all the same, right? You've got your spring water, your bubbles, and your tinted glass bottle. Certainly the folks who sell mineral water will claim *their* bubbles are more effervescent or their source is more pure, but to the untrained taste bud, it's all just so much fizz. So what is it that determines for the consumer which water to buy? In "Kicking Perrier in the Derrière," we find out that positioning, marketing the right image, makes all the difference.

The fine art of haggling—once the universal method of arriving at a price—has been relegated largely to flea markets and rummage sales in the United States. Not so at American TV and Appliances in Madison, Wisconsin. Shoppers at American TV are encouraged to negotiate their own prices on everything from color TVs to sofa-beds. "Name Your Price" investigates this free-for-all marketing strategy and how it works.

The final piece in this section looks at a real marketing coup. Two West Coast entrepreneurs have concocted a fruit juice and wine punch that brought in a comfortable $72 million in the first eight months of

1984. How did they do it? Easy—they positioned it as an alternative product in the already healthy beer market, and they learned their lessons from the leaders in that market—keep the stores well stocked and the stock well chilled.

As with all our anthologies, we have selected these stories to illustrate the infinite possibilities that exist for innovation in all aspects of business. One man's refuse, we've learned, is another man's fertilizer.

SOLE SUCCESS: From Army-Navy to Saks

It's easy enough, when you know a few tricks, to change a frog into a handsome prince. And it's not so amazing, when you know the right words, to turn an ugly duckling into a swan. But how do you transform an Abington Shoe Company into a Timberland? How do you pull a brand name out of a hat, or, in this case, out of a boot?

It happened once in Newmarket, New Hampshire, but even today, Herman and Sidney Swartz, the two brothers who own the Timberland Company, are slightly surprised that they brought it off. "Sure, we used a little brains," Herman says, "but you wouldn't believe the luck we've run into."

At one time, the Swartz brothers toiled thanklessly in private-label obscurity. Now their company is recognized nationwide for high-quality outdoor footwear. Once they advertised only in hunting and outdoor magazines. Now they tout their wares in *The New Yorker.* Once their products were displayed in the fluorescent hangers of the big discount chains. Now they're in the boutiques of Saks and Bloomingdale's. And once Herman and Sidney rode to work together in an aging, compact Plymouth. Now they make the trip in a gray Mercedes-Benz 300 SD.

Theirs is a real-life fairy tale that turns on a boot. That's right, a big, leather, waterproof, insulated boot with about a mile or so of thong to lace it up over the ankle. The brothers convinced folks that if they wore this knobby, rubber-soled boot they would be—and this is hard to say without a chuckle—fashionable.

"Once Saks used our boots in a window display right there on Fifth Avenue," forty-five-year-old Sidney says. "I guess we sent down an army of people to look at it and take pictures. I couldn't get over it."

A similar sense of wonder characterizes much of the Timberland story. Perhaps that's because, with what was an almost cosmic sense of timing, certain critical decisions coincided with certain critical events to transform the Abington Shoe Company into the Timberland Company. The story can easily make you realize that business success is often powered as much by a kind of magical coincidence as by rational planning.

In 1918, when he was twenty-one, Nathan Swartz, Herman's and Sidney's father, emigrated to the United States from Russia and got a job as an apprentice stitcher in some forgotten shoe company in Boston. As the years went by, he sampled a variety of responsibilities in the shoe business, including selling, managing, and manufacturing. "Throughout the thirties and forties," Herman says, "my father had a lot of ups and downs. The shoe industry was not as kind to him as it might have been."

But in 1951, Nathan found a niche for himself when he bought a half interest in the Abington Shoe Company, an existing business housed in a former piano warehouse in South Boston. In 1955, when his partner died, he bought the other half; that year, his two sons joined him. For the next fifteen years, father and sons struggled with the punishing economics and cutthroat competition of high-volume, private-label shoe manufacturing. They made a glossy oxford, a moccasin-toe work boot, and a functional, if not handsome, work shoe.

The principal attraction of Abington's products was price; they sold for roughly $4.95 a pair even in the middle 1960s, which made them very popular with discount stores.

"We were just a commodity," says fifty-four-year-old Herman. "We tried to make a nickel or dime on each pair. During those years we were just trying to keep our heads above water."

But low margins weren't the worst part of the experience. "There were no real roots set down," Sidney says. "You didn't know where your business was going. A buyer's loyalty lasted only as long as the last order he had written. It was always feast or famine."

The mid-1960s were particularly bitter: Too many competitors chased too little business. At the end of a typical day, as Sidney wandered through the shoe departments of nearby stores, he saw rack after rack filled with competitors' shoes. "They were literally giving them away, losing seventy-five cents or a dollar a pair, just to get into the chains. They were desperate for business. We didn't eat very well for a while."

For Abington, though, the hard times were a blessing in disguise. By 1968 many weaker shoe manufacturers had gone out of business as the persistent price war took its toll. That cleared the way for a business boom between 1969 and 1973. The tough competition also inspired the Swartz brothers to introduce a manufacturing innovation and convinced them that they had to break free of the boom-and-bust cycle.

For the first time, the story gets dusted with magical coincidence. Herman and Sidney were thinking economy, not brand-name marketing, when they decided in 1968 to buy equipment for injection molding. This process forms a thick rubber sole onto any leather upper without stitching, thus eliminating needle holes that leak. More important at the time, the process also eliminated the costly, hard-to-find hand-stitchers themselves.

"Injection molding," Herman says, "had the reputation of being used only on the cheapest shoes. But we decided that there was no reason we couldn't make a quality shoe by combining high-grade leather with injection molding. The labor savings were enormous."

But the brothers didn't have the $16,000 they needed to buy the molds. "Now here's one for you," Herman says, recalling the minor miracle. "Sidney and I had bought some stock in a small company at four dollars a share, and just when we needed the money for the equipment that stock went to sixteen dollars a share. Can you believe it?"

Labor was still a problem, even with the new machines. The old neighborhood just wasn't the same. Skilled help was scarce and often unreliable. When a few employees were mugged on the way to work, the brothers decided it was time to relocate. In 1969, they moved out of the old piano warehouse and into an old mill in Newmarket, New Hampshire, about an hour and a half north of Boston. Newmarket was a nice enough New England town. It was a little frayed around the edges, but it offered one major advantage: skilled labor, left over from the heyday of New England's shoemaking industry.

Once again coincidence worked to Abington's advantage. The company got the people and equipment it needed just as many of the big retail chains started major expansion programs. "Between 1969 and 1973," Herman says, "our sales almost doubled every year. The chains were opening new stores right and left. They had to have products, and there were a lot fewer suppliers, so we got all the business we could handle."

The drought was over, business was booming, but instead of whooping for joy, the brothers were gnawing their fingernails. "We knew," Sidney says, "that behind this fabulous feast was a door that could slam shut at any time. I mean we had lived through it more than once, and we were simply paranoid about it happening again."

They knew also that the only lasting way to escape the fickle swings of the private-label market was to develop their own brand name. Herman tells a story about how he and Sidney used to cool their heels with a gang of other salesmen all waiting to make a pitch to an important buyer. Then, Mort Meyerberg, the sales manager for Joseph M. Herman Shoe Company, would come into the crowded waiting room. "Mort never had to wait," Herman says. "That's the power of a brand name. You control your own destiny."

For years, all the brothers could do was wait. Then, in the early seventies, they glimpsed an opportunity moving in the background of their business. "Stores were telling us," Herman says, "that our leather construction boots were selling very well. When we visited the stores, we saw that a lot of young people, college students, were buying them. You don't have to be a genius to know that something's going on."

Although they didn't realize its full importance, Herman and Sidney had spotted the first flickers of what was to become a fashion bonfire called the "outdoor" or "survival" look. The corduroy pants, flannel shirts, down parkas, and rugged boots normally worn around backwoods campfires were soon to appear as any-day dress in the big city. And in a celebration of function, comfort, and durability, the survival look would even become fashion chic.

The commercial significance of this new fashion trend would be equally startling. Nearly every company that fanned the flame did extremely well. For example, L. L. Bean, of Freeport, Maine, perhaps the look's best-known booster, grew in sales from $9 million in 1970 to nearly $122 million in 1980. And the sales of a small shoe company in Newmarket, New Hampshire, would increase tenfold in only eight years.

Reports started trickling in to the brothers from their friends in the hinterlands that a competitor's boot was selling especially well. It was a leather, insulated, waterproof boot distributed by Dunham's, a century-old company based in Brattleboro, Vermont. "We started putting two and two together," Sidney says. "Dunham's had the market to itself, we had always made boots, and we had the injection-molding equipment already in place to make a waterproof boot. Dunham's became the focal point of our attack."

Magic was about to come to Newmarket. Herman and Sidney coaxed their father out of semiretirement to design their entry into the survival-market sweepstakes. They felt they had the right boot, but then they started to worry that they had the wrong name. "Neither of us is a marketer," Sidney says. "We're manufacturers. But at least we know what we don't know and we're willing to ask for advice."

So Herman asked his next-door neighbor, who owned a small advertising agency in Boston, what name would give the boot an "outdoorsy" image. After sifting through a dozen candidates, including Cherokee and Sioux, they settled on Timberland. The neighbor also came up with the circle with a multibranched tree in it that has served as Timberland's logo ever since.

Now that the brothers had their brand-name product, they couldn't decide when to cut it loose. Herman wanted to wait until the backlog of business already on the books was cleared up. Sidney wanted to start production immediately. "Sidney talked me into it," Herman says. "He always leads the charge."

Actually, the decision process was considerably more involved, because when either Sidney or Herman says they resolve differences by "talking" he has in mind something far removed from polite conversation. They have talked constantly for the past twenty-five years. This continuous dialogue picks up where it left off when the brothers meet in a parking lot in Danvers, Massachusetts, at 6:00 every morning. They both get in one car and proceed to jabber about business until, an hour later, they reach Newmarket.

Then they go to their office, where their desks are lined up side-by-side and jabber about business some more, moving the day along by overhearing each other's telephone calls in an absent-minded way and then amplifying the results with additional facts or considerations.

At first, this management style is slightly disconcerting, because the brothers know each other so well that either one can, and will, complete the other's unfinished sentence. But they are by no means interchangeable personalities. Herman is mellow, where Sidney is jumpy. Herman will sit and talk after dinner, while Sidney will be off trying to get everybody into the pool. "We trust each other implicitly," Sidney says. "That's what makes it work. I led the charge then, but I was just a little more paranoid."

Sidney leans forward in his chair at this point and confesses, almost conspiratorially, that although he didn't know it in 1973, their high-volume shoe business had hit its peak. In the years that followed, he says, a flood of imports that were coming from the Far East would decimate the market. "We talk about coincidence," he says, "but if we hadn't introduced a new product exactly at that time, things could've been very difficult for us."

In 1973, the brothers set up a subsidiary and produced 2,500 pairs of Timberland boots, compared to 490,000 pairs in the Abington line. "We intentionally started small," Herman says, "but we thought we should have done better. We began to realize that we had a product we didn't know what to do with."

Most of the brothers' initial problems with Timberland stemmed from their unfamiliarity with marketing. They were trying to reach a totally new market with the same methods of distribution and advertising they had used in the high-volume business. Most early sales were made in army-navy stores, and these sales were encouraged by occasional ads in hunting and outdoor magazines. Even the discount mentality was at work; they priced their boots at $25 a pair, slightly below Dunham's boots. "We thought we had to," Herman says. "After all, we were the new kid on the block."

Herman went back to his neighbor. But this time the neighbor said he had dropped out of the business because he wasn't feeling well. He said the man Herman needed now was Len Kanzer, president of the Marvin and Leonard Advertising Company in Boston.

Kanzer recalls that when Herman and Sidney first walked through his door, their basic pitch to the retailer was simply that they made a better product that was priced below the industry leader. "This was true," Kanzer says, "but it certainly wasn't enough. You could never have picked them out of a crowd. We had to tell them they were doing everything wrong in marketing."

According to Kanzer, Herman and Sidney were shocked when they heard his recommendations. And no wonder. Kanzer said the Timberland boot—heavy leather, mile of thong, thick rubber sole, and all—should be marketed as a fashion item. It had the outdoor look, he said, and the look was in. So take the boot to the "upscale" buyer, that growing crowd of well-heeled and well-educated urban backpackers that wanted the "look" and didn't care what it cost. Put it in Saks, he said, right up there with those sleek, imported slip-ons from England and Italy. Advertise it in, of all places, *The New Yorker.* And finally, he told them to increase their price by $5 a pair so they could put the difference in advertising. "Herman and Sidney reminded me," Kanzer says, "that it was their company I was fooling around with, and what was I trying to do anyhow—ruin them?"

In effect, Kanzer had asked the brothers to abandon twenty years' worth of business practices. "I can tell you," Sidney says, "that decision used up a lot of rides to Newmarket. We agonized over it. Even raising the price was hard to accept. I mean, we were used to raising prices by nickels, not by five dollars."

Neither Herman nor Sidney knows exactly why they agreed to try Kanzer's marketing strategy. It certainly had something to do with intuition, which, in turn, is arguably close to magic. Herman liked the approach, and Sidney thought it was taking the company in the right direction, which, for him, is forward, with vigor. "Let's face it," Herman says, "to a great extent we committed our profits from the volume shoe business to a flier. It was all up-front money. We couldn't be assured of anything."

On a spring day in 1975, Herman and Sidney were in their office trying to reassure their national sales manager that what they were about to do was best for the company. Sidney ended the futile conversation by telephoning Kanzer in Boston and telling him to go ahead with the plan. "We literally had to pick our sales manager off the floor," Sidney says. "He kept telling us that we had just ruined the company."

A few months later, the first Timberland ads began appearing in *The New Yorker.* They were masterpieces of creative advertising and eventually won more than fifty industry awards. They featured a colorful cast of straight-talking backwoods characters who clearly knew a good boot when they saw one. There was a family of moonshiners that included a mother whose face, even in wire-rimmed granny glasses, looked like a pick-ax, and her three boys sporting shotguns, suspenders, and outrageous high-water pants. They all thought Timberland boots were just fine.

And there was an old man testifying for Timberland from the seat of a log hauler. Not only was he satisfied with his own boots, but he also said he asked the Timberland salesman for "a pair of 13-wides for cousin Luther, double-wide on the left foot where the tractor run it over." Every ad closed with the refrain: "A whole line of fine leather boots that cost plenty, and should."

The ads had just the right touch of down-home sincerity to attract the "upscale" buyers—when they could find the boots. Unfortunately, the company hadn't yet signed up any of the big-name upscale stores where the upscale buyers are supposed to go. "Obviously," Kanzer says, "we wanted to include department store names in the ads, but we didn't have any."

Most of the company's salesmen didn't know how to sell to upscale department stores. "They were used to the army-navy store relationship," Herman says. "They didn't have the self-confidence to sell the department stores, except for a few of the younger salesmen who simply were too inexperienced to get scared. But it took Stanley to put the program over the top."

Stanley Kravetz, Timberland's forty-eight-year-old executive vice-president, originally introduced himself to Herman and Sidney with the idea that they might use him as a consultant. He had twenty years of experience in the footwear and sporting-goods industries, including positions in sales and management. He was, according to one industry observer, a "fearless salesman who would knock on anybody's door." "At the time," Kravetz says, "working for a small, family-owned business was the furthest thing from my mind. I thought I was going to find a sleepy New England shoe manufacturer, and then I saw what they were trying to do."

Kravetz was hired early in the summer of 1976. By July, he was tramping up and down Fifth Avenue in New York with a green plaid suitcase stuffed with samples. One day he marched into the shoe department at Bergdorf Goodman and found the manager in his office sipping tea. The manager looked on incredulously as Kravetz unpacked his bag. "Here I am buying women's shoes," the manager exclaimed, "and you want me to buy boots?" Kravetz sold him eight pairs of women's boots and, with that sale, he uncorked a gusher. In the next two years, Kravetz and his remodeled sales team signed up 2,000 new accounts, including a crowd of fancy department stores and an assortment of smaller, upscale retailers.

By 1979, company sales had reached $16 million. Out of a total production that year of 600,000 pairs of footwear, 500,000 bore the Timberland trademark, a complete reversal of the business mix only two years earlier. "With numbers like that," Herman says with a smile, "you don't have to be told that you've got a brand name that sticks."

Even the competition was properly amazed. Says Rick Sherwin, vice-president at Dunham's, "I was very impressed with their marketing approach. It's the kind of thing where you ask yourself, 'Now, why didn't we think of something like that? Why didn't we do more?' They simply did a fantastic job, helped the whole outdoor look, and created a tremendous market."

In 1979, as recognition that the subsidiary was now running the parent, the Abington Shoe Company formally changed its name to the Timberland Company. For all their success and notoriety, Herman and Sidney Swartz seem remarkably unaffected. Maybe it's the memory of all those lean years that keeps them humble, or maybe it's simply hard to believe that you've lived a real-life fairy tale where every dream comes true.

Battle of the Brands

Creating brand-name awareness is still more an art than an exact science. And even though some of the techniques are very well known—market positioning, pricing, advertising—there's a lot of room left for experimentation. Have you ever thought, for example, of getting yourself sued by an even bigger brand name?

In the spring of 1981, Timberland was faced with a lawsuit by the Stride Rite Corporation, of Cambridge, Massachusetts. Timberland had just launched an advertising campaign for a shoe it said would "blow" a Stride Rite subsidiary "right out of the water." The name of the subsidiary, Sperry Top-Sider, was in itself a brand name so famous that it had become synonymous with a nifty little item also called the "boat shoe." In 1980, Sperry Top-Sider's sales reached $24 million, more than all of Timberland's product lines combined. It was obviously an attractive market for a company looking to offset the seasonal sales pattern of rugged, outdoor boots.

Point by point, the Timberland ads compared specific advantages of their boat shoe with specific deficiencies of the Sperry Top-Sider. Some industry observers were shocked by what they considered to be a pushy, comparative advertising campaign unsuited to the generally low-key and fraternal relationships of the shoe industry. "I agree that comparative advertising is a risky business," says Stanley Kravetz, Timberland's executive vice-president, who engineered the introduction of the new shoe, "but when you have a superior product it can be very effective."

Naturally, Sperry Top-Sider uses other adjectives to describe the Timberland campaign. Says David J. Murphy, president of Sperry Top-Sider Inc., "We are the largest manufacturer of boating shoes in the world. We've been making shoes for forty-five years. To say that our leather cracks and eyelets rust is ludicrous. The whole thing's ludicrous."

After four months of legal wrangling, the two companies reached an out-of-court settlement. Timberland agreed, among other things, to revise its ad copy, and Sperry Top-Sider agreed to drop the suit.

Some people in the industry suggest the legal battle may have given Timberland the kind of notoriety it could do without, but Kravetz strongly disagrees. "They made an error in suing us," he says. "It put us on the map and brought us a lot more recognition than we probably deserved." The Timberland boat shoes produced revenues of nearly $8 million in 1980.

Even though there are conflicting opinions over who actually won the battle, the war rages on. A month after the original suit was settled, Timberland turned around and sued Stride Rite. The suit claims that the Top-Sider boat-shoe sole had been falsely marked and advertised as patented, when, in fact, the patents had expired. The suit says that this practice delayed Timberland's entry into the market and forced Timberland to "develop, at great cost, an alternative to the Sperry sole."

—LUCIEN RHODES

A NEW IMAGE FOR AN OLD PRODUCT

Richard Hendler, owner of Saxony Ice Company in Mamaroneck, New York, had always been impressed when such humdrum products as water, bananas, and chicken suddenly became big sellers after they were promoted under brand names like Perrier, Chiquita, and Perdue.

Why, he wondered, couldn't the same marketing strategy work for his own product? All he had to do was come up with a brand name that the public would automatically associate with clear, refreshing bags of ice.

Saxony Ice needed just such a boost. The company was founded in 1963 and, by 1975, sales were only $485,000. Hendler's customer base hadn't expanded much beyond the small set of stores that had been with him since the beginning.

Hendler realized early that a company the size of his couldn't afford to launch a widespread and effective marketing campaign singlehandedly. But there was nothing to stop him from joining forces with one or more ice companies to form a trade association, which would promote the member companies' product under a single brand name.

In 1975, Hendler and Harold Reynolds of A. T. Reynolds & Sons, in Kiamesha Lake, New York, formed a two-man trade association under the name "Leisure Time Ice."

The name Leisure Time was chosen to convey the convenience of packaged ice over homemade ice. The logo—a snow-capped mountain backed by blue sky and surrounded by green forests—suggested a clean and refreshing product different from traditional ice packaging, which featured scenes from the North Pole—igloos, Eskimos, and polar bears. Hendler and Reynolds had the logo printed on their bags, ten trucks, and company stationery. Total cost was approximately $5,000.

At first, other ice manufacturers were skeptical of Hendler's idea to give ice new status. "When it's hot, people buy ice," said the owners. "In the meantime, let's continue to advertise in the *Yellow Pages*."

But several months after the trade association was formed, another manufacturer, Richard Feingold of Bacu Ice Company, in Poughkeepsie, New York, began to think better of the idea and said he and some of his friends wanted to join the association.

During the next three years, Hendler, now president of Leisure Time Ice, made presentations at regional and national trade association meetings, gathering new members from Maine to Colorado. "The more people we have, the more exposure we get, and the bigger we appear," Hendler explained to each group.

Under the association's licensing agreement, a member company used the name and logo of Leisure Time Ice and contributed advertising dollars. In all other respects, however, a member company continued to operate as a separate entity, with its own buyers, suppliers, and pricing strategy. To join the association, each company paid a membership fee based on the number of bags of ice it sold annually.

By 1978, the Leisure Time Ice association boasted fifteen members and sixty trucks. Annually, it was selling about 13 million bags of ice with the new name and logo, along with the packager's name printed discreetly at the bottom of each bag. The next step was to hire a public relations firm to tell consumers about the advantages of packaged ice. The firm chosen—Creamer, Dickson, Basford Inc., of New York City—sent out fact sheets and news releases touting the association's message: Packaged ice is taste- and odor-free and is clearer and longer lasting than homemade ice.

The hearts of business writers and food editors from Boston to Los Angeles melted. Serious, lengthy articles were written on ice etiquette, including how many cubes to use with different drinks and how much ice to plan on per person. Hendler himself was interviewed by at least twenty-five editors and appeared on fifteen radio and TV talk shows, holding a glass of clear, pure Leisure Time Ice cubes in one hand and a glass of cloudy, homemade cubes in the other. *The Wall Street Journal, New York Times, Los Angeles Times,* UPI, and Associated Press have all featured items on Leisure Time Ice.

Meanwhile, association members' sales increased by at least 10 percent a year. Hendler's own company went from $458,000 in sales in 1975 to $1,700,000 in 1981. His new business increased by 40 percent, and his business with existing customers expanded by 60 percent. "We were the only ice manufacturers doing any advertising, and this gave us a considerable stature with buyers," Hendler says.

The association spent $50,000 for public relations in 1978, $75,000 in 1979, and $95,000 in 1980. In 1981, ads were placed in regional editions of such magazines as *Newsweek, Sports Illustrated,* and *Time.* One ad—a joint effort by seven members of the association—cost $24,000 to place. "It's very impressive to walk into the office of a buyer and say, 'Did you see our ad in *Newsweek?*'" remarks Hendler.

This summer the twenty-seven-member association will spend $100,000 to produce and air thirty-second TV spots in areas where it has membership—the Northeast, much of the Midwest, and some of the West and Southwest. The commercial's voice-over explains why Leisure Time Ice cubes are nicer than homemade cubes. Visuals show two beverage glasses—one with cloudy cubes and one with clear cubes.

Like Perrier water, Chiquita bananas, and Perdue chickens, Leisure Time Ice may or may not have something special to offer that sets it apart from competitors. But by banding together and using their imagination, a handful of small ice manufacturers with average sales of no more than $500,000 a year have given their product something that the individual ice companies never had—national exposure and a touch of class.

—Carol Rose Carey

IF THE CORPORATE IMAGE CALLS FOR A FACELIFT

When Dick Williams took over as vice-president at the Gardenia Cheese Company in South Gate, California, he had a number of urgent projects to undertake. Near the top of his list was the task of improving the company's image in the marketplace. The image was, at best, confused.

Gardenia, founded in 1946, makes mozzarella, ricotta, and string cheese that it distributes mainly to delicatessens and restaurants. As the company prospered and grew into larger production and distribution facilities, package designs and the company logotype, or symbol, periodically changed. At one point, when the company moved from the southern California community of Gardena, even the company name underwent a slight variation, from Gardena to Gardenia. To back up the new name, the two owners adopted the gardenia flower as a corporate symbol. "From that point on," says Glenn Lohstreter, president, "the original design grew like Topsy," as the owners experimented on the design with different typefaces and shades of color.

By the time Williams joined the company in 1980, there were, he estimates, at least fifteen different designs still in use for name cards, sales materials, and even product packages. All this made the company image confusing while competition was growing keener.

Too many companies pay scant attention to how their corporate symbol is perceived in the marketplace, and they worry even less about such things as graphic design, that is, the layout and color scheme of letterheads, brochures, and product packaging. Instead, they lump corporate design in the same category as interior decorating—an unnecessary expense until profits are so substantial that there is money to spend on making a good appearance. Few executives seriously connect graphic design with effective marketing.

Gardenia's problem was most acute because the company was then expanding its consumer market by stocking its products in the refrigerated cheese sections of supermarkets. Williams suspected, and confirmed with the help of Tauber & Tauber, a Palos Verdes, California, market research firm, that Gardenia's products were not clearly recognized by shoppers.

Williams went after professional help to deal with the problem and got bids from three design firms before choosing Harte Yamashita & Forest, a Los Angeles firm with expertise in packaged goods. He requested a completely new look for all company graphics, including logo, packaging, shipping labels, order forms, name cards, and even the decals for delivery trucks.

Gardenia, like its competitors, had always used the colors red and green. Most of the companies were started by Italian cheesemakers who had proudly adopted the colors of their native country—and whose graphics all ended up looking alike. The professional designers changed the name on the package from Gardenia Cheese Company Inc. to simply Gardenia—in large, easy-to-read type—and chose the color orange to give a feeling of freshness.

Williams, who recently left Gardenia to run his own company, warns that a company can have a slight and temporary drop in sales while customers become acquainted with the "new" product. Still, Gardenia is confident that the new design for the packages and all the supporting graphics will pay off.

In 1978, Gardenia became a subsidiary of Unigate PLC, of London, but, says Lohstreter, the change in ownership had no impact on the company's marketing or corporate identity program. Lohstreter estimates that 1982 sales will total about $25 million.

The national mania for physical fitness and recreation has been a boon for some sporting goods manufacturers. It has also made competition tougher than ever.

As a manufacturer of sporting goods, General Sportcraft Company, of Bergenfield, New Jersey, with annual sales of about $20 million, decided to review the way its products looked and were presented to customers. "The corporate design dated back about fifteen years," says Kenneth J. Edelson, president of the privately held company. "What looked great back then needed a facelift. We were looking for something clear and crisp that would stand apart from competitors on retail shelves."

General Sportcraft called in Selame Design, of Newton Lower Falls, Massachusetts, after Edelson had seen work the firm had done for a manufacturer of jams and jellies in Roseland, New Jersey. A roster of previous clients also impressed Edelson: Stop & Shop, Eastman Kodak, Siemens, and Amoco Oil.

Selame first evaluated the way Sportcraft looked to the public and to its retailers. Research confirmed that the line lacked identity and unity. For example, the company's name is written as one word—Sportcraft—but on packaging, Sport was positioned above Craft. Packaging colors also varied widely because no one had ever established precisely which shades and hues to use. Carton designs were cluttered and dated.

Selame designed a clean white package with red and blue stripes, "colors that connote sports and patriotism," says Edelson. The name of the product is in large, black, bold type, for quick and strong identification on store shelves. In some instances, an open window in the carton permits a piece of the item, such as a dart board, badminton racquet, bocce ball, or horseshoes, to protrude. The customer can touch the product without opening a sealed package.

Edelson reports that the striking packaging has helped Sportcraft land several major new accounts. "With more and more sports equipment being sold in chain stores and by mass merchandisers, there is much less personal selling and greater impulse buying," he says. "The package has become much more important in our business. It's the outer box that says 'buy me.' "

Rana Systems, launched in October 1981, in Carson, California, had more than its share of start-up problems. Just the same, the design of its corporate logotype, its trademark, and the package in which its first item—a floppy disk drive for Apple's home and small business computers—would be sold became issues of primary importance.

"From day one we wanted to be seen in the marketplace as a professional company with the look of an IBM or Radio Shack," says Fran Mulvania, advertising director. "The marketplace has changed. Not too long ago, the customer was an engineer or a computer hobbyist. He didn't care if the product came in a brown paper bag. He could decide for himself how good the item was. Now we're marketing to businesspeople, teachers, and others with less technical expertise. We need to attract them by having a package that reassures them that what they're buying is a quality product."

In selecting a corporate design firm, Mulvania took a close look at the graphics of other companies. She was especially impressed with a Los Angeles firm, Huerta Design Associates, whose clients include General Mills, Carnation, Rain Bird Sprinkler Manufacturing, Tyco Industries, Knott's Berry Farm, Bushnell Optical, Continental Air Lines, and AMF Voit. Mulvania asked several Huerta Design customers how well Huerta had followed through on projects, met deadlines, and stayed within budgets.

Satisfied with the responses, Mulvania and Michael Mock, Rana's executive vice-president, met twice with representatives from Huerta before signing a contract. "You should be sure that when you express an idea or feeling about what you want, the designers understand you," says Mulvania, who was particularly impressed by how thoroughly Huerta's people understood Rana's marketplace and competition. "Also be sure to have your budget set before you meet with the firm, and ask for estimates on any project they might undertake."

Mock and Mulvania established the criteria: "We wanted whatever design we adopted to work from the start and to last," says Mock. "We didn't want to change as new products were introduced.' "

Huerta prepared twenty different logo designs and three variations of color schemes before Rana's final approval. The chosen color scheme and design elements were incorporated into all company materials—price lists, brochures, trade and consumer advertisements, letterheads, cards, press releases, and, of course, the shipping containers and the products themselves.

In spring issues of consumer computer magazines, Rana's ads pulled 10,000 replies and outdrew competitors three to one, claims Mulvania. She credits the results largely to the impact of the company's design and layouts. So far Rana has spent about $40,000 for its graphics program, including the design of a portable trade show display booth. Rana expects to ring up sales of $3 million in 1982 and then hit $10 million in 1983.

While a change in identity can dramatically improve a company's appearance in the marketplace, it is no panacea, especially if not carefully researched and executed. Several corporate designers offer these suggestions if you decide to embark on a corporate identity program.

- Before selecting a design firm, get bids from several. Meet personally with the designers to review your objectives. Check with several references to find out how successful their programs have been and whether the relationship with the design firm was satisfactory.
- Don't decide overnight that you want a whole new look. You may be able to keep certain traditional elements of your image—recognized by loyal customers—while making subtle changes that give the company's image a fresher, more contemporary appearance.
- Know your objectives when you sit down with designers. For example, you may want to differentiate products while maintaining a strong family resemblance within a line. Provide as much information as possible about your marketplace and future strategies.
- Set your budget before talking to designers. Get estimates from them for all future projects. Make sure you and the designer are working toward the same deadlines. Good design cannot be done in a week.
- Choose a firm that is willing to spend time talking with you and analyzing your marketplace. Good design firms will study the packaging and design of competitors and will require more than superficial information about your company's history and plans regarding, say, new product introduction.
- Make sure key executives understand and support the corporate facelifting. Top management, not a secretary, should work closely with the designer.
- Check with professional design associations for the names of reputable firms. (Well-respected organizations include the American Institute of Graphic Arts, 1059 Third Ave., New York, NY 10021; Industrial Designers Society of America, 6802 Poplar Place, Suite 303, McLean, VA 22101; and Package Designers Council, P.O. Box 3753, Grand Central Station, New York, NY 10017.)

—NORM SKLAREWITZ

THEY MADE A $25-MILLION NAME FOR THEMSELVES

Rusty Jones, as television commercial watchers are learning, is a rangy, mustachioed redhead with a cowlick, suspenders, and an aw-shucks manner. Rusty Jones sells a product with the same name for a Chicago company called Matex Corporation. Rusty, the television salesman, isn't exactly real. He's an animated cartoon character. Rusty Jones, the product, is a chemical for rust-proofing automobiles.

Until 1976 the product was called Thixo-tex. It had been on the market for four years, and its retail sales had grown steadily to almost $3 million. When Thixo-text became Rusty Jones and Rusty, the redhead, started selling it on TV, sales shot up to $25 million in just over a year. And they haven't stopped climbing.

Today, because of that record, salesman Rusty wields a heavy hand in corporate policy. "We're careful to be consistent with his image," says Matex president Mike Mater. "It's common in our executive meetings to ask, 'What would Rusty do?' "

So far Rusty has done plenty. His creation was a major advance for Mater, whose goal is to build a major corporation and make it the industry leader.

Mater's strategy for building a corporation is to find flaws and eliminate them. "First you have to have a product with a real customer benefit," he says. "We had that in Thixo-tex, a clear, odorless liquid that was easily applied and was guaranteed to prevent rust. Then you have to search for all the reasons for customers not to buy the product. Those reasons are flaws in the system. Eliminate the flaws and you've got an easy sell for everyone along the distribution chain."

After four years, Mater thought he had all the flaws of his operation eliminated. Then he noticed a troubling phenomenon. When advertising of Thixo-tex was heavy, sales went up. But whenever advertising emphasis was off, sales were off, too.

After weeks of investigating, Mater decided the problem was the name. Thixo-tex had seemed right when the product was introduced. It was derived from one of the product's chemical properties, and it had a nice, scientific ring to it. But consumers obviously couldn't remember the name. In fact, Mater recalled, even his own employees and distributors often had difficulty remembering and pronouncing Thixo-tex. They sometimes called it Thermo-fax, or Thick-o-teck, or even Hick-o-thex.

The problem was critical. Mater was determined to make his company the industry leader. Being number one has enormous side benefits to a company, he feels. "When you have the greatest market share, you have greater flexibility in using your resources," says the thirty-eight-year-old president. "You can deploy those resources more cost-effectively and profitably, while those behind you have to play catch-up and put their resources into buying market share." To him, the name Thixo-tex was clearly an obstacle to gaining market share and reaching the number one position.

Mater and his advertising agency, Dawson, Johns, and Black, began looking for alternatives. They came up with more than 180 names sorted into four categories. First were those describing a function, process, or benefit, such as Rescue, Final Coat, and Rust Patrol. Next were names suggesting the product's reliability, like Nevermore, Secure, and Pledge. The third category was a variation of the existing name, Body by Thixo-tex, without the word *Thixo-tex:* Body by . . . Matex, Dover, Allen, Hogan, or any proper name. The last grouping was of "name names," as Mater called them—T. T. Newbody or Rusty Jones.

The search group set three criteria for the new name: (1) It had to attract attention and interest; (2) people had to be able to remember it; and (3) it had to sell the product. "Head and Shoulders shampoo does that," says Marion Dawson, the ad agency's creative director. "And DieHard batteries is a terrific name. It's the first time anyone ever named a battery."

Dawson first came up with Rusty Jones partly in jest, frustrated by the difficulty of finding an unclaimed name. "We would hit on something like Rust-Guard," he says, "and then we'd find it already registered for trademark."

But Rusty Jones fit the criteria perfectly. "We kept coming back to it," says Mater. "Finally we decided that it was right. The image was right, too. We saw Rusty as the kid down the block who knows everything about cars. If you have a question, he can answer it better than anyone else, and you have confidence in what he says and does. He's sort of a grown-up Boy Scout mechanic—the perfect salesman for this product and the perfect spokesman for the company."

Mater did have reservations about using the word *rusty.* He was afraid customers might be confused or put off by it. And because the name change would be a bold and costly marketing move, Mater ordered a market test to measure Rusty Jones's effectiveness. He wanted to be sure before revamping all the advertising, promotion, and signs.

Some of Mater's people didn't like the name-change idea at all. One sales manager called him and warned, "Mark this date on your calendar as the day of your biggest mistake. Rusty Jones doesn't represent our image. It's not what we're working for, and the disruption will hurt us badly."

Upstate New York is one of the company's major markets, and Buffalo was picked as the test location for Rusty Jones. Albany/Schenectady was chosen as the control test area for Thixo-text. The two markets had almost identical demographics—population, income levels, and kinds of employment.

The same quantity and quality of radio and newspaper advertising was purchased for Rusty Jones in Buffalo and for Thixo-tex in Albany/Schenectady. Radio would get the sales pitch across, and newspapers would list the dealers. The test was set for ninety days, to be extended to six months if early results were inconclusive. Dealers in both markets were asked to send in sales reports each Friday. A computer was programmed to analyze the results. The total cost of the test would be about $40,000.

In the first thirty days, Rusty's sales in Buffalo jumped 300 percent. In Albany/Schenectady, Thixo-tex sales rose by about 25 percent. That was enough for Mater and the search committee. Rusty Jones was it. Although the test continued for ninety days, a market-by-market roll-out began immediately.

Thixo-tex was sold through 500 new car dealers in sixteen markets in the nation's rustbelt—the coastal states and Midwestern snow areas where humid air and salt-laden roads take their heaviest toll on cars. Mater estimated the total changeover would cost $150,000—for new advertising, signs, and promotional material, and a road trip so Mater could introduce Rusty Jones to the dealers.

That was a staggering expense for a company Matex's size. So Mater ordered the roll-out to go one market at a time, starting in New England. Increased sales in one market would help finance the changeover in the next.

Mater's toughest sell was to his dealers. He had anticipated problems. In fact, he had scheduled the costly road trip "to salvage as many of the dealers as we could," he says. "Without them, we didn't have a business. I expected trouble."

But not as much as he got. At each of the dealer sessions, more than half of those present balked at the name change. Thixo-tex, they argued, reflected the quality and the highly technical nature of the product. Rusty Jones was honky-tonk, mass-market gimmickry. They were independent, community-involved businessmen, and their images would suffer with Rusty Jones.

Mater held firm. The customers just couldn't remember the name Thixo-tex, he told them. Rusty would stand for quality, but it also would increase sales. He bet several of the more recalcitrant dealers that Rusty Jones would improve the product's image, sales, and memorability. If it didn't, after six months Mater would buy back the dealerships. In the end, he didn't lose a bet.

The next step was a TV commercial. There was no money in the budget for production costs, but Mater went ahead with plans, believing that TV was essential for maximum impact. He decided early on that Rusty would be an animated cartoon, not an actor, even though animation was more expensive initially. "We would be spending millions of dollars on TV advertising eventually," Mater says. "And an animated character would never age, get a divorce, die, or hold us up in contract negotiations after he became a celebrity."

Mater commissioned several artists to come up with versions of Rusty. He picked the red-haired mechanic-down-the-street character that is the company's trademark. By late 1977, the substantial increase in sales enabled Mater to produce his $60,000 TV commercial. It followed the roll-out south and west out of New England.

In early 1977, retail sales of Rusty Jones were $3 million a year. By early 1978, as use of the new name and the TV commercial increased, sales jumped to $25 million, according to Mater. And by early this year, they had doubled to $50 million, he says. Mater owns the company he started in 1965 and will disclose only retail sales volume, not company revenues or income.

Mater has spent more than $4 million on advertising in the three years since Rusty was born, and currently is spending about $2 million annually. Both are huge outlays for a company the size of Matex, but Mater is after market share. He claims Rusty is the leader in most of his markets, if not all, and he will keep spending until the title is clinched. "We could be a lot more profitable without that level of expenditure," says Mater. "Once we dominate a market, we can bring our advertising expenditures more in line with sales."

But Rusty has become more than an advertising vehicle for Mater. The name and personification have given a benefit he didn't anticipate. "Rusty *is* the company. We're careful to keep all of our policies and procedures compatible and consistent with his image," says Mater. "We use him as a standard. He's not subject to the vicissitudes of life as we are. He doesn't have bad days or lapses that can affect decisions."

To guard against even the slightest change in Rusty's manner or countenance, Mater, Dawson, and two company executives regularly go over advertising copy and art. "The future of this company rests with maintaining the consumer and dealer perception of what Rusty Jones represents," Mater says. "We can't take the chance of a mistake."

ROLLING IN DOUGH:
From Commodity to Specialty

In 1966, Ron and Joe "Pep" Simek wrested a $5,600 loan from a local banker and bought a Chevy freezer truck that was big enough to carry 1,800 frozen pizzas to taverns, gas stations, resorts, bowling alleys, and other retail outlets. In the next four years, the Simek brothers transformed a tavern that sold dime brews into a producer of frozen pizza that folks around Medford, Wisconsin, said tasted pretty good.

Today, more than 140 commission route salesmen in the drivers' seats of Tombstone Pizza's fleet of trucks deliver, store-to-store, hundreds of thousands of frozen pizzas and a companion line of beefsticks. Many competitors regard such a delivery system as a relic of the horse-and-buggy days, but the Simeks stick to their way of doing business, saying that the control it gives them over their product's quality is worth it. Last year the family-owned company increased its sales 27 percent, from $49 million to $62 million, in line with a five-year compound annual growth rate of 27 percent to 37 percent. The numbers speak for themselves in a volatile industry that has been hurt by price wars and an influx of low-cost brands that promise but don't always deliver quality.

In the race to slice up the frozen-pizza market in the Upper Midwest, Tombstone Pizza Corporation, 250 miles northwest of Milwaukee, continues to win market share over such major corporate contenders as Pillsbury Company and General Mills, Inc. Like the tortoise in its race against the hare, Tombstone's success is based not on size but on singleness of purpose: to continue marketing frozen pizza—an item many companies treat as a plain commodity—as something special. "We're basically a single-product company," says D. David "Dewey" Sebold, Tombstone's executive vice-president and general manager. "We don't have the luxury of bringing out a new specialty product each week, and we can't compete with larger companies by cutting prices."

Robert Davis, a marketing professor at the Stanford University Graduate School of Business, sees Tombstone's marketing approach as an example of his "bent-arrow theory" at work. "The life of a product can be thought of as an arrow moving from left to right," says Davis.

"The product begins as a specialty and evolves into a commodity. While customers generally perceive value in a specialty product for reasons other than price—say service or image—they are more likely to choose a commodity simply because it is less expensive than another."

To "bend the arrow back," to inhibit the evolution of a product from a specialty into a commodity, says Davis, companies must develop effective strategies. They might, for example, introduce a more service-oriented delivery system, enhance their reputation in the marketplace through advertising and promotion, raise rather than lower prices, or produce a higher-quality product. The key to Tombstone's success is a combination of these strategies, including a commitment to producing a high-quality, higher-price specialty item and then selling this product through a tightly controlled sales network staffed with Tombstone's own salaried managers.

In the early 1960s, Ron and Pep Simek had no such vision of success. They had just opened a tavern in Medford, Wisconsin, and named it the Tombstone Tap, after the graveyard across the narrow tar road. Beer, the only alcoholic beverage the tavern was licensed to sell, went for a dime a glass. Because the business barely provided a livelihood for the two Simek families, Ron and Pep and their wives, Joan and Fran, broadened their offering by serving pizza, which they baked in the stove in the Tap's cramped six-foot-by-six-foot kitchen.

Pep virtually stumbled on the well-kept secret formula that is the basis of Tombstone's eight varieties of pizza. Dancing to the music of the "Peppermint Twist" one night in the Tap, he slipped and broke his leg, an injury that relieved him of tending bar for several months but allowed him the time to experiment with spices in the kitchen. Before long, the Simeks were freezing a dozen pizzas on request, then several dozen, and selling them wholesale to other taverns.

Brisk sales provided profits for personnel and capital expansion. In 1972, the Simeks began construction on their current 162,000-square-foot plant, where they make their own sausage and pepperoni and maintain a fleet of freezer trucks and trailers. As Robert Davis explains, "One of the best ways a company can provide a specialty product is to execute the manufacturing process better than anybody else in the business." To ensure quality pizza crusts, Tombstone moved its bakery operation in-house instead of relying on an outside supplier.

During the early seventies, Ron and Pep supervised every aspect of Tombstone's daily operations, down to making sure that the trucks were tuned and that just the right amount of tomato sauce was applied to the pizza crust. But, while they bird-dogged operational details in Medford, they lost their ability to oversee the growing sales operation, which included twenty-four commission route salesmen and more than a dozen distributors that they had signed on for expansion purposes. The specialty was turning into a commodity; the arrow was taking flight.

Without adequate supervision, the route salesmen built up profitable new accounts while neglecting established ones. Some salesmen and distributors fell behind in their payments to Tombstone. When Ron told one salesman to get his receipts in on time, the man replied, "It will ruin my credit rating." Many of the men, it turned out, were keeping $6,000 to $7,000 of Tombstone's receipts in their bank accounts. "If someone had to buy a car or a boat," says Pep, "he'd use three weeks of Tombstone receipts to pay for it. When we'd ask him to pay up, he'd get goddamned insulting."

"We had a mess out there," admits Pep, today fifty-five years old and Tombstone's chairman. "Everybody was selling pizzas, everybody was doing what they wanted. Because we had a good product, there was a demand and it was easy to sell. But the sales force was hard to control."

Signing on distributors had allowed Tombstone to expand its market into a dozen states. But many of the independent companies handled a smorgasbord of other items—ice cream, pot pies, potato chips—which they treated as commodities, without the special attention Ron and Pep had used to build their reputation.

Reports of poor service and sporadic deliveries reached Medford and confirmed Ron and Pep's worst fears: "I figured that for every written complaint or telephone call there had to be plenty more people out there who didn't take the time and just lived with that complaint . . . or went out and bought something else and formed a different habit," says Ron, fifty-two, the company president.

Without conceptualizing that they wanted to "bend the arrow back," Ron and Pep agreed that they wanted to regain control of Tombstone's sales. To do that, they would have to bring in management help. In 1975, they hired Grant White, thirty-two, as their first salaried sales manager. Within a year, they added Dewey Sebold, also thirty-two, who had an impressive track record at Ciba-Geigy, the Swiss-owned chemical company, where he had most recently managed the field sales group out of San Diego. Both men had served beer at the Tombstone Tap during college.

Sebold's experience with a well-structured field sales network quickly helped him see that Pep's assessment of the field was accurate—things were "a mess." Sebold argued that the best way to regain lost control was to replace the distributorships with Tombstone's own sale force.

Although the Simeks first resisted replacing distributors—which required no fixed expenses—with salaried managers, they finally agreed with Sebold's reasoning that the measure of control gained in the field would compensate for the cost of setting up the system.

Building a sales force in six years from 24 route salesmen with no supervisors to 143 routemen managed by twenty supervisors, nineteen district managers, and four regional managers was a slow, sometimes arduous process. White traveled often in those days, to places like Little Falls, Minnesota, looking for salesmen to service the routes inherited from former distributors. In 1976, he spent eight months commuting between Medford and Little Falls. During those months, he hired two local routemen and ran the third route himself until he could fill the position. The distribution system in 1976 was similar to that used by Tombstone today: A driver left Medford with a trailerload of frozen pizzas and either met up directly with a route salesman or dropped off the load at an eighteen-by-twenty-foot freezer warehouse where it would be picked up and delivered directly to retail outlets.

Tombstone's investment in its distribution system—in both its fleet and manpower—is only as valuable as the ability of its sales force to sell new accounts and to service established ones. In 1976, Tombstone introduced a sales training program for all route salespeople. Recruits receive field training for a minimum of four weeks, learning fundamentals about pricing, stocking shelves, and maintaining their vehicles. Then they spend a week in Medford, fine-tuning their selling techniques. The group reviews the classic points of a sales presentation: Determine the needs of the customer, identify the individual responsible for the buying decisions, make contact and explain the benefits, not just the features, of the product. After making the pitch, seek a commitment by asking for the business.

The training moves from general concepts to specific tips on selling Tombstone's products. In role-playing sessions, members of the group practice selling the pizza to one another and to the trainers. "If they can sell to their peers and leaders," remarks White, "selling to the guy in the field is a piece of cake." White throws out typical customer objections—"Not enough space," "Price is too high," "I'm already handling enough brands"—to prepare the salespeople for cold calls.

Tombstone's hiring record shows that the most successful managers have come up through the company, not from management jobs outside Tombstone. "We try to get salesmen into supervisory positions as soon as we can," explains Sebold. "Then, when we expand, we have company-trained people to travel to the new territory."

Today, all of Tombstone's sales managers in the seventeen states where Tombstone does business have paid their dues as Tombstone route salespeople, putting in as many as twelve to fourteen hours a day, five or six days a week. "That kind of work can grind on you," admits Grant White, although he claims that turnover is lower than it was five years ago.

An incentive for the salespeople is the opportunity to become salaried supervisors in as little as a year. From the supervisory level—the training ground for management—salespeople advance to district managers and are given authority over developing new accounts, hiring, and firing. "They're not puppet positions," says Sebold. "You have to give managers authority as well as responsibility to get things done. You delegate not because you don't want to do the job but because, if you've picked the right people, they can probably do it better than you can."

Besides its network of sales managers, Tombstone maintains five distributors in Michigan, Minnesota, South Dakota, Wyoming, and Hawaii. Hawaiian shipments are arranged through a broker who buys

Tombstone pizzas mainly for the military. Tombstone sends its freezer truck to Alameda, California, where the broker arranges to have the shipment picked up. Distributors conduct business in the same manner as Tombstone, sending their vendors directly to stores. White agrees with Sebold, however, that Tombstone's strongest card is its own sales force. "Being a one-product company can sometimes be a negative," notes White, "but it's also a plus, because it's hard to lose perspective on what we're selling. If you don't sell pizzas, then you don't sell anything." Although distributors' salespeople have taken the training program, he notes, they don't have the same focused aggressiveness, because they are selling a range of products.

Until the mid-1970s, the bulk of Tombstone's pizzas were sold to taverns, campgrounds, motels, gas stations, and other small outlets. When Sebold arrived, he led the Simeks through a formal, almost textbook approach to defining Tombstone's market. "We realized we weren't only in frozen pizzas, we were also in the convenience-food business. That opened up a whole new market segment for us. We could compete not only against pizza but also against pot pies, TV dinners, and other frozen entrees." Tombstone began to concentrate on developing new business among food stores—which today accounts for 75 percent of sales—holding to its original system of store-door delivery.

Sebold had advocated a direct sales force because it gave Tombstone the control over its product that no distributor network had. He and the Simeks stuck with direct store delivery for the same reason: It provided desirable control over their pizza. Tombstone's sales force goes directly into the stores, where they not only restock the shelves and take new orders but also provide product demonstrations—a key part of Tombstone's marketing effort to stand out as "special."

"As competition gets stiffer," notes Sebold, "every pizza producer claims to be selling 'quality,' so the word no longer has any relative value." Tombstone packages many of its products in clear plastic—most producers box pizza—so that the customers can see what they are buying.

Last year, Tombstone hired Charles Stoerzinger, formerly a marketing manager at Green Giant Company. Stoerzinger plans to make a modest shift in the marketing program by increasing demonstrations in new markets and focusing on more traditional forms of advertising—such as TV, newspapers, and couponing—in established markets. Under Stoerzinger's direction, Tombstone has also retained a new Minneapolis advertising agency, Campbell-Mithun Inc., which will, he believes, result in more creative advertising campaigns and better media buys.

Some food-store buyers—who prefer to work through brokers and to warehouse products themselves—have resisted Tombstone's direct store delivery approach. Dominick's Finer Foods chain, with seventy-four supermarkets in the greater Chicago area, opened its doors to Tombstone vendors only in May, after two years of negotiations. "Store-door delivery not only creates congestion," says Larry Nauman, vice-president of advertising and public relations for Dominick's, but "every time a driver opens the back door to enter or leave the store, it's an opportunity for theft" or for that person to rearrange the shelves to outposition competitors' products. But Dominick's finally agreed to carry Tombstone Pizza, because, says Nauman, "customers wanted Tombstone real bad. We were losing action without handling it." Notes Pep Simek, "When you're tied for the number one–selling product in Chicago, they have to start taking you seriously.

The Simeks see no reason why they can't continue to operate their store-door delivery system when they are two, or even twenty, times the size. After all, they point out, Frito-Lay Inc., the $1.9-billion-a-year company that has carved out a 40 percent share of the more than $5-billion-a-year salty-snack industry, runs a highly efficient store-door delivery system.

Tombstone is also girding itself for rising fuel costs. "You have to assume they'll increase," says Dewey Sebold. "But even if gas rises to three dollars a gallon, we're prepared to streamline our fleet, shorten our routes, and still call on our major, most profitable customers." So far, Tombstone has seen no reason to expand its use of brokers and distributors to carry its goods to retail shelves.

The belief at Tombstone Pizza that its product is special starts at the top. "At Tombstone, you know areas you don't tamper with," says Sebold. "You don't, for instance, screw around trying to make Pep's pizza sauce any different."

Such a commitment to maintaining product quality is at the heart of Tombstone's success. Without Ron and Pep Simek's fixation that pizza sauce must be applied just so, Tombstone would have found it difficult to bend the arrow back to continue turning out a specialty instead of a commodity product. "And once you've got a commodity," says Dewey, "there isn't much allowance for drift. It's difficult to ever turn back and develop market share in the specialty, high-quality end of the business."

"The risk a company runs when it wants to market its product as a specialty rather than a commodity," adds Stanford's Davis, "is that it may resort to all sorts of strategies at the expense of quality. The test, in the long run, is a good product."

—SARA DELANO

CHANGING TASTES:
Can He Keep His Customers Tuned In?

Thirteen years ago, Sandy Ruby spent a lot of his spare time selling stereo components, chiefly to fellow MIT students who dropped by his East Campus dormitory room. In a good week, Ruby and his partner found they could gross an easy $1,000.

Though Ruby insists he never intended to become a retailer, the little business seemed to take on a life of its own. Today, Tech Hifi has become one of the country's largest hi-fi chains, with sixty-five outlets that stretch in a fat arc from Michigan through New Jersey to northern Vermont. This year, Ruby's spare-time, spare-change business managed to rack up sales of $50 million, and next year he figures he'll come close to the $60-million mark.

Like many companies that serve often volatile consumer markets, Sandy Ruby's Tech Hifi chain has so far prospered by riding the crest of a moving wave—the baby boom following World War II. That wave inundated the country with eager young consumers just when Ruby began selling hi-fi equipment, and brought him quick success. But, like a surfboarder skidding precariously along the wave's foaming crest, Ruby has learned that keeping his balance takes constant attention and hard work. Tech Hifi's sales have always been concentrated in a narrow age group, and the company now faces a difficult challenge as its customers grow older, adopt new lifestyles, and change their buying habits. Still, Ruby has ridden the wave for thirteen years without toppling, and along the way he has learned valuable lessons in how to survive in the changing currents of the consumer marketplace.

Ruby himself, born in 1941, was one of the forerunners of the baby-boom generation, and he grew up in a world of crowded schools and teeming playgrounds. By 1963, when he reached graduate school at the Massachusetts Institute of Technology, a total of 80 million children had been added to the postwar U.S. population and were beginning to flood college campuses across the country.

At first, Ruby watched from the sidelines as the quiet of the Eisenhower fifties ended and an era of social protest, rock and roll, and unconventional lifestyles began. Thousands of businesses were struggling to serve the needs of the free-spending baby boomers; the entertainment business, fashion, and the media all reflected youthful tastes and enthusiasms.

But as the new youth market heated up, Ruby—who "grew up fascinated by electronics and small machines"—started his own business by assembling hi-fi component kits and selling them to college friends. Elaborate music systems were popular with MIT students, and soon Ruby and his undergraduate partner had to expand—into a vacant janitor's closet, where they stored their inventory.

In 1967, MIT officials demanded the return of their closet and booted the fledgling business off campus. A month later, Tech Hifi reopened in a public warehouse across the street from the main MIT campus.

Ever more customers for the twenty-by-twenty-foot store were drawn by word of mouth and amateurish ads in the *Harvard Crimson* and the MIT *Tech*. The store flourished, though Ruby is still amazed that his company survived. "We didn't do any market research," he says, "and we had no idea of how to run a business."

Ruby's indifference to conventional business management seemed to make very little difference in Tech Hifi's marketplace. More than 100,000 students were enrolled in the Boston area's thirty-three colleges, and the demand for good hi-fi equipment was urgent and practically insatiable. Ruby, a self-taught expert in audio electronics, by now knew exactly what kind of hi-fi equipment would appeal to his customers.

"We dealt strictly in components—turntables, receivers, speakers, tape decks, and the like—at a time when most other retailers were still pushing compact console units that tried to look like living room furniture and often didn't sound very good," Ruby recalls. "We felt an almost religious fervor about why people should buy components instead, and so did our customers."

In 1968, Ruby opened a second Tech Hifi outlet, then three more the following year, and four more in 1970, all close to college campuses. Tech Hifi outlets quickly gained a reputation as unpretentious, low-cost, comfortable places to buy hi-fi equipment. Ruby recruited salespeople straight from local campuses, creating easy rapport with college-age customers. Heavy advertising in student-oriented newspapers also stressed the chain's youthful image.

To Ruby's delight, eager young customers snatched components off his store shelves almost faster than Tech Hifi's salespeople could replace them. "We began to think everything we tried would be a winner," he recalls. It was a reasonable assumption: By 1973, six-year-old Tech Hifi had mushroomed into a chain of sixteen stores, with sales that topped $12 million.

The time seemed ripe for even more expansion. "Our plan," Ruby says, "was to locate key stores near college campuses, then move gradually into the suburbs as our original customers graduated and settled down. We always knew we should be going after more than just college students."

The strategy made good sense, but in his eagerness to keep up the momentum of growth, Ruby lost control. Within a year, he added fifteen new stores, almost doubling Tech Hifi's outlets. But sales stagnated and profits took a dive. Ruby's new stores were scattered all over the map, some in markets too isolated to manage effectively, others in suburbs where Ruby belatedly discovered there was far less enthusiasm for stereo components than in Tech Hifi's usual college locations. "We really didn't do a lot of thinking," Ruby now concedes sheepishly.

It was a sobering experience for the young entrepreneur. Overhead was rising faster than sales. Cash flow was down to a trickle. And the 1974–75 recession had begun to afflict the audio industry. "That period was about as grim for us as you can get without going bankrupt," Ruby now says. "The pressure from our creditors was awesome, especially to people of our age who hadn't been through this kind of thing before. We didn't know how to bob and weave. It was like being in a ring with a prizefighter and getting hit a hundred times over."

Ruby temporarily scrapped his expansion plans and went to work slashing overhead and boosting sales to Tech Hifi's traditional college-age customers. With agonizing slowness, the company pulled back into the black. Ruby now estimates the experience cost him the entire net worth he'd built up in the business.

But he also learned some long-overlooked lessons about his business and the market he served. That market was youthful, impulsive, quick to change direction. It was also, though a large one, a market of limited size—and declining in relative numbers as the baby boomers were replaced by smaller numbers of postboom teenagers. To keep growing, Ruby realized he'd have to find new ways to expand Tech Hifi's appeal to older consumers.

And that was a problem. More than age separated Tech Hifi's college-age customers from the older suburbanites Ruby wanted to reach, although he wasn't sure what the differences were. All he knew, he now says, was that he couldn't enlarge his older market simply by plopping down new stores in the suburbs.

To help find the answers he needed, Ruby went looking for a marketing expert to fill a new slot as the chain's vice-president of advertising. He found Rick Deutsch, twenty-seven, an ad agency veteran who was equally at home with creative concepts and computer printouts.

Deutsch began to assemble a small mountain of data about Tech Hifi's customers. He blitzed them with surveys, interrogated them in small focus groups, and sorted and resorted Ruby's customer records according to age, sex, income, buying habits, media preference, and other aspects of their lifestyles. Deutsch even staked out rival hi-fi stores to ask their customers why they weren't shopping at Tech Hifi.

Gradually Deutsch built up a sophisticated profile of Tech Hifi's marketplace—and it wasn't encouraging. The college market of the sixties and early seventies had leveled off, and would even begin to shrink in the eighties. Meanwhile, 85 percent of older households had no hi-fi equipment at all and showed little interest in acquiring it. "Stereo is a pretty essential ingredient in the life of a single individual," Deutsch concluded, "but once someone gives up dating, he seems to lose interest in hi-fi as well."

It might be possible to change that attitude, Deutsch pointed out, by finding ways to promote the idea that listening to music is fun. But that was a huge effort for a retailer to undertake, especially with no guarantee that new converts to stereo would shop exclusively at Tech Hifi outlets. "Unlike college students," Deutsch says, "older consumers cost a lot to reach with any advertising message. They read more expensive media, and they need more repetitions of the message before it sinks in. It can easily take five years to prime this kind of market, and very few retailers are prepared to make the investment."

Ruby took Tech Hifi's market research to the major equipment manufacturers whose lines he carried, arguing that only they could sustain a national campaign to develop a broader market for hi-fi equipment. He pointed to the makers of small cameras, who took a specialized hobby and transformed it into a major new consumer market. "The camera manufacturers doubled their sales in three years," Ruby points out, "but the stereo manufacturers figure it's easier to grow by knocking off weaker competitors. "They've ridden the baby boom all the way through high school, college, and graduate school, and all they understand is getting the easy sales."

Since the manufacturers wouldn't help bring new customers to Tech Hifi, Ruby and Deutsch realized they would have to find their own strategies for expanding out of the college market. And they would have to do the job within the limits of Tech Hifi's still-fragile balance sheet. They would have to develop new sensitivity to the prejudices and preconceptions of their maturing customers, be ready to anticipate new trends, and occasionally try some adventurous strategies.

"Tech Hifi got started simply by doing a good job of filling a demand," Deutsch says. "Now we had to learn how to create a demand, sell hard and keep moving."

Deutsch went back to his market studies and looked for fresh ways to bring in customers. One reason some would-be hi-fi enthusiasts never showed up at Tech Hifi, he found, was "the intimidation factor." Stereo equipment scared people—it was complex, expensive, and hard to evaluate because for years manufacturers had been stressing minute technical comparisons. "We countered with an ad campaign that invited people to come in and just fiddle with our systems," Deutsch says. "It was all very relaxed, and we ended up by reminding them that 'all you have to do is listen' to pick a good system." The campaign struck a responsive chord: Tech Hifi's sales jumped 50 percent in the six months after the campaign broke.

The campaign proved to Ruby and Deutsch that they could find ways to bring into the stores customers who weren't part of their traditional college market and that market research could provide the clues to reaching those customers. But they also realized that it would take more than a single ad campaign to change the chain's youthful image. "In a way, we're victims of our own success," Deutsch admits. "Tech Hifi is so closely identified with the college-age market that it can be hard to get anyone else to take us seriously."

Deutsch began revamping Tech Hifi's ads and promotional materials to show a broader range of customers, particularly women, "who are an audience we've neglected terribly." The new look is clearly visible in the half million color catalogs Tech Hifi hands out every year, illustrated with sometimes fanciful scenes of typical customers and their systems. One $189 system shows up on the front porch of a college fraternity house during a party; a $4,000 system graces a spacious parlor where a silver-haired *grande dame* and her poodle enjoy music with their afternoon tea. Other apparently representative customers include housewives, teenagers, a pair of brandy-drinking chess players, a gospel choir, modern dancers, a florist, and a vampire. "The point we're making, of course, is that stereo fits into anyone's lifestyle," says Deutsch.

While Deutsch was hard at work changing Tech Hifi's traditional image, Ruby was using a different strategy to attract older customers. Two years ago, he began opening two entirely new kinds of stereo outlets—Tech Hifi Bargain Centers, aimed squarely at the same buyers who frequent suburban discount stores, and a slick minichain of Music Systems Limited stores, designed to appeal to the second-time buyer. "MSL prices are a bit higher," says Ruby. "The brands aren't mass-marketed, and the cosmetics and extra features are better. And we try to have salespeople who know more and can spend more time on individual customers.

"So far, I've got to admit that MSL hasn't been one of our more brilliant successes," Ruby adds, "but it is one way we have of holding on to a customer as he grows older."

Tech Hifi's market research has given Ruby and Deutsch a degree of insight into the minds of their customers that is unmatched in the hi-fi industry. They know who buys their equipment, and why; they know what part of Tech Hifi's $3-million advertising budget brought the customer in; they know which competitors lost the sale and what qualities about their own stores that same customer didn't like. "There's virtually no marketing question we can't answer," Deutsch boasts.

But market research alone won't predict the future, Ruby and Deutsch insist. Sometimes, they say, you've got to get a jump on the market, anticipating a demand that few consumers have begun to feel. Ruby's latest guess is that video disc equipment will be the magic that unlocks a wave of enthusiasm among older, more affluent consumers, and he's betting heavily on this hunch. In the spring, he bought a retail video center in Boston, and is beginning to stock Tech Hifi outlets with video disc equipment.

It's a risk, says Ruby, because the video market right now is "infinitesimal," and it may never get much larger. Or Ruby may have bet on the wrong system, or he may get squeezed out by price-cutting competitors. "Video may even wreck the hi-fi business," he concedes. But if video discs are going to revolutionize home entertainment, Ruby is determined to be waiting for the wave when it catches up to him.

So far, his efforts to keep pace with the changing tastes of his maturing customers seem to be paying off. In a $2-billion industry plagued by bankruptcies and devastating price wars, Tech Hifi has sustained an enviably healthy growth rate—and Ruby intends to keep developing his market regardless of what setbacks the rest of the industry may suffer. "You've got to keep moving with the market," he says, "or you'll be left stranded on the beach when the tide runs out."

—Jeffrey Tarter

THE BABY BOOM: Where Have All the Children Gone?

When demographic experts show how the maturing baby-boom generation has affected the American population, they often point out that their charts look somewhat like "a python swallowing a pig." The huge bulge in their charts—which will slowly pass along the "python" until its members reach old age—is the result of a burst of post–World War II fertility. For about twenty years the birth rate shot up to record levels, then it dropped precipitously.

As children, the baby boomers left a wake of overcrowded schools; as young adults, they strained the economy's capacity to find them jobs. Unemployment, delinquency, and other forms of social stress peaked as the baby boomers struggled toward maturity.

But that maturity is now close at hand, and in fact a good part of this troubled generation has now reached its late twenties and early thirties. As adults, say the experts, the baby boomers will bring a good many blessings to the economy of the next few decades. Here, briefly, are what demographers foresee for the baby boomers and other key elements of the U.S. population.

The Baby Boomers Grow Up

As youth-oriented retailers and manufacturers, such as Tech Hifi's Sandy Ruby, have discovered, the ranks of the young are already beginning to thin out appreciably. The result is a change in patterns of consumption and in the workforce that will gather momentum steadily throughout the eighties. By 1990, say the demographers, the most populous segment of society will consist of people aged twenty-five to forty-four—men and women in the prime of their lives, at the peak of their earning abilities, mature and affluent consumers.

These changes are generally good news for employers. Young workers bring few skills and little job experience to the workforce. Instead, they suffer from abnormally high rates of unemployment, low productivity, and rapid turnover. In addition, the surplus of young baby boomers hit the American workforce at an especially sensitive moment, just as the supply of traditional entry-level jobs had begun to decline. Hardest hit of all were young black and Hispanic baby boomers, who found themselves least able to compete for scarce career-oriented jobs.

In the eighties, the workforce will still have to absorb many millions of young workers, but by now the bulk of the baby boomers have found their way into stable jobs and productive careers. As a result, the coming decade should see less turbulence in the job market, combined with a healthy supply of workers with the advanced skills and knowledge necessary to man an increasingly complex, service-oriented economy.

Similarly, the increasingly affluent baby boomers are good news for most consumer-oriented businesses. Inflation and high energy costs may take a hefty bite of the baby boomers' rising incomes, but enough should be left over to sustain a healthy improvement in living standards. Moreover, the consumer demands of most baby boomers are likely to reflect stable, maturing tastes—a welcome change from the costly, unpredictable zig-zagging of the sixties and seventies.

Where Have All the Children Gone?

Nineteen sixty-one set a historic high-water mark for the number of children born in this country; thereafter the tide ebbed swiftly. In general, this decline in the number of children that our society supports is welcome: It frees resources, including the labor of parents, that traditionally must be invested in the raising of a new generation. Still, the declining birthrate may be a mixed blessing. The makers of products as diverse as textbooks, bicycles, and baby food are already bracing for sharp declines in sales. And those who employ teenagers and young workers—including newspaper circulation departments and the U.S. Army—see their pool of available employees slowly drying up.

As for what will happen to the birthrate in the future, that's still one of the mysteries of demographics. Unlike some European nations, the United States is unlikely to see its birthrate drop below replacement levels. One possibility is that today's baby boomers have simply deferred childbearing and will shortly begin to catch up—setting off yet another baby-boom generation. But other experts say steady and modest growth is likely until at least the beginning of the next century.

The Vanishing Housewife

Old-fashioned stereotypes notwithstanding, more than half of all American women over sixteen have already turned in their aprons and gone off to join the labor force. Moreover, predicts the Bureau of Labor Statistics, the rate will be even higher by 1990—around 60 percent—and more of the jobs women hold will require specialized skills. In the academic year 1977–78, for example, women earned 26 percent of the law degrees and 21.5 percent of the medical degrees awarded in this country.

The large number of women who work outside the home is a historical novelty, and it raises controversial questions about future trends. If most of these women elect to pursue long-term careers, devoting little time to childbearing and housewifery, they are likely to continue making gains in salaries, experience, and responsibilities. These gains will directly benefit the American economy, which will acquire millions of new productive workers and millions of new well-paid consumers.

But there is no way to be sure that this trend will continue. Many of these working women may finally choose the rewards of homemaking and motherhood over those of the office and factory. The decision is likely to be based partly on economics, a subtle weighing of their own incomes and their husbands' earnings against their rising expectations. Another factor is that few women are eager to start families after their midthirties—a deadline that is rapidly approaching for millions of the country's female workers. No one, least of all the demographic experts, pretends that this part of the future can be predicted with any certainty.

The Amazing Shrinking Household

As the birthrate shrinks and women go off to work, the size of the American household continues to shrink. When the first census was taken in 1790, the average number of people in an American family was six; today, the average household contains only 2.8 people. And by 1990, say the demographers, two-thirds of all households in this country will have no children at all under the age of fifteen.

What has happened is a steady splitting up of the "extended family" of recent generations. More than half of all households now consist of only one or two people—the childless, the unmarried, the divorced, or the widowed. These small households are increasing rapidly in number, and this change will have profound effects on housing and consumer markets. Small households, for example, mean a greater demand for small apartments, condominiums, and townhouses; they also point to a rosy future for those in the business of outfitting households with pots and pans, toaster ovens, microwave ovens, and dishwashers.

At the same time, the country is seeing a sharp increase in the number of households that are made up of two income-producing adults. About half of all households headed by married couples now have two paychecks to spend, and consumer marketers view these couples as the most promising segment of the economy in the eighties. For many, of course, two incomes have become necessary simply to keep even with inflation. But the double paycheck is also a strategy that provides fairly easy entry to the ranks of the affluent. Already, families with two incomes make up 40 percent of all households with more than $50,000 income, and the rate continues to rise steadily as more baby-boom couples acquire a taste for the good life.

Gray Power

Not all of the optimism is generated by the newly affluent baby boomers. Among the remnants of older generations, there's also a surprisingly strong and relatively growing part of the population. During the coming decade, more than a third of all adult Americans will be aged fifty or older, and they will be an economic force to be reckoned with.

Though it is true that a good many of the nation's elderly suffer from eroding fixed incomes, there are still millions who are debt-free, with no children to support and a taste for long-deferred pleasures. In fact, the spending power of the fifty-plus generation already outpaces all other age groups; its members hold enormous equity in corporate stocks and bonds, and they account for more than 80 percent of all the capital in savings and loan institutions. Like the armies of baby boomers and working women, these Depression-era oldsters can be counted on to lend new vitality and new strength to the American economy of the eighties.

—JEFFREY TARTER

SELLING TO THE NEW AMERICA

Nineteen years ago, Mark Roth left his job as manager of the food division of a chain of discount stores to take over a dying food market in a working-class section of Los Angeles. Within a week, he had doubled sales at the store, which now serves as the base for a specialty-food business with customers throughout the Southwest.

In 1981, orthodontist Ron Greenspan assumed ownership of a lackluster Volkswagen dealership on San Francisco's "auto row." With a radical change in marketing strategies, he transformed it into the second largest dealership in America.

Harriet Nickolaus, a mother of three from Greenwich, Connecticut, had virtually no marketing experience when she started peddling her homemade Muscle Medic ointment. Yet with a healthy advertising budget and a change in market focus, she increased her sales last year tenfold and opened up important new export markets.

These three entrepreneurs have two things in common. They are all white, native-born Americans of European descent. And they all have positioned their businesses to ride a wave of recent immigration that is radically changing the complexion of the American consumer marketplace.

Forget seniors. Forget yuppies. Forget female professionals. For sheer numbers and purchasing power, it is immigrants, most of them now from Asia and Latin America, who represent the fastest-growing domestic markets. While Asians and Hispanics were only a few drops in the national melting pot just twenty years ago, they now account for nearly 10 percent of the American population. And at some magic moment in the next century, they and their offspring—together with America's black population—will constitute an absolute majority of American consumers (see charts).

You don't need a futurist's crystal ball to catch a glimpse of the new America. In New York City, Hispanics are about to become the largest minority group, surpassing blacks, while in cities such as Miami, San Antonio, and El Paso, they already constitute an absolute majority of the population. San Francisco's Asians, about 15 percent of the population in 1970, already outnumber the local Anglo population by some estimates. And Los Angeles, once jokingly dubbed "the largest city in Iowa" because of its ethnic homogeneity, now boasts a hodgepodge of ethnic and racial minorities who together easily outnumber its residents of European descent.

These new demographic trends represent just the latest chapter in what sociologist Nathan Glazer calls the "permanently unfinished story" of America, a nation that continues to take in more immigrants each year than all the rest of the countries of the world combined. Immigration has always been the source of the remarkable self-renewing power of the American economy—the source of new people, new ideas, new products, and new markets. Similarly, it has always been a source of social unrest and political discord. For U.S. business, that presents both challenge and opportunity.

The challenge is to resist the temptation to write off each wave of new consumers as a fringe or niche market, insignificant and impecunious. Such nativist insularity is nothing new—the economic history of the nineteenth century is littered with now-defunct businesses that clung bitterly to their familiar customs and customers rather than adapt to the waves of Italians, Germans, and Russians who swelled the populations of the great cities of the East and Midwest. Today the Sunbelt cities of the South and West are favored ports of entry for the American dream. And it is no coincidence that these are the cities enjoying the highest rates of growth and newfound wealth.

To those who embrace the new America comes a rare business opportunity—the opportunity to sell into rapidly growing, untapped markets largely free from competition. Although a handful of companies such as Anheuser-Busch, Coca-Cola, Kraft, and Campbell Soup have made special efforts to sell to the new America, big business still largely ignores it. By and large, these are still local and regional markets, and as Mark Roth, Ron Greenspan, and Harriet Nickolaus all happily discovered, they are markets just craving to be served.

"It's a whole new ball game out there," states Ed Escobedo, a Los Angeles consultant who advises businesses on marketing to Hispanics. "People have to start realizing that these new immigrants have a lot of buying power. Instead of thinking of them as undocumented aliens, maybe it's time to start thinking of them as undocumented consumers."

The new America arrived in the Los Angeles suburb of El Monte in the late 1960s. Like many communities in the San Gabriel Valley east of downtown, El Monte was changing rapidly from a predominantly white community to one that was predominantly Hispanic. To the owner of the local Mars Market, it was a transformation he wanted no part of.

"The guy simply wanted no Mexican trade," recalls Mark Roth, who purchased the failing business in 1969 for $72,000. "He didn't carry the products they wanted or the cuts of meat they could afford. He just wanted to cater to the so-called elite of El Monte. And he was starving to death."

But where the old owner saw a mere rabble, Mark Roth spotted opportunity. Back in his native Belfield, North Dakota, Roth had watched his father build the family grocery store by catering to the community of Ukrainian refugees who had settled there in the early 1920s following the Russian Revolution. The majority population in Belfield—German, Dutch, and Scandinavian in origin—generally looked down on the Ukrainians and kept them at a distance. The South Side Mercantile Company was one of the few places where the immigrants were not only welcome but courted.

Working with wholesalers in Minneapolis, Adam Roth took pains to import the foodstuffs traditional to eastern European cuisine. And when products like kielbasa, the Polish-style sausage, were unavailable, he made them himself. If harvests were lean, Roth would extend credit to the immigrants as best he could. He even taught himself Ukrainian—and in the process, taught his son a valuable lesson about markets and marketing.

"My father always said that the new arrival was the best customer," the son remembers. "They are settling down, so they need pots and pans and staples. And they are people on the way up. The Ukrainians dominate the whole area back there now."

Mark Roth sees in today's Mexican immigrants grocery customers every bit as ideal as the Ukrainians of the twenties. They represent a growing market, both in terms of numbers and affluence—Los Angeles Hispanics today constitute a consumer market roughly the size of metropolitan St. Louis. And they spend more on food than Anglos—$20 more per week than other shoppers, according to a recent supermarket study.

To appeal to this market, Roth started by hiring local Spanish-speaking employees, both as a way to facilitate communication with non-English-speaking customers and to tie the market to the community. Today, about two-thirds of the employees at Mars Market are Spanish-speaking. And the community ties are more than simply commercial: A former box boy once counted relations to fifty-two different families in the area.

The focus on family has been the key to Roth's marketing efforts. Because Hispanics spend relatively more of their free time with their extended families, shopping is often a group affair, not a lonesome chore. From the start, Roth hoped to turn that cultural reality to his advantage. On the first weekend after taking over the stores, he brought in Ray Walston, star of the popular TV show "My Favorite Martian," as a celebrity draw. A Mexican mariachi band provided music, and there were balloons and prizes for the kids. Some of the Anglo customers were bemused, others offended. But when the week was over, Mars Market's sales had doubled.

It is not surprising that such fiestas are now regularly featured at Roth's store. And even on weekdays, Mars Market has more of the feel of a Mexican town square than a sterile American supermarket. Aisles are gaily decorated in bright colors, and customers mingle at the complimentary salsa and chips table. Although Roth himself never learned to speak Spanish, he is a friendly and familiar presence with employees and customers.

Product selection, too, is geared toward Hispanics, who now account for nearly three of every four customers. Next to the lettuce and onions in the vegetable section are cactus leaves, hot chilies, and other Mexican ingredients. The meat department has long since stopped pushing high-priced meats, such as porterhouse and London broil, in favor of large displays of the chuck steak and neck bones used in many traditional Mexican dishes.

But perhaps Roth's most clever and important move was to install a *tortilleria*—a bakery for making tortillas—just inside the main entrance to the store. By producing hot, fresh corn tortillas, the staple of the Mexican diet, Roth gave every Mexican family in El Monte a reason to shop in his store. Fresh burritos, tamales, enchiladas, and other Mexican specialties soon followed, and continue to give him an edge even as the large supermarket chains have finally begun to make a push for the Los Angeles Hispanic market.

Although most of the techniques for marketing to Hispanics are fairly obvious, Roth has found that nuances can also be important. Early on, for instance, Roth thought it would be a great idea to print up posters and fliers for the stores in Spanish for his growing clientele of non-English-speaking customers. But to his surprise, this offended not only his Anglo clients, but also many Mexican-Americans who had already been in the United States for a generation and resented being lumped in with the recent arrivals. His solution: Print fliers in English, but use large pictures to illustrate the items on sale.

"When we started all this, people asked us, 'Why are you catering to those wetbacks?'" Roth explains, "The payoff is that we have built credibility with these people over all these years. They may not speak the language, but they sure learn fast how to use the currency."

Mark Roth's success in El Monte reflects the more traditional side of marketing to ethnics—selling specialized food and everyday low-cost staples to first- and second-generation Americans right in their neighborhoods. But today's immigrants are not all huddled masses yearning for entry to the middle class. Many of them are already there.

Asian-Americans are perhaps the most populous such group. They are two or three times as likely to hold a college degree as the average American adult. They are also more likely to hold positions as managers, executives, or professionals. And among the Japanese, Chinese, and Filipinos, average family income already exceeds that of whites.

San Francisco has long been the capital of Asian America. During the past fifteen years, Asians have more than replaced the whites who fled the city for surrounding suburbs. But the San Francisco Chinese are no longer the poor immigrant FOBs ("fresh off the boat") of the popular imagination, washing dishes in a small Chinese restaurant or stitching garments in a stuffy sweatshop, living in crowded flats on the quaint but squalid streets of Chinatown. Today they constitute a prosperous consumer market, with 41 percent owning their own houses. When the Brahmins of the city's Nob Hill complain about the Chinese these days, it has nothing to do with poverty, crime, or prostitution. The fear is that the Chinese are "taking over too much" of the city's property and businesses.

For Volkswagen dealer Ron Greenspan, word of this newfound affluence came straight from the horse's mouth, you might say. Greenspan, you see, was an orthodontist who opened a small practice in a comfortable San Francisco neighborhood in 1969. Back then, 70 percent of his practice was white. A decade later, at least 70 percent was Asian, mostly Chinese. "I learned fast that these folks had money when they began paying with cash," recalls Greenspan.

Straightening teeth, however, was never Greenspan's great love—cars were. And in 1981, he bought one of San Francisco's two VW dealerships for $250,000. At the time, this was a business going nowhere. The flocks of youthful, white San Franciscans who had bought up "Bugs" by the boatload now were opting for more expensive German imports or cheaper cars from Japan. Once one of the strongest VW operations, the San Francisco outlet had dropped near the bottom of the list of the country's 900 dealerships.

It was natural that Greenspan would find former patients among his new customers. What was not so predictable is that this Jewish dentist from Cleveland could build a booming trade selling German cars to the Chinese. That required a good deal of ingenuity.

Greenspan started out by placing ads in such outlets as the *Asian Yellow Pages*, a popular Chinese-language advertising medium. He mailed fliers into middle-class Asian neighborhoods such as the Richmond section of San Francisco, and the nearby suburb of Daly City, with its large concentration of Filipinos. Taking his cue from his salesman father, Nat, who had encouraged him as a youth to sell everything from shoe polish to toilet deodorizers door-to-door, Greenspan sent his salesmen out into the streets of the city to visit shops and hangouts frequented by the Asian bourgeoisie.

Bringing Asian customers into the showroom, however, was the easy part. Persuading them to buy was where the real challenge began. And it was here that his experience in the dentist's office began to pay off.

"The problem is that a lot of people don't really see Asians as people," Greenspan explains. "There's a great mystique about the Asian, and how hard he is to sell. Salespeople tend to be intimidated by them."

Most intimidating was the Chinese penchant for tough bargaining over price. To the Chinese, this is simply a normal part of the business culture. But to someone more accustomed to American business—even a car salesman—the exchange can seem downright cutthroat.

"When the guy comes in here and makes a ridiculous offer on a car, you don't get mad," Greenspan instructed his salesmen. "You come back with something equally ridiculous and have a good laugh. Then start your real negotiation."

Another facet of Greenspan's "Asian Sensitivity Training" focused on dealings with the family. The Chinese prefer shopping in large family groups, with buying decisions usually made by the family elders. Greenspan explained to his salesmen that while the car might be for a teenage schoolgirl or a middle-aged engineer, the successful sales pitch may have to be directed to the grandfather or elderly uncle. To help things along, seventy-five-year-old Nat Greenspan is often on hand to make the generational connection.

"I introduce the father to my father, and there's an immediate bond there," Greenspan explains.

You may think all this is fairly subtle stuff, but Greenspan's Chinese customers apparently appreciate the considerations. Largely as a result of sales to Asian-Americans, Greenspan has now boosted car sales from only twenty a month to more than a hundred. In 1984 and 1985, Ron Greenspan's dealership ranked second in the nation in terms of VW sales. And in 1986, it was sixth.

Three thousand miles away in Miami, Toyota dealer Richard Goldberg has had a similar success. These days, much of Miami's white business establishment has turned its back on the city's new Hispanic majority—a popular bumper sticker of the early 1980s asked bitterly, "Will the last American to leave the city please lower the flag?" But Goldberg didn't buy the conventional Anglo version of what makes for a good American, or a good customer. Growing up in Newark, New Jersey, Goldberg counted blacks, Italians, and Jews among his friends. So why, he asked himself, couldn't his customers be Cuban or Colombian or Salvadoran?

Goldberg, in fact, was so convinced of the future of Miami's Cuban market that he upped and moved his dealership from the city's north side, with its concentration of black and Jewish populations, into a heavily Hispanic neighborhood just east of Little Havana. If other car dealers wanted to continue to compete for the 20 percent of the city that was still Anglo, so much the better, he told himself.

"We came here because it was a growing area, not because it was Hispanic," Goldberg explains matter-of-factly. "We wanted to go where there would be the most people with the bucks to buy Toyotas."

In the five years since the move, Goldberg has used most of the familiar techniques for marketing to minority consumers. Nearly 90 percent of Expressway Toyota's 150 employees, including much of his top sales staff, are Hispanic, and the predominant language on the showroom floor is Spanish. And on weekends, he has used every family draw he could think of—Latin singers, clowns, acrobats, even an elephant.

But perhaps the most important changes were in Goldberg himself. When he made the move, he looked on Hispanics as business prospects. Today, he thinks of himself and his business as part of the

Hispanic community. Over the past few years, Expressway Toyota has poured thousands of dollars into Latin community events, including beauty pageants and the annual *Calle Ocho* festival in Little Havana. Goldberg also sponsors youth baseball and soccer teams. And if, as the French philosopher once said, you are what you eat—well, you might as well call him Ricardo Goldberg.

"Give me a Cuban holiday and we'll sponsor it," jokes Goldberg between gulps of *sopon,* a spicy Cuban fish soup. "I really like this culture. And I think they can tell that."

In the last analysis, that may be what marketing to minorities is really about. Be it the Mexicans of El Monte or the Chinese of San Francisco or the Cubans of Little Havana, what "minority" consumers respond to most eagerly is a level of respect that, too often, is missing in their transactions with mainstream businesses. Targeted advertising, bilingual salespeople, and special events all help to break down barriers. But their long-term value is to confirm for minorities that they are genuinely welcome and valued not just as consumers, but as people—and as Americans.

"If the Hispanic respects you and you respect him, I think he's a better customer than the Anglo," says Goldberg, whose business from repeat customers is now twice what it was in North Miami. "With the Anglo, you're always bargaining. They are interested in only one thing—the price. They'll go across the state to save fifty bucks. But with Hispanics, if you earn credibility, that's it. Sure, we sell the car as cheap as anyone. But what makes it work is that we've created the image that if you're Hispanic, you buy your Toyotas here."

Today, Goldberg lays claim to more than half of Toyota's Hispanic market in Miami—not bad for a city where Hispanics are an undisputed majority. As a result, sales have climbed 400 percent in six years, to $75 million last year. Once only number 350 in sales among the 1,100 Toyota dealers nationwide, Expressway Toyota so far this year is ranked number 22.

It's true what they say: If you pitch your company openly to minority consumers, some of your traditional Anglo customers may go somewhere else. The vaccine for bigotry hasn't yet been discovered. But it is also true that minority marketing can have just the opposite effect, providing an effective and inexpensive access to a wider, mainstream marketplace.

That's the way it has worked out for Harriet Nickolaus. A dance teacher from Greenwich, Connecticut, Nickolaus backed into business after concocting a homemade muscle pain–relieving lotion for her choreographer husband. Later, several friends tried and liked her mixture of water, herbs, and spices, and it was only then that she began to think of selling it to the public.

Her idea was to position it as a "natural Ben-Gay," and the logical market, she figured, was New York City health-food stores. But for two years Muscle Medic languished on the shelves, in need of the kind of promotion Nickolaus could not afford. In 1985, sales barely reached $48,000.

Then, on the strength of the response she'd received from a few Haitian friends, she placed Muscle Medic in some local *bodegas,* small markets that cater to Hispanics. In contrast to the health-food stores, the *bodegas* seemed able to move the product among Hispanics. When she learned that Hispanics have traditionally been enthusiastic customers for a variety of home remedies, she decided to abandon the health-food stores and New York and to move to Miami.

"I realized that Miami was a large Latin market with a lot of local media," she explained over drinks at the Alexander Hotel in Miami Beach. "It was a market we could really reach." Gambling with a $200,000 advertising budget, she invested most of it in Spanish-language television, appearing herself before the camera to explain her product. Her ads were every bit as homemade as her product—she had taught herself just enough Spanish to make the spots. But however awkward her presentation, Hispanic viewers seemed to respond favorably to an Anglo woman attempting to sell to them *cara a cara.*

"When I got on and said in Spanish, 'You have nothing to lose but the pain,' it really caught on," said Nickolaus. "I use a very personal approach, like Frank Perdue and his chickens. I go on and say that I made this for them. They seemed to appreciate that an Anglo woman would do that—and say so in Spanish."

Sophisticated marketeers might sneer at Nickolaus's analysis, but not at the growth in her sales figures. By the summer of 1986, she was selling more product in a month than she had sold in a year through New York City health-food stores. At the same time, visitors from Latin America—who number in the millions each year—started picking up the product, and orders soon began arriving from such places as Guatemala, Panama, and Costa Rica.

The response from the Hispanic market was encouraging. But more encouraging still were the calls that began to come in from the large Anglo-owned stores whose managers had seen the ads and heard of the customer response. Today Nickolaus counts among her customers 150 Anglo stores, including Eckerd Drug Stores, a major chain in the Southeast, which now carries Muscle Medic at all of its Florida stores, even those located outside Hispanic neighborhoods.

"I never expected it, but our success with the Latins in Miami opened everything up for us," says Nickolaus, who now reports sales of $400,000. "It was the Latins who led us to the Anglo market."

Is this simply a fluke, an isolated case of good luck? Not to hear it from the business owners themselves.

Take the case of grocer Mark Roth in El Monte, where our story began. Although Roth's Mars Market continues to be profitable, he finds these days that he is facing increasing competition from large supermarket chains that have begun to employ some of the same strategies he has long used to attract Hispanic shoppers. At certain key locations, these chains are now stocking large quantities of Mexican-style meats and produce. Some have stepped up the hiring of Spanish-speaking employees. A few have even installed their own *tortillerias*.

In the long run, Roth figures he cannot prevail against the giants in an industry that measures profit margins in tenths of a percent. So he has found a way to turn the trend to his advantage. Instead of remaining a competitor to the chains, Roth has decided to become their supplier.

It all started several years ago, when Roth, celebrating the opening of his new *tortilleria,* asked one of his employees to make a little salsa to go with the corn chips. The response of the customers was so enthusiastic that he started packaging some for his Mexican-food deli counter. Later, he happened to bring some of the salsa to a meeting of area independent grocers. The grocers ate it all—and left him with orders for their stores.

Soon the workers in the backroom of Mars Market were churning out not only the original hot sauce, but other Mexican specialties such as guacamole and green chili sauce. Some of it he sold under his own El Burrito brand name, the rest he provided on a custom-label basis. Now, with sales last year close to $1 million and doubling annually, Roth is already making more money on his packaged foods than he is from the market. He has moved much of his production to a separate manufacturing plant several miles away. And he counts among his customers supermarkets as far away as Montreal and as close as El Monte.

All this started out of a calculated interest Roth and other grocers had in serving a growing Hispanic market. But it has now gone far beyond that. For to Roth's surprise, the largest orders for the packaged foods are not coming from stores in predominantly Hispanic sections of Los Angeles or San Antonio—they're coming from Anglo merchants serving mostly upscale Anglo shoppers. Roth estimates that Anglos now account for 60 percent of the market for his packaged Mexican foods. Setting out to sell to Hispanics, he has found himself on the forefront of the latest *American* food craze.

It is, of course, a familiar story. It is the story of pizza and pita pouches, of the bagel and the croissant, of sushi and chop suey. It is a story of minorities that become majorities, minorities—of Ukrainians and Mexicans and Cantonese and Cubans—who constantly define and redefine what it is to be American. *E pluribus unum*—from the many, one—is how it reads on the seal of the United States. For 200 years it has been the motto of American democracy. Now it is a political creed that translates nicely into a marketing strategy for American business.

THE LESSON OF MONTEREY PARK

Only a decade ago, Monterey Park was a sleepy, all-white suburb on the eastern fringes of Los Angeles. Each morning businessmen gathered, as in a scene from a Norman Rockwell painting, at a coffee shop to discuss local goings-on. And come election time, it was the same group who often dictated who would serve as mayor and city councilor.

Since those days, Monterey Park has taken off. Spurred by an influx of well-educated, affluent new residents, there are today scores of new office buildings, shops, and restaurants in the downtown districts and in new outlying shopping centers. Commercial space that went for $5 a square foot back in the early 1970s now goes for $45 and more. Deposits in local commercial banks jumped $400 million.

Yet if prosperity has come to Monterey Park, few of the merchants who once gathered at the coffee shop are still around to enjoy it. For rather than welcoming the Chinese and Southeast Asian families who now comprise more than 40 percent of the city's population, many of the city's white businesspeople have spent the better part of a decade fighting them. Some have sold out grudgingly—and greedily—to Chinese interests and moved away. Others tried to hold on to a shrinking base of white customers before closing down or going bankrupt. And those still left behind spend much of their energy still trying to push back the Chinese tide, pressing for restrictions on further development and a ban on signs written in Chinese characters.

"You have a group of suburban, uneducated people out here who would like to turn the clock back to 1950 and hang a Chinese from every lamppost," explains George Ricci, past president of the local Chamber of Commerce. "These people didn't do anything to market to the Chinese. They left themselves open to be replaced."

Not everyone sees it quite that way. Marie Purvis, one of Ricci's predecessors at the chamber, runs a small art gallery and framing business and still longs for the good old days when "American" rather than Chinese restaurants lined Garvey Avenue. In fact, Purvis insists there is a Chinese conspiracy brewing to drive the white businesses out of town.

"It's deliberate. They have a plan, not that I know what it is . . ." says Purvis, who moved to Monterey Park from East Boston thirty-five years ago. "I am not used to being prejudiced against. We've always been discriminating against the newcomers, but no one has ever turned the tables on us before."

But if there is a conspiracy, Kelly Sands has not found it. Seven years ago, Sands took over Bezaire Electric Company, his family's contracting business. Sales seemed to have peaked at $300,000, and virtually all of the developers and major contractors who had worked with Sands' father and grandfather had either gone out of business or left town.

But Sands, a college dropout in his early twenties, noticed the rising number of Chinese developers around town. And rather than disdain these often well-heeled new players, he courted them. He hired a staff of young, aggressive Chinese managers to help communicate with his new market and adjusted his schedule to accommodate the hard-working Chinese entrepreneurs, who often held business meetings late into the night.

As a result of his efforts, Sands is one of the few white entrepreneurs to cash in on Monterey Park's demographic boom. He estimates that Bezaire gets at least half of the area's Chinese-related electrical contracts, which have boosted sales to $3.7 million. Nearly 80 percent of his customers are Chinese. His biggest project these days: a Buddhist temple going up several miles east of town.

"I think it's all in the mind-set," says Sands. "Either you adjust your mind-set to reality, or you'd better get out of the way."

—JOEL KOTKIN

FUTURIST LAUREL CUTLER

Laurel Cutler is perhaps Madison Avenue's most powerful woman. She counts among her current clients the food processors at Campbell Soup, the brand managers of Colgate-Palmolive and Procter & Gamble, and the tobacco and cereal merchants of RJR Nabisco—as well as the top brass at Chrysler and Citicorp. What they all want is a glimpse into the future: Cutler's prediction of where the consumer marketplace is headed and what that means for their once and future businesses.

"This whole business of calling the future is either a lot easier than most people think it is, or we've been very lucky," says Cutler as she surveys the consumer landscape from the vice-chairman's office of FCB/Leber Katz Partners, forty-two stories above Manhattan. While others in her trade retain a slavish devotion to market research, Cutler and her staff travel through more distant precincts in search of evidence of change in the sciences and art, in fashion and in retailing, in technology, and in demographics. The patterns that emerge from these anecdotal impressions become working hypotheses that are shopped around in draft form to Cutler's clients, who collaborate in refining the good ones and rejecting the bad on the basis of their own experiences. It is only years later that there will be any hard evidence with which to confirm the hypotheses that emerge from that process. "There is," she tells skeptics, "no data on the future."

Cutler began her career as a *Washington Post* reporter and unpublished novelist before switching to writing advertising copy for J. Walter Thompson Company during advertising's salad days. Now sixty and very much the industry veteran, she is a self-described "tough cookie" who delights in confronting and challenging her buttoned-down corporate clients. She spoke about consumers and the changing consumer marketplace with *Inc.*'s Paul B. Brown and Steven Pearlstein.

INC.: There has been a lot written about the disappearance of the mass market and the rise of ever more specialized market segments. Chicken-or-egg question: Is this happening more because consumers have changed or because business has changed?

CUTLER: Actually, the consumer has less to do with it than the increased competition in the marketplace. New competitors offering highly differentiated products—these are the people who have changed the rules. Today, if you try to appeal to everybody by being bland and inoffensive, somebody is going to come in and begin to pick off significant chunks of your market. What that means is that as a marketer, you have to figure out exactly who your audience is: What are their aspirations, and what differentiates them—and your product—from the mass market?

INC.: Is it big business or small business that is driving this segmentation?

CUTLER: The more common pattern is that the ideas are developed by smaller companies that get to the point where they need more money, and they are bought by the larger companies. General Foods, for instance, has never created much of anything—they have simply bought up the Posts and the Jell-Os. There are some large companies that have never lost the ability to think entrepreneurially—IBM, Hewlett-Packard, 3M, Frito-Lay. But these are more the exceptions than the rule.

You have to stand for something, and you have to stand for it very, very firmly, because if you don't, somebody else is going to come along and take it away from you.

INC.: What's a classic example of a market that's been segmented?

CUTLER: Shampoo. Back twenty years ago, the market leader in shampoo was probably protecting a market share of 45 percent or 50 percent, and all shampoos were pretty much priced the same. Today, the market leader—Head & Shoulders—has a share of less than 10 percent, and there are all sorts of tiers and segments. You even have a market now in $30 shampoos, if you can believe that.

INC.: So it's come full circle—the market leader now is the product that started out to fill what was considered an uninteresting niche—dandruff control.

CUTLER: But the more important point is that the market leader has only a small percentage of the market. You see, up until even four or five years ago, companies such as General Foods would think only in terms of $200-million sectors—if the business couldn't get to $200 million in two years, they weren't interested in pursuing it. And by definition, that almost always meant mass market—bland, undifferentiated. Nowadays, if they can identify a $50-million opportunity, they're thrilled.

INC.: What is it about their management that distinguishes those companies from the pack?

CUTLER: Several things. They give their people the right to be wrong. They have compensation systems that pay people at least as well for creating new business as they do for maintaining old business. And—this may be the most important of all—they are willing to pay for the breakthrough. New ideas can't pay out in the first year.

INC.: Can you give an example from your own experience of a big company that did it right?

CUTLER: Well, let's talk about Prego, which has become a $200-million business and a very great success for Campbell Soup. What Prego had going for it was that it was a fabulous sauce in a jar—that's not just my opinion, that was the opinion of two out of three consumers in taste tests who preferred it to Ragú, the industry leader. Two other agencies had been given the assignment of coming up with a concept to sell this sauce, but neither could come up with a scoreboard above 25. Campbell's action standard is 80. So they turned it over to us somewhat in desperation, and it turned into a wonderful collaboration.

INC.: And how did you size up the situation?

CUTLER: Ragú was sitting out there very successful and very vulnerable. It had 64 percent of a market that was unsegmented, offering a product that was puréed, untextured, orange, and bland—to a marketplace that was becoming increasingly sophisticated about its food. So here comes Campbell with its sauce. It was textured, not puréed. It was very spicy, not bland, with little flecks of herbs and spices in it that you could see and taste. It was ruby red, not orange.

INC.: So you have a gloppy red sauce with little specks that any five-year-old would think were little insects floating around in it. How do you sell such a product?

CUTLER: It turns out that there is only one promise in spaghetti sauce that generates any interest among consumers, and that is that it is closest to homemade. We tried fifty different supports to that promise, and there were two winners when we tested them. The first was, "Closest to homemade because it's naturally thick with tomatoes, not starch." The other was, "Closest to homemade because it has spices and herbs that you can see, smell, and taste." In both instances, what was seen as a product deficit—the lumpy tomatoes, the yucky spices—was turned into an advantage. And it worked.

INC.: How did Ragú respond to the strategy initially?

CUTLER: They really didn't react much at all. You have to understand that Ragú had just faced down Hunt-Wesson's Prima Salsa by coming out with their own "extra-thick and zesty" sauce—they spent a fortune and very quickly got Hunt-Wesson to withdraw its sauce from the market. So a year goes by, and now comes Campbell with Prego, and the folks at Ragú say to themselves, "They'll never stick with it; they'll never spend the money, so why should we spend ours?" But they were wrong. Campbell did stick with it—they kept the spending up—and they now control 26 percent of the market. And most of it is coming right out of Ragú.

INC.: Is there any one thing you consider your major contribution to that effort?

CUTLER: There are probably thirty-nine things, all of them small in their way, and all of them important. Probably the most important was convincing them to change the name from Campbell's Very Own

Spaghetti Sauce, which was very much a 1970s concept, to Prego, which was much more eighties.

INC.: Talk some more about that, if you would—the changing character of American consumers that makes them more receptive to all this differentiated marketing.

CUTLER: There are a number of themes we've developed over the years that have anticipated changes in the consumer market—forecasts that have held up very well. The first, which we did back in 1972, talked about "emerging lifestyles" before that term became debased. The second, in 1978, we had the presumption to call "1982." And the third, in 1985, talked about the "Europeanization" of the American marketplace. The notion was that if California had been the spawning ground for much of what was new in America in the seventies, then Europe would be the source for the eighties—a period in which the United States finally reached the age of limits. Europe had to deal with questions of limits long ago, and so we thought perhaps we could learn from the European example.

INC.: What in particular could we learn from Europe?

CUTLER: Three things. First, that the marketplace would become much more polarized, with all the growth at the top and bottom of the market, with deep erosion in the middle. Second, that American business would move from being marketers and manufacturers to being global trading companies, making products where they could make things the cheapest and selling where they could make the most money. And finally—and this was perhaps our wildest prediction—was that there would no longer be any discrete markets called upscale, middle, and downscale, but that the very same people would buy at Neiman-Marcus in the morning and K Mart in the afternoon, depending on whether they cared about the category or not.

INC.: So the consumer would become much more strategic as a shopper.

CUTLER: Exactly. Indeed, for a whole variety of reasons, this is the best time that I can recall to be a consumer. There have never been so many choices, not only of what to buy, but where to buy it and how to shop for it and how to pay for it. You don't have to be a big corporation or a government any longer to have good access and good information: The information is often as close as the nearest personal computer, and the access is only a telephone call and credit card number away.

INC.: Are there some demographic trends that are also redefining the consumer marketplace?

CUTLER: There are the obvious things—people are better educated, more affluent, and because of travel and television, more sophisticated.

They are also, on average, more mature. By that I mean that after a rather prolonged adolescence, the big baby-boom generation is entering middle age, and its outlook is changing very quickly. The adolescent says, "I am sixteen years old, and I belong to a club called teenagehood, and I want to look like every other teenager—maybe a little hipper, maybe a little quicker to spot a new fashion, but for God's sake, not different."

Maturity is quite the opposite: "I don't want to be like everybody else. I want to be independently and distinctively who I am. And I am certainly not part of any mass market. I am a unique human being, and I express uniqueness by the things I buy." That means cars, clothing, cigarettes—those are the public things that have always been very ego-intensive consumer choices. What's fascinating now is that so many private categories are becoming more ego intensive as well.

INC.: Like shampoo.

CUTLER: Shampoo, toothpaste, even toothbrushes—that's the newest one. Stanley Katz, our chairman, and Les Wexner [founder of The Limited] get together, and they compare notes on their $15 imported French toothbrushes. The other day Stanley walked in and announced that somebody was sending him a $100 toothbrush.

INC.: Somehow, if I owned a $100 toothbrush, I don't think I'd run around telling anyone about it.

CUTLER: I don't think you can buy a $100 toothbrush and *not* tell anybody about it. And that's just the point. That's how the toothbrush got out of the medicine cabinet.

INC.: Yet if everyone is so interested in defining their individuality through their consumer purchases, then why do you suppose everybody is wearing Reeboks?

CUTLER: Well, I'm not sure they are. You have to be careful to distinguish between large markets, such as Reeboks or Grey Poupon mustard, and mass markets, which are undifferentiated and appeal to everybody: Keds and French's mustard. But I don't mean to dismiss your question, because it is a good one. Markets, especially in trendy fashion categories such as running shoes, are difficult to maintain. It's like a club, and when the club gets too big, watch out—or you'll find yourself like Izod's alligator.

INC.: And what do you do if you're Reebok, and your market gets so large that it looks like a big, fat target waiting for somebody to come along and differentiate a little more?

CUTLER: You anticipate it and splinter it yourself—you introduce a super-Reebok, or a stripped-down Reebok.

INC.: Which one?

CUTLER: Maybe both. Although I'll say that it is always easier to start at the top and then broaden than it is to come up from the bottom.

INC.: Why is that so?

CUTLER: Call it the law of marketing gravity.

INC.: And who is the Sir Isaac Newton of that idea?

CUTLER: Maybe me.

INC.: Can you give us an example of how this law works?

CUTLER: The perfume business: The advertising is done for the $200-a-bottle pure essence, the business is done in the toilet water. Occasionally somebody has come along who has been able to defy the law—right now, for example, Honda is trying to move up the ladder with its Acura, as is Toyota, but they are both finding it extremely tough going. Mercedes-Benz, on the other hand, found it very easy to move down with the 190. Another example is in a category I've been working in recently—frozen foods. Swanson has come out with a fancier line that they call Le Menu, and I think that they may have lost Swanson in the process.

INC: What happened?

CUTLER: What happened is that General Host came into the market with a lower-priced line called The Budget Gourmet, and it's beating the pants off everyone in the top and middle of the frozen-food market.

INC.: What's their secret?

CUTLER: My hunch—and it's only that at this point—is that consumers decided that, in the end, frozen food is frozen food, and none of it is really very good, so they might as well go with Budget, which offered the same upscale varieties at a lower price. First they came after Stouffer's and Le Menu and hurt them very badly. And now The Budget Gourmet has come out with a line called Slim Selects, and it has taken Lean Cuisine's share down—24 percent at one point—and I would have thought Lean Cuisine was impregnable.

It's been a great drama, and it's another indication of what I said before: We are dealing with the smartest consumer we've ever dealt with. She'll pay the difference if she can see it, taste it, smell it, feel it, or show it off somehow. But if she can't, she won't.

INC.: Campbell Soup, which owns Swanson, is a big, experienced consumer packaged-goods company. Why didn't market research tell it that?

CUTLER: Perhaps it did. But you have to remember that most market research is a crock of . . .

INC.: What kind isn't?

CUTLER: Example: You have an idea to import this lovely green bottle of bubbly water from the hills of Umbria, in Italy. So what do you do? You take your water and a carton of paper cups to a shopping mall—the right shopping mall—and say to people, "Would you mind tasting this water? Do you like it? Do you think your husband would like it? Would you buy it? Would you pay two dollars a bottle? How about one-fifty?" That kind of market research is indispensable. What is useless is hiring some survey company out of Chicago to call people at random on the telephone and ask them, "What would you like to drink?" or "Do you want some Italian bubbly water?" That kind of market research will always tell you why you can't do something. It is a substitute for decision making, for vision, for guts. In all the years I've sat listening to them, consumers have never come up with new product ideas.

INC.: You seemed to be saying two things just then about market research—do it right, but also do it yourself.

CUTLER: In this marketplace, you're crazy to interpose anything between you and the consumers. If you want to know what they think, *you* go, *you* ask the questions, *you* watch the faces, *you* watch the body language, *you* decide whether the people are just being polite and want to say yes because they are in a rush to finish their errands.

This is the undelegatable part of giving birth to any new product. Remember, we're not talking about mass products and mass markets anymore. You're looking for 10 percent, and you're looking for intensity. It's not good enough any longer that 80 percent think it's nice. Nice is nowhere. You need 10 percent who love it.

INC.: What qualities distinguish the clients who can operate effectively in this consumer environment?

CUTLER: Maybe the best way for me to answer that is to give you my two parameters for taking on a piece of business. Number one, I want to work with the top people, because only they have the courage and the confidence and the risk-seeking profile that you need. Number two, I look for a deep sense of urgency, which is the name of the game. There are some companies that will take eighteen years to get something to market, that will use research to give them report cards rather than insights. Use research? By all means, use it to check things out, revalidate assumptions. But for heaven's sake, move, get out there and test. And always fix—fix the little things.

INC.: Is it best, from your standpoint, that the person you're working with come to the project with a marketing background?

CUTLER: Actually, I think the ones who come up from R&D make for the best partnerships. They're more creative. And often they're more articulate. Scientists can be the most extraordinary users of words and builders of dreams—many of them are poets, really. They're inventive, but they're rigorous, which is the way I like to think we operate.

INC.: And what about marketers? They would seem to be your natural allies.

CUTLER: The marketer is too often caught up in research, which is oriented more to the past than the future. Creative people have much more confidence in their imaginative leaps, in their intuition.

INC.: What about salespeople?

CUTLER: Salespeople can be fabulous to work with, but they're usually not as rigorous. The process is usually a seesaw—you dream, then you check, dream, check. And salespeople tend to be somewhat insufficient, as a class, on the checking.

INC.: And the worst people?

CUTLER: Literal, linear thinkers. CFOs, lawyers.

INC.: You are known for your predictions about the future. Could you tell us about the general theme or themes of your next report?

CUTLER: Without going into too much detail, I think we're coming into the age of trade-offs. We were talking before about the difference between the teenager and the adult. Well, one thing that is different about adults is that they defer gratification. They plan, they work in longer time frames, they are more cautious, more scared. They think of the downside.

INC.: Most people seem to agree that the big downside just waiting to happen is a recession of some severity and duration. How will that reshape the consumer market?

CUTLER: Again, I can't answer a question about the whole consumer market, because it matters whether you're talking about the haves or the have-nots, the top or the bottom.

INC.: Well, let's start with the haves.

CUTLER: Let's face it: The haves have been on an orgy in this country over the past decade, and that means that most people already have everything they want now. They're probably going to manage perfectly comfortably during a recession just by retrenching a bit. Their compromise will be on quantity—how long you'll keep the car or how many vacations you'll take. It will be a very European response: I'll buy one nice blouse, and I'll wear it for years.

INC.: And the have-nots?

CUTLER: In its way, the low end loves quality, too, and these people will probably be forced to part with it very reluctantly. One of the really extraordinary things is the power of premium brands in the disadvantaged black marketplace. Hennessy cognac, Bristol Cream, Pepperidge Farm cookies—these have tremendous power. Affordable luxuries at some level are how people get through depressions. Everything else gets eliminated or deferred: restaurants, flowers, vacations . . . desserts.

INC.: And if you're running a consumer business—as a manufacturer, as a distributor, as a retailer—what is the age of trade-offs going to mean in the broadest terms?

CUTLER: This will surprise you, coming from a futurist, but the best guidepost to the future is the past, particularly now, when we are hurtling into the future at such a frantic pace. We must help our customers find something to hang on to—to sink roots into. One hundred percent quality, real service, unique design, style—these are the product values that deliver the human values that never change: love, pride, joy, the family, self-esteem.

—PAUL B. BROWN
STEVEN PEARLSTEIN

MARKETING WIZARDRY: Consumers Push WD-40's Profit Button

Push the button on the blue and yellow spray can labeled WD-40, and out comes a multipurpose lubricant and rust inhibitor. For WD-40 Company, located in San Diego, what comes out is earnings of $5 million on $34 million sales in fiscal 1979, just completed. Yet the product is the same as it was ten years ago, when sales were only $2 million.

What's made the difference? Marketing, merchandising, and promotion. The effort has increased both sales and earnings at a ten-year compounded rate of nearly 35 percent. The company, close to disaster in its early stages, is now cash-rich and debt-free.

WD-40, the product, has been around since 1953, when it was invented by an independent chemist seeking a substance that would prevent corrosion on the Atlas missile. On his fortieth attempt (hence the 40), he discovered a water displacement (WD) formula that did the trick. With the formula and three investors, he launched the Rocket Chemical Company to serve San Diego's aerospace industry.

For the first ten years, Rocket was satisfied to do mostly that, although employees did discover that the product could also protect guns and fishing reels, silence squeaky hinges, and dry out sticky carburetors. A rudimentary retail and industrial distribution system followed, using manufacturer representatives, and WD-40 flowed through several hundred retail outlets.

In 1969, with the company showing modest growth, Jack Barry was signed on as president. He is the brother-in-law of one of the three original investors, but he brought with him solid marketing experience that included stints at 3M, Avery Label, and Adams Rite.

Barry's mandate was to accelerate growth, both in sales and in earnings. He felt that the best way to do that was to market the company's one product to its full potential. The basic problem was to get millions of consumers to understand the glories of WD-40 and to use it. There would be no diluting of the effort by diversifying into other product lines.

"Our strategy was to diversify the uses of the product, not the product itself," explains Barry.

To emphasize that, the name of the company was changed from Rocket Chemical to the name of the product. "After all, we weren't making rocket chemicals and we weren't going to," says Barry. The goal was to make WD-40 a household word.

Barry quickly recruited a national sales manager from Johnson's Wax to join him and a newly appointed marketing manager from Upjohn. Among the three of them they had more than sixty years of sales and marketing experience. They also had a huge task ahead.

Consider the situation. The product was virtually unknown. Except for a single entry from Du Pont, the market was virtually untapped. There was no capital for investment in a sales organization or a media campaign, nor for plant and equipment or inventories.

On the business and manufacturing side, this meant that expansion would have to be financed strictly with cash generated by sales. There would be no in-house packaging, no production machinery, and a minimal investment in plant, equipment, payroll, and inventory. The company would stick to its plan to mix concentrated WD-40 formula at San Diego headquarters and ship it in bulk to independent packagers. They, in turn, would add a mineral spirit, package the product in spray cans for consumers and in larger containers for industrial users, and ship to wholesalers.

On the sales side, manufacturer representatives would be the sales force, selling to wholesalers. Wholesalers would stock the finished product and move it into retail outlets. Barry and the headquarters sales and marketing staff would concentrate on working with the reps and on building product awareness.

To make the strategy work, several crucial policy decisions were made early on and have been adhered to rigidly.

The manufacturer reps were offered exclusive sales territories and commissions of 10 percent on the billed amounts of all shipments into their territories. Annual sales forecasts and quotas would be mutually agreed upon, but there would be no written contracts. The relationship between a manufacturer representative and WD-40 Company could be terminated by either party on thirty-day notice.

Sales would be to wholesalers only, never to end-users. Excluded would be catalog houses, single retail outlets, firms that export only, and accounts that place orders solely for drop shipment. "We didn't want to compete in any way with our customer base," says Barry. In short, WD-40 determined to deal only with accounts that buy the product with the intention of stocking it and reselling it.

And there would be one price for all. "Wholesalers and retailers can charge whatever they like," says Barry, "but when they buy it from us there's only one price." A fifteen-case minimum order was established, with no quantity price breaks. Wholesalers were promised that their orders would be processed immediately upon receipt in San Diego. Packagers, in turn, would ship within three days direct to the wholesalers' warehouses.

With the ground rules established, all Barry and his headquarters staff had to do was line up the manufacturer reps, keep product flow and packaging capacity in balance with orders, and build end-user awareness and demand. That's all!

Barry can point to no single breakthrough element in the plan that accounts for the spectacular growth of the past ten years. "Essentially, we had a strong product and a single objective. What we needed were policies for reaching that objective," says Barry. "We saw it as an evolutionary process, taking a long-term approach and not betting the store on some wild scheme to triple sales in a year."

With one product, one price, and one type of account, WD-40 management made it a policy to teach its reps new trade channels. Many were heavily oriented toward sporting goods outlets and needed exposure to mass merchandisers, grocery chains, and industrial distributors. Working with more merchandisers and retailers led to policies on co-op advertising and display allowances. The minimum order was changed to 20 cases and later to 24. And, finally, quality price breaks at 720 and 1,200 cases were introduced a year ago.

"We've changed policies very slowly," points out Barry. "As a result, however, any imitators who enter the market end up competing not only with our product but with our policy. That plus our trademark and trade dress—the spray can with the blue and yellow label and little red top—is the most valuable thing we have, and it doesn't even show up on our balance sheet. Like Coke, the value of our trademark goes up every day, while the value of the formula goes down."

In sum, the spectacular success of the company reflects a superb job of orchestrating a diverse mix of rather familiar marketing elements—such things as fliers and giveaway samples for wholesalers, special sweepstakes and discount programs, participation in trade shows, print and electronic advertising. The company annually spends from 7 percent to 8 percent of sales for media campaigns and merchandising aids. This year the promotion tab topped $2 million. In all, some 28 percent of sales is spent on selling, marketing, and administration.

Sales and promotion built slowly at first, gathering real momentum in the past five years. But it's been strictly a pay-as-you-go approach. There has been no debt, and the payroll has been, and still is, lean and clean.

Today the company has only thirty-two employees in all, and nine of them are in selling or marketing management. Twenty of the employees are clerical, handling orders, credit, and data processing related to selling.

WD-40's entire manufacturing operation consists of one part-time production worker, who stirs up concentrate for the end product by mixing a handful of off-the-shelf chemicals. The concentrate is blended and stored in ten 20,000-gallon tanks behind the San Diego plant. It's shipped by tank truck or rail from there to five independent packagers spread from Los Angeles to Piscataway, New Jersey.

The sales force is up to sixty-five manufacturer reps in fifteen organizations throughout the country. The majority make more than $100,000 a year from their WD-40 accounts.

The wholesalers now number 14,000—double the number five years ago. Their orders are received by mail at San Diego headquarters, which handles all processing and billing.

In response to orders from San Diego, subcontractors package the product in spray cans or bulk containers and ship directly to the wholesaler customer via common carrier or UPS. They handle all the warehousing but have no marketing responsibility.

Some 35 million spray cans of WD-40 go into consumers' hands each year. There are no figures on total retail sales, since retail sales prices are determined by wholesalers and retailers. But spray cans account for 90 percent of WD-40's total dollar volume. The other 10 percent is sold in one-gallon, five-gallon, and fifty-five-gallon sizes.

The wholesaler accounts range from mass merchandisers to retail drug and grocery chains, hardware and sporting goods stores, automotive jobbers, industrial distributors, dairy suppliers, and farm co-ops. Although many are giants, such as J. C. Penney, K Mart, Sears, Western Auto, and Woolworth, no single wholesaler accounts for more than 3 percent of WD-40's total sales.

Also included in the company's customer base are stocking distributors and licensees in more than two dozen foreign countries. International sales, however, currently represent less than 5 percent of total volume and, with the exception of the Canadian market, are not a major factor in the company's growth strategy.

Ultimately, the company's revenues are derived from millions of WD-40 end-users, ranging from household consumers to mechanics, plumbers, farmers, and industrial maintenance engineers. About 55 percent of the WD-40 sold is used by homeowners and sportsmen, with commercial and industrial users accounting for the other 45 percent.

The rule remains "wholesalers only," however. A giant industrial consumer recently placed an order for a truckload of WD-40, seeking to bypass distributors and buy at a better price. The company turned it down.

With a highly diluted customer base and with millions of end users, WD-40 considers itself well insulated against the loss of a particular account or a turndown in a particular market. But what about the competition?

Barry doesn't hesitate to usher visitors to the San Diego headquarters into a small office lined with competitors' products. It offers a kaleidoscopic array of also-rans and also-running, manufactured by both fly-by-night operators and billion-dollar conglomerates. "We can't really worry about competitors—there's a new one every week," Barry says. "And we always assume that there are at least twenty-five out there making a strong bid for a share of our market."

The WD-40 formula, which has not changed since its invention in 1953, is not patented, but it is a closely guarded secret. "If you patent your product it winds up in the public domain, and sooner or later your closely guarded secret becomes a widely circulated seller," says Barry.

With no product evolution and no intention of broadening the line, WD-40 has no R&D expense. Research consists of simple product comparison. Basic equipment is three test tubes filled with San Diego water and some ungalvanized nails. Packagers' batch samples of WD-40 and samples of each newcomer on the market are submitted to the "nail test." The nails are sprayed, dropped into the test tubes, and monitored for corrosion. Sometimes the process lasts only a day (never with WD-40, of course), and sometimes it takes eight weeks (never with a would-be competitor's product, they hope).

Except for the nail test and the guarded formula, management takes little notice of competitive threats. When the silicone sprays hit the market, they barely caused a ripple at WD-40. "Silicone is not a good water displacer—it simply builds up a film," says Barry matter-of-factly.

Similarly, the company did not panic when the aerosol crisis struck in the spring of 1974, making Freon a dirty word. Widespread shortages were predicted. WD-40 simply switched to another propellant. "In retrospect, Uncle Sam did us a big favor. We shifted to hydrocarbon as a propellant, which is far more cost-effective anyway," reports Barry. "And we simply started phasing the word *aerosol* out of our corporate vocabulary."

WD-40's management prefers to devote its competitive energies to building greater brand awareness and backing up its wholesaler customers with prompt deliveries and vigorous promotion.

When a serious disruptive threat does surface—such as last spring's truck strike—management's reaction time is such that crises are quickly defused. With the truckers threatening to grind to a halt, for example, WD-40 sweetened its credit terms by sixty days and enticed its larger accounts to submit oversized orders for immediate shipment.

As sales and profits have risen, WD-40 has been able to hold its prices relatively firm. Prices on can sizes went up 15 percent to 16 percent September 1, the first increase since August 1974, when prices were bumped up 10.6 percent. "Passing on higher costs once in a while can't be avoided," concedes Barry. "But when you rely on it as a regular tactic, you begin pricing yourself out of the market."

WD-40 is now established in a modern 15,000-square-foot plant and tank farm, but it has almost no capital equipment. The only inventory there is 200,000 gallons of concentrate that is kept churning. That, added to the finished product stocked in packagers' warehouses, results in an inventories-to-sales ratio of 2.5 percent.

Internal cash generation finances all of the company's needs, which, beyond working capital for day-to-day operations, are primarily cash dividends. Cash represents half of the total assets on the balance sheet, which boasts a current ratio of 4.16 to 1. Some $4.4 million of cash is in certificates of deposit. After-tax net earnings are about 16 percent, and net-income-to-average-net-worth is about 60 percent.

The company went public six years ago. Some 40,000 shares were offered at $16.50, which generated net proceeds of about $590,000. Of that, about $350,000 was earmarked for a new plant and about $240,000 was added to working capital.

But that was not the main purpose of going public. The real reason involved tax and estate planning considerations by the selling shareholders. Prior to the offering, the company was a Subchapter-S corporation. To loosen up their estates and adjust personal tax bites, the selling shareholders went public, giving up their Sub-S election in the process.

The firm remains closely held. Currently there are about 1,300 stockholders and about 2.5 million shares outstanding, following a two-for-one stock split last October. More than 50 percent of the stock is held by officers, directors, and relatives of the original three investors.

With sales soaring from $2 million to more than $34 million in ten years, what does management do next? Continue to build brand awareness, which National Family Opinion currently pegs at about 50 percent. It's a matter of getting more nonusers to use the product, and getting those who already use it to use more.

"We'll have to keep up our intensive advertising and merchandising programs, but refine them," says Barry. "They should no longer include such heavy sampling, for example," referring to the practice of generously handing out free samples of WD-40—more than a million last year, in fact. "The idea is to get 'em hooked, not feed the habit."

Upgrading the current account list, rather than continuing to build it, is another goal. "Perhaps, at fourteen thousand wholesalers, we ought to shift gears and concentrate more on improving existing accounts than attracting new ones," suggests Barry.

And, finally, management must consider WD-40's growth and its effects on suppliers, reps, and packagers. There are alternative sources and services in each case. But they are not necessarily the answer to some of the more nitty-gritty problems, such as a chemical industry that is no longer a bottomless pit or a packager who suddenly runs out of storage capacity.

"At this point, we have to determine what it will take to sustain WD-40's growth in the *next* five years," concludes Barry. At the moment, the only sure answer is a multipurpose lube in a blue and yellow can.

CHANGING HOW THE GAME IS PLAYED

Each spring, before the dogwood blooms at the nearby Jack Daniel Distillery, the white Dodge vans—emblazoned with the Worth Sports Company logo and filled with bats and balls—pull out of the company headquarters in Tullahoma, Tennessee, and hit the road. Before spring training in March, through the season, and past the World Series in October, Worth's salesmen travel, mile after mile, ballpark after ballpark—singing along with Willie Nelson over the hum of the fuzzbuster; packing and unpacking the Tennessee Thumper and Ball Buster bats, the patented Poly-X balls, and Doc Joc batting gloves; preaching the company's gospel.

"Let me show you this," the salesman will say, bouncing the ball in front of him. The company has pictures and statistics to document the ball's liveliness and durability. But bouncing the ball a few times still seems to work best. Then he will cut one open, slicing through the hand-stitched leather to the patented polyurethane core.

"Try this," he will insist, thrusting two thirty-four-ounce bats, handle first, into the prospect's hands. "Both bats feel the same, don't they?" That is the old way to buy a bat: total weight.

"Now try this," he will say, retrieving the bats, reversing them, and thrusting the barrel end into the outstretched hands. "One feels heavier, doesn't it? That's how much weight you can put behind the ball." Worth calls it Swing Weight. It is a trademark, and it is the new way to buy—and sell—a bat.

A few bats and balls given away, a visit to the local sporting goods store, a promise to check back next time he comes through, and back on the road. For a few days in spring training the salesman may rub shoulders at camp with the Carlton Fisks and Mike Schmidts of the world, but that is the extent of the glamor. For every overpaid pro in center field's sunshine there are thousands of would-be Reggie Jacksons on college campuses, on Little League fields, and on neighborhood softball diamonds. That is where the real market is. In 1982, the estimated 30 million softball players in the United States bought roughly 12 million balls. Nearly 5 million bats (for both baseball and softball) were bought the same year. So the salesman will drive, and he will talk with coaches and athletic directors, park and recreation officials, and every player he can find.

"We're a small company," marketing manager Ted Savage insists. "We can't afford a huge advertising budget—the dollars just aren't there. So we had to become backwoods evangelists instead."

The technique may be old-fashioned, but it fills the company coffers. Last year Worth had more than $30 million in sales, up from $4 million—about 650 percent—in just over a decade. Ten years ago Worth's main market was in low-grade baseballs, but that market disappeared. The baby-boom generation grew up, changing from Little League players to slow-pitch softball devotees, with dollars, not dimes, to spend for equipment. But Worth thrived, introducing new products for the newly quality-conscious consumer, products innovative enough to let Worth leapfrog such well-know competitors as Hillerich & Bradsby Company, the manufacturer of Louisville Slugger, and Dudley Sports Company.

The Worth salesmen may travel like itinerant preachers, but they carry Space Age sporting goods in their vans: swing-weighted aluminum alloy bats and patented Poly-X softballs. John Parish knew that Worth could never compete with Louisville Slugger bats and Dudley softballs at their own game. So he changed the way the game is played.

Tullahoma, Tennessee, halfway between Nashville and Chattanooga, is hardly your typical sleepy southern hamlet. You can still buy overalls in the Dollar General Store and savor hickory-smoked ribs at Piggy's Place Pit Bar-B-Que over by the Church of Christ, but the tract houses, Taco Bells, and shopping malls of today have grown up around the core of the old town. The Arnold Engineering Development Center, an Air Force research and development facility, employs nearly one-third of the town's 15,000 people. That craggy-faced man in the Caterpillar hat, driving the Jeep down Jackson Street, is more likely to be a Ph.D. engineer than a dirt farmer.

Lannom Manufacturing Company, Worth's corporate parent, has grown in much the same way as the town, grafting the new to the traditional for three generations. In 1912, when George S. Lannom bought the tannery that still stands, ramshackle and redolent, on Rock Creek near the center of town, his goal was never simply to sell leather. The tannery was to be his supplier, first for the manufacture of horse collars, then, when the automobile killed that market, for the baseball manufacturing facility he set up in 1919 on the second floor of a Tullahoma drugstore. He believed in vertical integration—raw materials from the tannery and the mill, a manufacturing facility, and a strong sales force. Eventually Lannom would expand into gloves and shoes to maximize use of the tannery, and he would buy a wool mill to produce the baseball windings. While the glove and shoe line have been sold, the concept remains. The tannery still operates, and the company has added two sawmills to provide wood for the bat division. The development of new product lines—the sport bag developed eight years ago, for example—builds on this supply and manufacturing strength.

John Parish—president of Lannom Manufacturing, who has temporarily stepped aside as chief executive officer to work as Commissioner for Economic and Community Development for the state of Tennessee—has kept many of Lannom's old-fashioned values. The company has stayed family-owned, governed with a stern financial hand. Parish preserved the vertical integration that was his grandfather's creed and the aggressive salesmanship that was his father's faith. But he added his own belief in the blessings of R&D.

Chuck Parish—later to be George Lannom's son-in-law, John Parish's father, and the CEO and owner of Lannom Manufacturing—brought his own changes to the company after he arrived in 1930. Parish was an old-fashioned salesman. Known in the trade as "the baron of baseballs," his sales technique would boost sales tenfold. "He'd sell a baseball by bouncing it, by cutting it open, by getting up on his soapbox," his son says. But he attacked new markets as well. "Before Chuck came we'd been selling to small sporting goods retailers," Jess Heald, Worth's president, says. "Chuck got us into the major retail chains—Sears, Penney's, and Montgomery Ward—which generated high volume and significant sales growth." To provide product at low cost, Parish became one of the first U.S. executives to manufacture offshore, setting up ball-sewing facilities in the Caribbean. To keep sales high, he insisted that company salesmen carry Worth products exclusively, rather than represent a variety of product lines, something unusual for a company so small. Worth employs its own sales staff, and products are still made in both Tullahoma and the Caribbean.

Young John Parish joined Lannom Manufacturing in 1959, after graduating from Vanderbilt University, and spent his first three years overseeing the company's Caribbean facilities. When he came back home, however, he was eager to put his own imprint on Worth. "I went on the road selling, and I could see new trends emerging," Parish remembers. "We were primarily a manufacturer of junk baseballs for the carnival and domestic trade. We'd always sold price, not quality or service, things consumers were starting to want. Sporting goods was becoming a big business. Our company was built on good foundations—our small aggressive sales force, for example. But a few good salesmen weren't enough anymore. We needed sales technique. Then, to compete into the nineteen seventies, eighties, and nineties, we needed product innovation along with vertical integration—and the marketing to go with it."

Conflict was inevitable. Chuck Parish's management style was as old-fashioned as his salesmanship. He kept the books in his head and monitored inventory from clipboards hung behind his desk. John Parish wanted to introduce more modern techniques. Chuck Parish wanted to keep the company small. "I hope we never grow bigger than a million," Heald remembers him saying. John wanted to see the company grow. "We'd usually end up hollering at one another," John remembers. But young Parish persevered, and, in 1969, his father finally agreed "to let a young buck try his wings," seeding him $50,000 for a foray into bat manufacturing.

It was a fortuitous time to venture into the bat business. In 1969, production of Louisville Slugger, the brand leader, had dropped because of labor troubles, so there was a market demand that wasn't being met. Adirondack Industries Inc., the number two manufacturer, had just been purchased by a conglomerate, so Parish was able to persuade Frederick Juer, Adirondack's former president, to join the Worth team, where today he is president of Worth Bat Company, a Lannom subsidiary. More important, however, 1969 marked the introduction of the first primitive aluminum bat, developed by a Pittsburgh inventor, and the approval of the aluminum bat by the Amateur Softball Association of America. Parish recognized that he couldn't compete over the long run with the brand identification built up by the Louisville Slugger, but aluminum was a whole new ball game. "All the other bat companies were resisting it," he says. "But given our situation it was obvious we had to be innovators in something." So back he went to his father. After all, he said, we are already in the bat business.

Enter Jess Heald. John Parish and Heald had met through their local church, where Heald, a United States Naval Academy graduate with a master's degree in aerospace engineering, then working at Arnold Engineering, had volunteered to help Parish run a local Boy Scout troop. "John knew I had done some metal and structural work in the aerospace industry," Heald says. "So he asked me to do a little analysis as a consultant on the prospect of making a bat from an aluminum tube."

Although Heald was "unimpressed" by the original aluminum bat, the study convinced him that the technology was available to produce a bat that was "far superior" to any product then on the market. The original had a wood knob handle, likely to shear off under stress; Heald recommended a welded metal knob. The original had a rubber plug at the hitting end; Heald suggested a single-piece construction. The original came in just one size, "kid's size," he called it. By using different forming equipment and stronger alloys, Heald said, it would be possible to provide the variety of handle and barrel sizes the market demanded. "I decided that aluminum bats would be worth the risk," Heald says. "Then I outlined a way to get into it with a minimal investment. John turned around to me and said, 'Okay, but you'll have to do it.'"

Worth's start-up was cautious—an initial investment of some $20,000, with most of the manufacturing subcontracted in order to avoid premature capital expenditure while Heald perfected the design. At the end of the first year, convinced that the bat had exceptional promise, Heald recommended a major five-year development program, an investment he was sure would give Worth a tremendous advantage over the traditional manufacturers of wood bats.

The gamble paid off. "We became the first company to make wood softball and baseball bats and aluminum softball bats," John Parish says. "We went from less than four million dollars in sales in 1971 to over six million in 1972. We grabbed fifty percent of the aluminum-bat market almost immediately."

Chuck Parish sniped from the sidelines—and sold bats. His rapport with the mass marketers permitted his son to find immediate volume markets and record a profit for the overall bat line in the first year. "He referred to us as 'the Young Turks,'" Heald remembers. "But we would never have been able to expand into the bat business without his strong endorsement. He would never have made the move himself, but he was backing his son, whom he very much wanted to see take over the business."

While Chuck Parish was selling bats, John Parish and Jess Heald were refining the product. Besides gradually introducing the innovations recommended in his initial study, Heald made further changes in the Worth bat. "We weighted the heavy end for extra power for the slow-pitch softball game. And this made us even more competitive against wood bats," explains Heald. "The traditional wood bats were lighter, and not as effective in the slow-pitch game. We kept waiting for the traditional manufacturers to follow us—but they didn't." To compound Worth's success, the National Collegiate Athletic Association approved aluminum bats for college baseball starting with the 1974 season. "Louisville Slugger was already back in the wood-bat market in force. So we needed an edge again—and this gave it to us. We rode that crest for another four years."

Metal bats now account for an estimated two-thirds of the total bat market. Worth claims an estimated 20 percent of the total bat market. The company refuses to disclose a more exact breakdown of sales or market share per bat type. In any case, Heald argues, the company's early entry and continued innovation have given it a strong product identification. "Having a product name where you're first in your field means you'll be the one people ask for, regardless of how many other products like yours come into the market. For us, it's almost like a patent."

The death of Chuck Parish in 1975 left his son in control of the company, free to modernize management and to pursue further growth. "We took stock of our situation then," Heald remembers. "We asked ourselves what we had done to be successful so far. And it finally came to us: When we came out with aluminum bats, we surprised our competition by changing the rules of the game."

Market research pointed the way to the next move, into top-line softballs. "We had eighty percent of the low-end ball market," Heald says, "but we could see that that market was going to come down." The slow-pitch market, on the other hand, was flowering. Players were willing to spend top dollar for a top-quality product, a product that offered a baseball with a healthier profit margin.

The problem, as it had been with wood bats, was that another company already dominated the market. Traditionally, softballs had been filled with kapok. But slow-pitch is a hitter's game, and a kapok ball could rarely last a full seven innings. So Dudley had introduced a cork-core ball—harder, livelier, and more durable—and captured a 50 percent market share. Worth also had a cork ball, "but Dudley had gotten too far ahead," Heald says. "Even when our product was as good we couldn't sell it. Their brand identification was just too strong. So I realized I'd have to do exactly what Dudley had done. I'd have to find a new material, something that would make a better ball than cork."

The answer was polyurethane foam. Heald was familiar with the material from its use as an aerospace insulator. Not only was it hard and impact-resistant, but since it would rise and harden on exposure to air, Worth could avoid costly injection molding. Worth first began selling the Poly-X polyurethane-core ball in 1975, and a patent was granted in 1976. Heald kept working on new compounds. "By 1978, I knew I had a winner—it was harder, livelier, and more durable than cork. So we became very aggressive in our marketing," he says. "We've ridden that crest ever since, selling every ball we can make. In 1983, I expect we'll have some forty percent of the market—or even more."

Even while developing its new softball, Worth continued its bat research. Having changed the product, Worth next changed the way consumers thought about the product, introducing innovations in marketing to parallel the innovations in design. In 1979, the company began marking its bats with Swing Weight, a measure of the weight at the point of impact with the ball. Top-line golf clubs have always been sold with a comparable measure, but Worth, currently selling bats in ten different Swing Weights, was the first to bring the concept to the softball diamond.

In 1982, the company followed with Swing Ray, a laser timing device to record a player's bat speed. "I'd always dreamed of an instrument that could help a player find the bat that would give him the most power," Heald explains. "It's a nice engineering problem. How much power you have when you hit the ball means how much bat weight you're swinging and how fast you're swinging it. But no one ever knew the trade-off between bat speed and bat weight.

"So for every player there exists an optimum bat. The perfect bat." The Swing Ray let Worth help players find that perfect bat.

So far the Swing Ray has been primarily a research and promotional tool. Last spring, for example, a Worth van carried the prototype, a cumbersome thing, through eight major league training camps, generating newspaper stories and an appearance on NBC-TV's "Today" show (see box, pages 71–72). This spring, however, the company will take a simplified version on the road, to set up at sporting goods stores and softball tournaments each weekend.

"Grass-roots promotion is the key to our success," insists sales manager Doug Bennett. "A retailer doesn't want to have to spend the time convincing people a certain bat or ball is best. He'll only handle a line if the customers ask for it."

"There are guys that play softball tournaments every weekend from the first of April to the end of August," marketing manager Savage says. "And guys that spend every weekend playing softball don't read a lot. They don't have the time. You can't get through to them with printed material, long detailed explanations of what makes Worth better. You've got to go talk to them one on one."

To make sure its salesmen can carry their end of the conversation, Worth insists that its promotion and sales staff be softball experts before they take to the road. Each salesman must spend time working in every step in the manufacturing process, right down to hand-stitching ball covers. "That way they know what's involved in making the product," Bennett says. "So they end up knowing more about balls and bats than any of their competitors."

"First of all you hit the parks and recreation departments," explains salesman Mike Cunningham. "They're the ones that buy the bulk of the softballs. You take a ball in and explain that it will save money because they can use that one ball over and over again.

"Once you sell them, you go to the sporting goods stores. Then you go talk to the players, to create the demand. You put a ball in their hands and let them beat it up. Once you get them to hit the ball—boom. You've got 'em."

It is the kind of salesmanship that Chuck Parish excelled in, personal and substantial. And it works. "The leagues and college teams call us now," says Heald. "They want to win and they know we can help."

Making baseballs, softballs, and bats is still a handicraft industry, much as it was in the days of George Lannom, although the company can now turn out 20,000 balls and 5,000 bats a day. Inside the aging ball factory, recently refronted in brick, countless cartons of fresh softballs share floor space with modern polyurethane molds. But there are no machines to replace long-time employees like Doris Phillips, an eighteen-year veteran still hand-packing some 600 dozen balls each day, or gray-haired Stella McEwin, one of Worth's eighty-five ball stitchers, who laboriously hand-sews the eighty-eight cross-stitches in the hand-cut and hand-graded leather cover of Worth's patented softball. "I've been sewing balls for nearly forty years," she says. "My mother used to sew, and my daughters still do—it's kind of handed down from generation to generation."

Over the past three generations, Worth, too, has built on its past. Vertical integration has given the company exceptional flexibility to attack new markets. Eight years ago, for example, Worth test-marketed leather sports bags stitched at the company plant with leather from the tannery. Today most of the bags are made from vinyl and nylon, some with leather handgrips. But Suzy Heald, general manager of the accessories division and Jess Heald's wife, reports that her division has nearly doubled sales annually for the past five years. More new products will be developed in the same way—probably something that can be stitched, Heald hints, or perhaps wood and leather furniture—then sold with Worth's traditional aggressive marketing.

Worth's growth plan remains conservative. "We've always spent our money circumspectly," Heald says. "We aren't high rollers, we want to make sure we have enough money to stay private." Growth planned for the future will be "a bootstrap operation" financed by cash flow.

Innovation, however, remains the key to the company's future. While ball division manager Charles Dale insists that his product is technically "about six years ahead of the nearest competitor," and while no one else yet markets bats with Swing Weight, Herald insists that Worth will make its way into the future through product innovation. R&D has been established as a corporate division in its own right, with a budget of roughly 0.5 percent of sales. "We've got some things on the drawing board that might well usher in another new era," Heald promises. "I don't want to let any secrets out, but we're looking closely at weight concentration—the sweet spot that is the batter's target area."

After all, innovation has kept the company alive. "There used to be a tremendous market for low-price softballs and baseballs," Heald says. "But that market doesn't exist today.

"But when we went into the bat business, we actually went into new markets as well. You can't make just low-grade bats like you can balls. When you cut a tree it yields twenty percent top-grade wood, and you've got to sell it. So if you're going to sell bats you've got to compete across the spectrum. And aluminum bats are all top grade. So by going into bats we thrust ourselves into top-grade sporting goods, where the company had never been before.

"We look back now at the low-end ball market and think, Wow. If we'd stayed there the company would have been in serious trouble."

MAJOR LEAGUES—MINOR MARKETS

It was the high point of Worth Sports Company's spring tour: Bryant Gumbel, of NBC-TV's "Today" show, resplendent in the inevitable navy blazer and gray flannel slacks, interviewing Jess Heald, on the sidelines of the Yankees spring training camp in Fort Lauderdale, Florida, about the Swing Ray. "It won't sell bats to the major leaguers," Heald acknowledged later. "By the time they reach that level of play they know what is the best bat for them." But for the millions of Americans watching the "Today" show it was another indication of the exciting research that Worth Sports Company puts into its bats. And that promotional value—more than product sold—is the point of sending the Worth van to visit the major league camps.

For the past three seasons, Worth vans have made a limited foray into the world of professional baseball. "It's no problem getting major leaguers to use the product," bat division manager Frederick Juer says. "They need good wood, and since the wood-bat business is only half of what it used to be, less timber is being cut. So there is a scarcity of major league timber." Worth currently supplies some bats to twenty to thirty players, including the Philadelphia Phillies' Mike Schmidt and the Detroit Tigers' Lance Parrish, who last year set a home-run record for catchers. Unlike other bat manufacturers, however, Worth hasn't tried to get players to sign contracts or endorse bats with an autograph. "The cost is unreasonable," Juer explains. "And historically a player will use what he likes and advertise what he's paid to advertise."

"You can't get excited over spending a lot of promotional dollars for professional baseball, because of the limited value of what it can do for you," Heald agrees, although he acknowledges the promotional boost of the "Today" show story on the Swing Ray. "And the amount of goods we're able to sell pretty much offsets the costs."

Besides bats, those goods include pitching machines and junk baseballs for "ball days," the junk baseballs with which Chuck Parish once built the company.

—CURTIS HARTMAN

JUST A POOR, DUMB DIRT FARMER

The Colonel—that's Colonel S. Stone Gregory, Jr., owner of Gregory General Farms—feels something close to loathing for the Internal Revenue agents who visit periodically after he's been written up in a newspaper or magazine. That's why he'll only say that Gregory General Farms sells a "nice seven figures" annually. He insists that the lessons he has to offer don't come from how much he sells, but rather from how he sells. "I've got no staff," he says. "There's just me, Stone Gregory, a poor, dumb dirt farmer."

Truth is, Colonel Gregory is neither poor nor dumb. The Colonel and his two brothers do own a lot of dirt in Java in Virginia's Pittsylvania County, 125 miles west of Richmond. But the Colonel doesn't so much farm it as he does promote its natural bounty, bit by bit, piece by piece, and drop by drop.

There's Gregory's White Hickory Smoke Bits, Incense Cedar Bits, Sassafras Root Bits, Combination Manure-Mulch-Compost-Peat, Creosoted Posts and Poles, and Virgin Spring Water. There's the Gregory General Store and, just down the road, Gregory's Hog Hotel, where some 1,200 Yorkshire hogs fatten for market while producing Gregory's Virgin Hog Crap, billed as Nature's Perfect Plant Food. "With the proper romancin' and merchandisin'," the Colonel says, "you can sell anything."

The Colonel just isn't the hard-scrabbling clod-busting dirt farmer he makes himself out to be. He's more an idea man, a born promoter with a dirt-farming background. It's a background that drives him to get the most out of what's available. He finds markets in industry directories and telephone books; he writes his own sales brochures, designs his own ads, and types his own letters. He pays his bills by return mail, goes to bed at nine, and sleeps very soundly.

The Colonel will argue all day that any business can be run his way. If it's not, it should be, especially when interest rates are going up and money's tight and every little bit counts.

"All you need is a little common sense and ingenuity and internal ability," he says. "If you want to find a good idea, get out there and talk to people and listen. I never met a man I couldn't learn something from. Pretty soon you'll spot a need, and then you keep thinking until you find a way to fill it. Maybe it's a crude operation, but I want to keep things simple."

Outwardly, everything about the Colonel is simple. "A smart man doesn't put everything in the showroom window," he says. "He also keeps the warehouse full."

He wears baggy corduroy trousers, a brown, short-sleeved work shirt, and a khaki hat darkened with sweat around the brim. He's sixty-three years old and rises six feet six inches off the floorboards in an impressively straight line, looking slightly faded but dependable and sturdy.

His office is a small rectangular room attached to the Gregory General Store. The store was opened by his father in 1900 and has changed very little. It's a shuffling, friendly collection of freshly painted white clapboard with a long shade roof across the front and narrow double doors. Just inside the door is a handmade wooden counter with Ball jars on it filled with seed: Heart of Gold Cantaloupe, 95¢ an ounce; or Seven Top Turnip, 60¢ an ounce. Another big seller is Big Duke Chewing Tobacco, and there are Wolverine work boots and meats and groceries. A sign says, "Everything for everybody."

The Colonel works at a small gray metal desk. There's a typewriter on the desk, but the phone, an old, black finger-dialer, is hidden in the second drawer. The walls of his office are papered with hundreds of yellowing business cards, and stacked near the window are 400 new telephone directories.

Outside his office, the early corn is already four inches high. Gregory farmland ripples slowly toward the horizon in every direction. The Colonel's two sons, "the hardest-working two young men in Virginia," John and Stone III, are in fields nearby, tilling and fertilizing. His brothers, Jim and Lewis, are working with their boys, planting tobacco a mile or so away.

Lewis Gregory, the Colonel's great-great-great-grandfather, first planted family roots here in 1840. "He came from Scotland," the Colonel says. "We think he was about to be hanged for stealing horses or mules—anyway he was stealing something." All Lewis had with him, the story goes, was an oak barrel holding his worldly possessions. But there must have been a little extra sandwiched between the pots and pans, because Lewis soon bought 200 acres of fertile Virginia farmland and began the endless round of tilling, planting, harvesting, and adding a few more acres every now and then that has occupied six generations of Gregorys.

According to Gregory custom, the Colonel was given responsibility early. He pulled his first commercial tobacco crop when he was only twelve. The original receipt—for $48.80—from Planters Warehouse in Danville, Virginia, dated January 27, 1930, hangs on his office wall. That was his first encounter with the tough economics of farming. "Even then it didn't seem like much money for all the work," the Colonel recalls, "particularly when I had to take out the twenty-five dollars I owed for fertilizer. What's more, I couldn't help worrying about what would happen to me if my crop failed after I'd spent the money for fertilizer." He says this experience taught him to avoid products whose sale price he couldn't control and "never to put all my eggs in one basket."

It was during World War II that the Colonel spotted the need that would later launch him into business. He was twenty-four years old, a freshly minted colonel in the U.S. Army's armored artillery serving in the North African invasion force. In November of 1942, he was talking with two Egyptian Army officers over dinner at Shepheard's Hotel in Cairo. The Egyptian officers were reminiscing about visits to the United States. They told the Colonel that one of the experiences they had never been able to duplicate was the gastronomical delight of a Virginia ham. How was the unique flavor achieved? they asked. The Colonel explained that the hams were cured in the smoke of smoldering white hickory. "It's the smoking, not the heating," he said, "that's the secret."

In January 1947, the Colonel retired from the regular army with fourteen American and foreign decorations. He was twenty-nine when he returned to the Gregory farms. A long line of his forebears had been content to work the land and they had prospered, but the Colonel already had a different approach to prosperity. He wanted to develop products that, unlike wheat, rye, and barley, would be free from the pricing constraints of agricultural commodity markets.

One afternoon, on a tour of the Gregory reserve, he found himself studying acre after acre of flourishing white hickory trees and thinking about a dinner conversation in Cairo five years earlier. He cut down a tree, sawed it, and chipped it into small bits. Then he sent a generous sample to the two Egyptian officers, telling them that more was available at a modest price. Some time later, they sent him his first order for $28 worth of white hickory smoke bits.

"I knew there was a need for it," the Colonel says, "and I knew the market was a lot bigger than two friends in Egypt, if only I could let the right people know."

The Colonel drew heavily on his dirt-farming self-reliance and set to work concocting the right blend of "romancin' and merchandisin'." He sent for a variety of industry directories published by trade associations, private companies, and the federal government. Before long he had a list of meat packers, sausage smokers, food processors, charcoal manufacturers, and many others who could be potential users of white hickory smoke bits. "You'd be surprised how much information is available for free if you take the time to look," he says.

The Colonel's wife, Helen, describes what happened next: "One afternoon, Stone came home with a big sack of hickory bits. At the time, we had three children and they were still pretty young. Stone sat them down at a table in front of the television and told them to fill these little cellophane envelopes with hickory bits, put on his business card, and then staple the two together. It was a regular production line. I can still see the kids sitting there with their feet dangling off the floor and their heads barely poking over the tabletop."

The Colonel took his samples back to the office, hired a part-time assistant, and spent the next two weeks organizing his customer lists and mailing 2,000 letters with samples to the president of each company. "I only deal with the top man," he says. "Life's too short for anything less."

In the same letter promoting the unparalleled excellence of Gregory's white hickory smoke bits, the Colonel also asked for some advice. He wanted to develop a company logo, something that would give his products a little color, a little romance. "I felt there were two things most people think of when they think of a Southern farm," he says. "One's a Kentucky colonel with a wide hat, mustache, goatee, and a string tie. The other's a mule. But I couldn't decide what to use, so I asked these presidents which one they liked. Why should I pay some consulting firm to ask for me?"

It must have been one of the more unusual letters a company president ever received. But its combination of gritty determination and old-fashioned honesty did the job. The Kentucky colonel image was elected unanimously, and ever since, the smiling Southern gentleman has graced all of Colonel Gregory's sales literature and letterheads.

Along with the ballots came more than a hundred orders for bits. The Colonel hastily constructed a wood processing and storage shed and built his own hickory chipper from old saw blades and other spare parts lying around the farm. The facility was completed just in time to show visiting customers and to produce enough bits to meet the first shipment dates.

Five years after he shipped those first orders, the Colonel estimates that he was chipping his way to annual sales of between $50,000 and $70,000. To his way of thinking, this wasn't a bad return at all, because his homemade brand of market research, advertising, and promotion only cost him about $3,000. "Sales have been growing ever since," he said. "Now it's a nice six figures."

Based on the success of the White Hickory Smoke Bits, the Colonel fashioned a highly personalized business strategy that he has repeated time and again. Its motivating idea is the complete confidence in his own abilities, and its chief characteristics are his determination to do as much as he can by himself, to extract the greatest benefit from what is at hand, and to offer honest value—no gimcracks, gewgaws, or modern flapdoodle.

He also matches the bluntness of his marketing with an equally straightforward billing system. His terms on any product he handles are 2/10/net 30 and no volume discounts. If a customer doesn't pay in thirty days, the Colonel calls him collect every day until he does and then kisses him goodbye. "I can have a past due account," he says, "but only once. Everybody gets one chance. If you go back on your word, that's it. Life's too short. Remember, you haven't accomplished a thing until you have a check in your hand—a good check."

In 1953, five years after introduction of hickory bits, the Colonel tried his hand at diversification and got burned. It started on a rainy Saturday afternoon. The Colonel was working at his desk when a man stepped into his office and announced himself as one A. S. McQueen of Johnston City, Tennessee, inventor of a revolutionary tobacco curer. Most Virginia-grown tobacco is heat-cured for five days in smokehouses. McQueen said that his curer burned sawdust only and could save farmers a lot of money in fuel costs. He said he needed $500 to have a prototype built, but no one would give him the money. The Colonel agreed to finance the prototype. "A month later," he says, "McQueen showed up with his contraption stuffed into the backseat of his old Hudson and tied onto the roof. We wrestled it out and fired it up. It worked fine."

The Colonel ordered a hundred more and the two men drew up a handbill that looked like a wanted poster for a member of the James Gang and started hawking the curers, which sold quickly. The Colonel, sensing something big, ordered 800 more. Then he made what he considers a fatal mistake; he hired an MBA, newly graduated from a well-known Southern university, to market the new curers. "I don't know what came over me," the Colonel says. "Farmers want to see things in operation, but this guy never wanted to leave his office in Richmond. One day I just got fed up. I called him and told him to get his butt out in the field. And the next day his wife called me and said she didn't want her husband doing any manual labor. I reminded her that I hadn't hired her, and then I fired her husband."

But it was too late. The sales campaign never regained its momentum. The Colonel still owns 732 revolutionary tobacco curers. "I lost sixty thousand dollars on that one," he says, "but I haven't given up yet. With the price of every other fuel going up, sawdust is looking better all the time."

After the curer fiasco, the Colonel quickly returned to his do-it-yourself brand of romancing and merchandising and scored a big hit with Gregory's Virgin Spring Water. He knew there was a need for the stuff, because as he traveled to trade shows in various cities, he often found that he couldn't drink the local water. Instead, he filled Thermos jugs with spring water and took them along on his trips. "I ask you," he says, "what would you rather drink: recycled sewerage or my Virgin Spring Water?" So back he went to his dog-eared directories and telephone books, this time looking for private-label bottlers with established distribution networks. He sent out his letters, distributed his samples, and took visiting customers home for dinner. As a result, the Colonel's elixir is now sold to bottlers in twelve eastern states.

The Colonel added another winner in the early seventies when he introduced Gregory's Incense Cedar Bits. These flakes are made from the stems of a highly aromatic species of cedar tree that grows naturally on Gregory land. The Colonel always knew they were there, but it wasn't until he started running the Gregory General Store that he discovered there might be commercial use for the fragrant stems.

As part of his "everything for everybody" policy at the store, the

Colonel used to sell handmade pine coffins at $49.50 each to local tenant farmers and personally deliver them to their homes. Usually, when he arrived, the traditional "sit-up" was already well under way. A "sit-up," the Colonel explains, is a funeral observation, something like a wake, that was peculiar to tenant farmers in the area. It could last a week or more, the Colonel says, because it took that long for all the family's friends and relatives to arrive from distant farms. The Colonel often saw large bundles of cedar stems smoking in the family's yard. When he asked what they were used for, he was told that they were a kind of ceremonial incense long known to ward off evil spirits.

"The custom died out in the late forties," the Colonel says, "but those cedar stems stuck in my mind. When I bought the big chipper, I knew that I could process them just like Hickory Bits."

Today the fragrant chips are sold to chemical and pharmaceutical companies for use in a number of products, including deodorizers, detergents, and cosmetics.

Even though the Colonel has become increasingly proficient over the years in spotting and filling needs, occasionally he still hits a snag. Recently he ran into some unexpected marketing difficulties with his Virgin Hog Crap. The Colonel first used this fertilizing miracle on his own lawn. He thought it was great stuff and convinced some golf course and park groundskeepers to try it on their green sward. The grass loved it. Unfortunately, for two or three days after application, there was this disturbing odor in the air, which greatly offended local authorities.

The Colonel had even gone so far as to send out his habitual promotion letter to several lawn and garden centers. One owner of a New Jersey store, he relates incredulously, actually called him up and asked how the powerful fertilizer was made. But the Colonel remains convinced of his product's merit and thinks that he may have solved his marketing problem. "I've come up with a way to deodorize the stuff," he says, "using dolomitic limestone and a couple of secret ingredients that I can't describe because my competition will no doubt capitalize on it."

When asked if he thought his product's slightly indelicate name might be a drag on sales, the Colonel said he saw it as a personal challenge. "Anyone can sell manure," he says, "but how many people can merchandise crap?"

That's Colonel S. Stone Gregory, Jr.—maybe the last of his kind, maybe the only one of his kind. He says that right now he has five or six new product ideas, and he points to the stack of new telephone directories as proof of his claim. Then he leans back in his swivel chair and sighs, "But I'm still just a poor, dumb dirt farmer trying to keep his head above the waterline."

You be the judge.

—LUCIEN RHODES

PUTTING THE CUSTOMER IN THE DRIVER'S SEAT

Not so many years ago, when cheap oil flowed from Texas wells and good citizens worshipped their sleek V-8s, there were 48,000 automobile dealers in America. Now, when the Shatt al-Arab waterway is our tenuous gas tap, and prudent consumers value a high m.p.g. rating more than a fast four-on-the-floor, there are a little more than half as many. From 1980 to 1982 alone, some 3,400 dealers went out of business.

The reasons for this exodus vary. Some franchises disappeared as part of a natural evolution toward fewer but larger dealerships. Others, unable to keep pace with changing tastes and the growing popularity of imports, were victims of a market that in recent years has been as treacherous as a locked differential. Still others fell prey to the recession.

And some, it must be said, were done in by the automobile dealer's traditionally cavalier attitude toward the customer—an attitude rooted in righteous belief in both Detroit's invincibility and their own.

"For years we were taught that we could do no wrong," explains Robert P. Mancuso, president of Mancuso Cadillac-Honda Inc., a $15-million-a-year dealership in Barrington, Illinois, not far from Chicago. "I remember having a violent discussion with my father, a thirty-year Chevrolet dealer. I was working in his service department, and I told him I was embarrassed because we'd just had to tow in a car that had been in for a tune-up the week before.

" 'What are you embarrassed about?' he asked me.

" 'Well, the guy spent eighty-five dollars here, and now his car won't start. You know, we screwed up.'

" '*We* don't screw up,' he informed in no uncertain terms."

In the automotive landscape of the 1980s, the experts agree, such an attitude makes little sense. "Better service for the customer is undoubtedly the name of the new game," notes Carver Hendrix, Chicago zone manager for Cadillac Motor Car Division. "Dealers are going to have to get a lot better at managing their businesses," adds Robert Daly, executive director of communications and industry relations for the National Automobile Dealers Association.

These are lessons that Rob Mancuso, thirty-three, has already learned—the hard way. "When everyone was making so much money, there was no need to innovate, to manage your dealership better," he observes. "The best thing that ever happened to me was learning how to run a business without cash." His dealership, one of twelve in Barrington, was founded in 1974, a scant five months after the first Arab oil embargo. Since then, it has bumped along from one disaster to another.

All the hardships have left Mancuso with a rule of business so simple that he smiles as he says it: "Make the customer happy." But what sounds trite as a maxim is in practice a sophisticated sales strategy that has helped him maneuver his dealership through obstacle after obstacle. So compelling is the strategy, in fact, that Mancuso has begun to package parts of it for sale. And other dealers, some of his competitors among them, have lined up to buy it.

Mancuso is a fourth-generation automobile dealer. His great-grandfather, Charles, began selling Studebaker Series-18s more than sixty years ago, and until recently his father, Jim, owned a Chevrolet dealership in nearby Skokie. But Rob is hardly an offspring of the old school. A 1973 graduate of Princeton University, he dresses in three-piece suits and exudes the lean glow of a vegetarian and veteran marathon runner (he placed number 1,557 among 3,624 in Chicago's 1980 marathon). And in a business known for its back-slapping camaraderie, he favors the soft sell of an Alan Alda, whom he somewhat resembles. His office, like his showroom, is chicly efficient: an Apple Macintosh on one corner of his desk, a photo of the Porsche 928-S he is buying thumbtacked to the wall behind, bottles of wine stored in the adjoining bathroom. As he tells his story, he gestures airily, impersonating the people he describes, and the conversation takes the form of a series of acted-out anecdotes. Sales, he admits, was always his forte.

Fresh out of Princeton, Mancuso became sales manager of his father's Skokie dealership, where his older brother, Rick, was minding the store. It was a case, he recalls, of three "aggressive, individual, and stubborn" men locked in good-natured combat. "After that argument with my father—the only one we ever had—I began to think that maybe I did have a different attitude about this business." In 1974, when a Cadillac dealership became available in Barrington, a horsey suburban "village" of 9,000 residents with a median income of more than $50,000, Rob set out to get it. Jim Mancuso financed the deal for his younger son, with the understanding that the new grad would buy out dad at the end of five years.

"On April 22, the day we signed the agreement," says Mancuso, "my father pulled up out front, threw me the keys, shouted, 'Good luck,' and drove off."

It was a little bit like getting the keys to your family's old Edsel. Village Cadillac was a small, aging dealership ($4 million to $5 million in annual sales) with twenty-two older employees, no retail business to speak of, and a fleet business that the former owner had taken with him. And it was Doomsday: 1974, the year that new car sales would plummet from 11.4 million to 8.8 million units, largely because of the oil embargo. Cadillac, the most luxurious of the old-style land arks, virtually sank from sight. Unit sales dropped 65,716 in 1974, a 23 percent decline, contributing in a major way to General Motors Corporation's 3 percent loss of market share.

Mancuso, at twenty-three the youngest Cadillac dealer in the nation, felt his age acutely. "When I walked in, the employees looked at me as though I were from another planet," he says, conceding that they had legitimate cause for concern. "I knew just enough to be dangerous." The new dealership made money its first month. But it soon slipped into the red, quickly worked its way through $150,000 in certificates of deposit, and began bouncing checks.

"In all the years I'd been at my father's store I'd never heard the word *overdraft*," Mancuso admits. "I quickly learned how to turn frozen assets into liquid assets. We bailed out of used cars, sent new cars back to the factory, and cut back on parts to the point where, if a guy came in for a tune-up, we'd have to run down to K Mart for spark plugs."

These were desperate measures, and Mancuso knew it. Slowly, as though he were fashioning a dealership from scratch, he began to put together a new way of doing business. He moved to Barrington and joined the Rotary Club and the Chamber of Commerce. He fired his old salespeople and hired new ones. He also began a series of imaginative promotions: a coupon good for the use of a Seville for a day; catered new car introductions with salesmen dressed in tuxedos; copies of the *Wall Street Journal* with a special insert—a fake front page of the *Village* (Cadillac) *News*—handed out to Chicago-bound commuters each morning at the Barrington train station. "They loved it," Mancuso recalls. "That one sold forty-five automobiles."

Some of the changes were more radical than others.

"There was a belief in this business," says Mancuso, "that if a guy didn't buy his car from you, and he came in for warranty work, that you had the right to insult him, to abuse him, to toss him back out on the street. I was taught that by my father, and I used to do it. Then one day, I was out back in the shop, watching two mechanics twiddling their thumbs. I asked my service manager, 'How many warranty jobs came in today that we threw out?'

" 'Eight,' " Mancuso replies, acting out the shop manager's part in this little drama.

"Now, Cadillac pays for warranty work—we make money on it—and we could probably have sold some of these cars an oil change or other legitimate work that they needed. And I thought, 'Why am I doing this?' "

The result was fresh ads in the *Barrington Courier-Review:* "We want your warranty work. Trained technicians. Free loaners."

"All of a sudden, the place started filling up," says Mancuso. In the service department, which many dealers regard at best as a necessary evil, sales climbed from an average of between $30,000 and $40,000 to between $50,000 and $60,000 a month.

The dealership slowly edged its way back to profitability. Still, like the rest of the auto industry, it suffered from recession and lingering gas-shock until 1977. Then the economy began to recover, the oil embargo receded, and pent-up demand for large cars resurfaced. Encouraged by this market, Mancuso moved. The new quarters of Mancuso Cadillac, as he renamed his dealership, were a 20,000-square-foot facility of red brick and exposed wood beams on the crest of a country road connecting Barrington with I-90, Chicago, and the world beyond.

The move proved to be a disaster. It doubled Mancuso's monthly overhead, from $50,000 to $100,000, and it meant paying the higher cost of advertising in the Chicago metropolitan market. Customers hadn't yet discovered the new location, and Cadillac couldn't supply him with the new cars he wanted. In June, its first month there, the dealership once more fell into the red, losing $30,000. In July, it lost another $20,000. Mancuso tried every trick he knew. He plugged away with original ads ("Who's the young punk on TV selling Cadillacs?") and marketing ploys (a drawing for the free use of a Caddy for a year). He even resorted to such tried-and-true techniques as overloading the showroom with salesmen. "It works," he comments, a bit regretfully. "You throw enough guys out there, everybody begins to starve, and they start finding business . . . but it's blood and guts."

None of his maneuvers, however, worked well enough: For two years his losses continued. Then, sure enough, things got worse. "Each time it got bad, I thought that that was as bad as it was ever going to be," observes Mancuso, "but there was always worse times to come."

In 1979, after his two losing years, the planned buy-back from his father began, significantly increasing Mancuso's already onerous expenses. "The figure that we'd settled on," he explains, "was four hundred thousand dollars cash, but I was also paying my father a salary of more than fifty thousand dollars a year." Adding it all up, Mancuso calculated, it cost him something like $900,000 to get the business back.

A radical move, he decided, was definitely in order.

"In seventy-nine," he says, "I didn't know where this product [Cadillac] was going to go. It had its ups and downs. I couldn't bank on allocations, and the United Auto Workers had targeted GM for a strike that year. I'm thinking, My God, if supply is bad now, what happens when they go out on strike?" When Mancuso learned that a Honda franchise had become available for Barrington, it seemed the answer to his anxious prayer.

American Honda Motor Company had been in the United States since 1969, and by 1979 it had 740 dealers around the country, including 21 in the Chicago area. But not one of the 23 Cadillac dealers in the metropolitan Chicago market had dared to "dual" with a Japanese import; indeed, only one handled an import of any kind. Honda, Toyota, and Datsun were more than déclassé; they were an outright affront to Cadillac's image of itself as the standard of the world.

"I thought it might be a nice hedge," says Mancuso, with a sly smile. He put together an elaborate package—dealership history, sample ads, customer testimonials, proposed media plan—and flew off to Honda's U.S. headquarters in Moorestown, New Jersey. Two weeks later, the franchise was his.

"We were selling thirty to thirty-five new Cadillacs a month, and I figured we'd do ten to twelve Hondas," he recalls. "We did twenty-five in our first month, thirty the second, then thirty-five." Although Honda provided the insurance he needed, Mancuso is convinced that other Cadillac dealers regarded him as something of a turncoat. "Before, I was the new kid on the block. Afterwards, I was guilty of a little bit of treason." Today, more than half of the Cadillac dealers in Chicago "dual it." The largest, Mancuso jokes, has more Japanese lines than the Tokyo telephone exchange.

Positioning Mancuso Cadillac-Honda required some delicate shifts. "We had to walk a fine line," says Mancuso, "between that of a prestige operation . . . and getting down and dirty." Mancuso succeeded by treating both cars as class acts: The glistening white Honda Civic-S sits beside a regal black Cadillac Cimarron in his showroom, and the classic script of the Cadillac sign out front plays off a restrained but eye-catching orange Honda logo. Occasionally, though, the novelty—some would say the incongruity—slips through, as when Mancuso ran a two-for-one sale: Buy a Cadillac at list, get a Honda for free. The campaign attracted national attention and sold cars, but it raised eyebrows even at Honda headquarters. "The head of the company cornered me at a party," Mancuso recalls, "and told me, 'Don't you *ever* do that again.'"

Although Honda gave him a much-needed shot in the arm—and his active imagination continued to find new ploys like the two-for-one deal to tempt and satisfy customers—Mancuso still wasn't making it. Free rust-proofing, picnic lunches, and private sales could accomplish just so much, and extra advertising—a quick fix—was becoming an unconscionable expense. "I was operating under a discipline imposed by my financial condition—that of having no money." Mancuso laughs. And indeed, the bottom line remained intransigent. His business's continuing losses in 1979 and 1980 were the sorry legacy of the untimely buyout.

At that point, six years into his dealership, Mancuso reassessed his strategy. His fundamental concern, after all, was not simply promotion, but also giving customers what they wanted. And since he couldn't buy any more promotion anyway, he had better be sure he was meeting the needs of the customers he had.

Many dealers, he explains, keep rather informal records of their traffic, often estimating what percentage of their "ups," or potential buyers, they sell. Industrywide, this closing ratio averages from 14 percent to 18 percent. Mancuso wasn't sure of his. So he hired a greeter to welcome arrivals, see that they were taken care of, and record the eventual outcome. His goal was simple: "We had to get our slippage down."

To the same end, Mancuso began to make regular use of "shoppers"—counterfeit customers who come in to look at a car, then report back to him on how they were treated. He discovered that there was considerable room for improvement and that a host of small details, all of them having to do with customer satisfaction, were holding back sales.

It is not his favorite anecdote, but it makes his point. "The very first time I did it," Mancuso recalls, "after I'd had the shopper fill out a questionnaire. I asked him, 'Did you notice anything in particular about the salesman?' And this guy says, 'His breath—his breath smelled like death; I wouldn't have bought a car from him if it was free.'

"It was something that we'd all noticed about this salesman, but we'd never considered that a customer might. And I thought, 'What have we found out here? What has this cost this guy? What has this cost the dealership?' "

The problem was solved with a 69¢ bottle of Binaca, and the close ratio inched up.

Shopping, Mancuso explains, has been around in a variety of guises for more than fifty years. Automotive Profit Builders Company, a sales and management consulting service he uses, sends in shoppers when it first begins working with a dealership. Both Ford Motor Company and the Chevrolet Motor Division, General Motors Corporation use shoppers as well. But all of the programs, Mancuso felt, left something to be desired: They were expensive, sporadic, and generally geared to the manufacturer's rather than the dealer's needs. "I really didn't care whether a salesman told a customer about the Twilight Sentinel on the Cimarron," he explains. "I wanted to know what the customer thought about me, about my dealership."

As he developed his program, he learned more and more about these matters. Demonstration rides weren't being given. The quality of his service department wasn't being stressed. Cars weren't priced in accordance with his instructions. Gratified that he now knew enough to correct such situations, Mancuso decided to formalize his system—and to sell it.

The idea for selling the system came to him, oddly enough, on a beach in San Diego. "About two years ago, I wasn't too happy with the business—GMAC was pressuring me because of the financial condition of the dealership, and Honda, because I was selling so many of their cars, was pressuring me to put up a separate building." So he went on vacation, sat on the beach, and outlined a shopping service he called Consumer Concepts Ltd. Then, not one to procrastinate, he picked up a telephone and called Kent Allen, a dealer at Team Nissan-Datsun, in nearby Encinitas, California.

"Rob just showed up one day," recalls Team controller Edward Kaiser, "and told us what he was doing. We signed on the spot because it fit in so perfectly with our philosophy of customer treatment."

Under Mancuso's system, shoppers are recruited by Manpower Inc. and sent to visit the dealership twice a month. They then produce a computer-scored, 50-point questionnaire and a taped interview. The dealer pays $250 for each pair of visits and the information they generate.

"It's been incredibly helpful," says Allen, noting that Team now enjoys a close ratio of 46.7 percent, one of the highest in the nation. One of Team's first revelations, for example, was that customers had a hard time finding the dealership. "We had a nice, well-laid-out facility," explains Kaiser, "but even though we were next to the freeway, we were difficult to spot." Team responded with extra signs.

Since than, Consumer Concepts has signed up fifty independent dealers. Recently, it signed a pilot-program contract with Cadillac to shop fifty dealers in ten metropolitan areas. CC grossed $75,000 in 1983, will do $250,000 in 1984 (returning to break-even after absorbing significant start-up costs), and, as far as Mancuso can see, has a promising future. "I'll be talking to Honda next week, to Ford the week thereafter. . . ."

For Mancuso, CC is more than a sideline or a tool to use in his own dealership. It is the embodiment of his evolving philosophy. "Ninety percent of the dealers I know haven't really committed themselves to customer treatment," he says. "They all pay it lip service, but they beat up a guy when he comes in a day over warranty. And in the evenings, they congratulate themselves on how well they're doing.

"We're saying, 'Let's stop measuring the gains—they're already in the bank. Let's do something about the losses.' It's an entirely different approach."

While he developed Consumer Concepts, Mancuso continued to look for ways to pull in customers and satisfy existing ones: a "New Age Thinking" motivational program for employees; a free car wash with every service; a computer campaign that let customers price their own cars (that one, he says, was good for more than fifty sales); and undercover shoppers who not only continued to show up in the showroom but also ventured into the shop. "I found out what sort of efforts were being made to sell additional service," says Mancuso. After his service people were briefed, the average service sale went from 1.8 to 2.1 hours.

Thanks to such measures, Mancuso Cadillac-Honda nosed back into profitability in 1981, and remained there for the next two years. To be sure, pretax return was a matter of fractional percentage points. But the important thing was that the dealership was in gear, warming up and ready to go.

Finally, after nine years, all of the planning and market conditions came together. The economy improved, and the market for Cadillacs came back, eventually climbing to 300,337 units in 1983. Exactly one year ago, the buyout was concluded, and Mancuso's dealership took off.

Mancuso slides a Macintosh-generated chart—"Year to Date Comparisons"—across his desk. During the first two months of 1984, new car profit has increased by 189 percent, used car by 11,132 percent, service by 79 percent, parts and accessories by 3,250 percent. Overall dealership profit is up a remarkable 2,500 percent. The close ratio has risen to 32 percent, and Mancuso expects to earn a healthy 4 percent on sales this year. With an average daily balance of from $250,000 to $350,000 in the bank, Mancuso is using his working capital to build a separate building for Honda and to pursue a Porsche-Audi franchise.

"I'm beginning to enjoy this business for the very first time," he says. "Now that we're making real money, it's a lot easier to make more."

On the management side, ideas that in the past went begging for time or money are now being implemented: extra loaners, a greeter for the service department, ads that offer free car washes or oil changes, service writers in ties and jackets, extended hours, videotaped evaluations of salesmen's presentations. And there is renewed emphasis on innovative management—regular strategy meetings, department heads with virtual autonomy, "true turn" inventory figures from the parts department. "Management is the new growth area," observes Mancuso, echoing industry experts.

Although most of his fifty employees have gotten used to his brand of business as unusual—"I think they'd come in wearing shorts and tennis shoes if I asked them to"—old ways still die hard. "In the past, I'd warned my people never to sacrifice pennies," he explains, "and now that I want to *give away* money, they find it hard to adjust to."

Mancuso recently told his sales and service managers that they each had $500 to give away each month, but they didn't understand. So he acted out an explanation in the shop. "There was a customer there who had been coming in for years," he reconstructs. "'Ah, Mr. Abbate, how you doing?'

"'Just great.'

"'What are you in for?'

"'Grease, oil and filter, and rotate the tires.'

"'How much is the bill going to be?

"'About sixty-five dollars.'

"'Mr. Abbate, you've bought a lot of cars from us, and we love having you around. I'm going to pick up that bill.'

"'What do you mean? You're going to charge it?'

"'No, I'm going to pay it. Thanks for coming in.'"

The resulting goodwill, Mancuso explains, is something no advertising can buy. "We have one central operating philosophy now," he adds, "and that's to make the customer happy . . . right now."

THE DEALERSHIP BUSINESS

Automobile dealerships are rarely the money machines they are sometimes thought to be. Their profit margins are often so narrow, in fact, that some people have suggested labeling them auto supermarkets.

Like a supermarket, the typical dealership is a modest-size enterprise. In 1982, the most recent year for which complete National Automobile Dealers Association (NADA) figures are available, the average dealership had twenty-eight employees, total sales of $5.8 million, and a gross margin of $799,000 (13.9 percent of sales). Net pretax profit on average came to $74,820, or 1.3 percent of sales.

New-car sales accounted for 61.4 percent of the average dealership's revenues in 1982, and the average new car sold for $9,910. Used cars contributed 22.8 percent of total sales, while parts and service made up the remaining 15.8 percent. A dealership is relatively capital-intensive, with the typical dealer carrying a new car inventory worth close to $700,000. In 1982, March, May, and November were the peak selling months.

Although sales figures have risen fairly steadily since 1976 (1980 was the only year in which they actually fell), dealerships have experienced a significant drop in profitability over the years. Measured in constant 1967 dollars, for example, the average dealership netted $42,881 in 1976 and just $25,880 in 1982. Only recently, with the recession over, has the market snapped back. According to estimates, dealers are now seeing an average 2.2 percent return on sales. Most, moreover, seem to expect the good times to continue: In January of this year, NADA's "Optimism Index" stood at an all-time high of 180.

—Craig R. Waters

PAYTON'S PLACE: An American Brings Pizza to the U.K.

"Being American is the only thing I'm good at," booms Bob Payton, ripping a meaty pig bone from the rack of ribs on his plate. He is sitting in the Chicago Rib Shack, one of his four favorite restaurants in London. The others are the Chicago Pizza Pie Factory and two joints called Henry J. Bean's But His Friends All Call Him Hank Bar and Grill. He owns them all. He also owns his favorite restaurant in Barcelona, Spain, and his soon-to-be favorite restaurant in Paris—both Chicago Pizza Pie Factories.

The restaurants are knockout examples of how to export American culture. The Rib Shack, for example, where the proprietor has chosen to eat today, is a $1.2-million piece of Chicago on Raphael Street in the Knightsbridge section of London. There is a huge curved mahogany bar where Payton enjoys watching the British, refugees of wretchedly cramped pubs, negotiate for drinks without the embarrassment of having to elbow one another aside to get at them.There are stained-glass windows and a flashing light sculpture that reads BONE APPETIT. No other sign is needed: Rib-bones—smoked and marinated in a secret barbecue sauce before being given a final spin under the broiler—are the principal entry on the menu.

The Rib Shack opened in 1982, to just the sort of notices an American (if he was good at being one) would hope for. "Carnivorous," huffed the London *Times*'s critic. "Artless," sniffed the London *Evening Standard*. "A horribly jaunty menu," lisped *Tatler* magazine. The word-of-mouth reviews were more balanced. "I can see why they call Chicago the Windy City," said one British patron. "The food is quite good, but, how shall I phrase it . . . Let's just say that there are certain gastric consequences after enjoying one of Mr. Payton's meals."

Payton smiles, stabs a fork into a creamy banana cheesecake, and says loudly, "I call this place the Chicago Rib Shack for the same reason I named the Pizza Factory after Chicago. I wanted to give the product a birthplace, a heritage." Europe, you might suppose, has quite enough heritage of its own, and in truth the continent is strewn with the bones of American products that failed to "take" in that alien culture. General Motors Corporation went into Belgium, only to discover that its famous "Body by Fisher" slogan translated into Flemish as "Corpse by Fisher." General Mills Inc. bombed in the U.K. by putting cute freckle-faced, carrot-topped kids on its cereal boxes, failing to foresee that the English would associate them with Irish Republican Army terrorists. Pepsi-Cola flopped in Germany because "Come alive!" was misunderstood in German as a call to rise from the grave.

Bob Payton, however, has foisted his Chicago heritage on Europeans with appalling success. He has taught Barcelona sophisticates how to devour two-inch thick hunks of Chicago pizza while listening to the Ronettes. In London, 14,000 Brits a week shed a century's worth of inbred dining propriety as they tear into Payton's slithery ribs, their dignity guarded by one simple plastic bib. In Paris, thousands of patrons will soon be instructed by Payton himself in the sophomorically American art of chugging a pitcher of beer without causing a brawl.

This is no Harry's Bar phenomenon—a little corner of America in Europe where, in the 1920s, expatriates like Ernest Hemingway and F. Scott Fitzgerald would huddle together out of the Old World cold. Payton's restaurants and gin mills are the avant-garde of a cultural takeover bid. Between the pizza place and the rib joint, he sells one and a half tons of ribs, 230 cases of beer, and a Niagara of pepperoni every week. The Queen herself is rumored to have dined on his tender ribs. (Without the plastic bib, however. A Buckingham Palace source revealed that "H.R.H. used a knife and fork.") Through a trust called Boogie & Pal Ltd., Payton enjoys the benefits of a tax haven in Bermuda. His return on this invasion, which he launched in 1977 with $120,000, is already some $9 million a year.

"I must go back to the States for about a month a year to eat and recharge my batteries," exclaims this 240-pound Yankee at Elizabeth's Court. He finishes his meal now, wiping his greasy fingers with a scented towel. "But I get excited when I land at Heathrow [Airport] and see the long lines of black London cabs. . . . I love the smell of diesel smoke in the morning. It smells like victory!"

At age forty, Bob Payton has led the weird sort of life that lends itself to successful fantasy marketing. In the early 1960s, he was just another kid from Miami Beach trying to be Troy Donohue, when he went off to the University of North Carolina in Chapel Hill. There he became a drummer with Little David & the Wanderers, and, by his own account, learned "the dance steps from every musical Hollywood ever made." At Northwestern University, where he went next to earn a graduate degree in advertising, he learned Chicago—and fell madly in love with the city.

The advertising degree got him into J. Walter Thompson Company's Chicago office. "Back in those days, Bob was very ambitious and very personable," recalls Burt Sloan, who at that time was an account executive at a Chicago soul-music radio station where Payton placed Hamm's beer ads. "I'll tell you, though, when the guy wasn't working, he was out eating pizza." Thompson also liked Bob Payton. More fatefully, the firm liked his prodigious Americanness—and sent him to London, where it might be better appreciated than in the heartland of his country.

It was not Payton's first tour abroad. In the summer between his sophomore and junior years at Chapel Hill, Payton had landed a job, through an incredibly twisted series of events, as Xavier Cougat's assistant for the production of a television show filmed in Portugal. "It was Lisbon, it was 1964," Payton recalls," and nobody is going to believe this, but I was hired to drive around Portugal with Cugie and Charo, and to hold Cugie's idiot cards for him while he stood in front of the camera."

Six years later, in Thompson's London office, earning $20,000 a year, Payton took off after bigger things—flogging razor blades to the European masses. "Payton showed great creative leadership from the day he started," recalls Thompson executive Walter O'Brien. "He always had a high energy level." The firm cast him as its rock 'n' roll messiah, defying clients to get into the blue-jean culture of Europe's rolling youth market. "I would dress up in my best ad-agency suit and go tell our conservative clients that it was time for them 'to get down and boogie' if they wanted to capture the new money," Payton says. "The clients could not believe that a guy in a suit would stand up in front of them and do dance routines."

They believed in the message, though. Payton did very well being an American for Thompson in London. But after four years of research meetings, alternately falling asleep and passionately declaiming the merits of Chicago Bears football helmets as the perfect headgear for British motorcyclists, Bob Payton decided to quit. The giant agency had offered him $75,000 a year and an office in New York City—in vain. Payton had found his mission in life. He would spread the gospel of American gusto where it was needed most. He would open a pizza place for the English.

Bob Payton's path to glory, however, was pitted with more craters than Omaha Beach. "I knew that London needed a good pizza restaurant and that I was the one to do it," boasts Payton of the ordeal he went through in 1977 to get the first Chicago Pizza Pie Factory open. "The only problem was that I didn't know the first thing about the restaurant business or how to make fabulous pizza for hundreds of people." So he went to school. More accurately, he paid $5,000 to Laurie Soll, owner of Chicago Pizza Works in Los Angeles, to teach him the art of cooking deep-dish pizza by the hundreds. Before he left for Los Angeles, however, Payton concluded what looked like a solid deal with EMI Records to back him in his London venture. He also had a place lined up, on Jermyn Street, and had arranged for $3,000 worth of pizza ovens to be airlifted to Britain.

Then, just back from pizza school, he found out that the Jermyn Street location had fallen through. (He subsequently found another location, this one in Crown Passage, an alleyway around the corner from St. James's Palace, the home of the Queen Mother.) He also received a terse little note from EMI, saying it was out of the deal. It looked as though the once and future "Lord of the Pies" would be denied his crown.

"It was time to drop back ten and punt," the Lord recalls today. He is in his office across from Harrod's department store, reclining in the comfort of a candy-striped lounge chair. "I went to my girlfriend."

She was English, and was well-enough connected to introduce the man in her care to a principal of Norton Warburg Investments, one of England's first venture capital outfits. With their help, and Payton's pizza ovens, they formed My Kinda Town Ltd. The initial investment was $120,000, with Norton Warburg controlling 60 percent and Payton's offshore Boogie & Pal controlling the rest.

The original Chicago Pizza Pie Factory opened on Thanksgiving Day 1977, the first American restaurant in London since Isaac Tygrett started selling hamburgers at Hard Rock Café in 1971. Chicago was on hand in the form of rock 'n' roll tapes provided by one of the city's FM radio stations. It was an immediate success. Certain ladies in waiting to the Queen Mother, from around the corner, were among the patrons. But the Crown Passage place was too small, and within two years Payton had moved the Pizza Factory to a larger location on Hanover Square. His sales volume at the new stand: $4 million a year. A sign on the door proclaimed, "Purveyors of Chicago Pizza to London and the World."

By 1981, Payton's annual sales were more than $4 million. He was indisputably the most notorious, the most influential, and the richest American restaurateur in London. He then fell prey to a series of disasters, only one of which, strangely enough, stemmed from pride.

The city of Bath is an ancient and elegant resort, about 100 miles west of London. Its leading citizens cherish the architecture and ambience of their town with the sort of desperate protectiveness that mothers devote to an invalid child. Bath, in short, was My Kinda Town, the perfect site for cultural invasion. As Payton put it at the time, "I'm creating a Disneyland of food and other attractions in Bath." He spent $610,000 on his Pizza Factory there, figuring that in the first six months he could feed about 100,000 mouths at $10 each. He figured wrong. The 100,000 did not materialize. Never mind that the figure was considerably more than the city's population; the trouble was more a matter of taste. The residents simply did not want pizza on their jewel of a Georgian city.

So the Bath venture bombed. Then, in the fall of 1981, it burned. Payton rebuilt it. Then he unloaded it, quickly, for $375,000.

Meanwhile, as the Pizza Factory burned, the parent company of Norton Warburg Investments, Norton Warburg Ltd., went belly-up. The managing director, Andrew Warburg, had bolted to the beaches of southern Spain, allegedly taking with him most of the investors' money. What was left of the venture capital outfit, including 60 percent of My Kinda Town, went into receivership.

Payton took this disaster as an opportunity. He would buy back the

60 percent at fire-sale rates. "I went to the banks," he recalls, "American banks—First National Bank of Chicago, Continental Illinois [National Bank & Trust Company of Chicago], and Harris [Bankcorp]. They turned me down. I was in the process of opening the Rib Shack and these American bankers just didn't believe that the British would wear plastic bibs." Undaunted, Payton did something that no American with a trust called Boogie & Pal would have dreamed of doing. He went to Coutts & Company.

Like the royal household, whose bankers it is, Coutts & Company is something of an anachronism. But it is an anachronism cunningly devised, beautifully preserved, and skillfully marketed. It was founded in 1692 by a fierce Scottish goldsmith, and the bank still requires its male employees to be clean-shaven and to wear long frock coats. The atmosphere is that of a marble-and-glass tomb, which a lock of the Duke of Wellington's hair, prominently displayed in a glass case, does nothing to dispel. If there is anything left of the Empire, Coutts seems to say to its approximately 40,000 customers, it is the privilege of banking at 440 Strand.

Payton entered Coutts & Company with the reverence of a Cubs fan racing for a good seat in the bleachers of Wrigley Field. The first words out of his mouth (directed at banker David Jones) were: "You guys always wear those silly coats?" But when he left, it was with a $600,000 overdraft and the respectful wonder of the bank's senior management.

"We have very clear ideas about the market we serve," explains A. Julian Robarts, deputy managing director, in very clear tones. "We serve the top end of the market. But it is clear that we must also serve the smaller businessman like Bob Payton. The banking business is changing, and it is quite stimulating, I must say, to be associated with the success of the My Kinda Town group of restaurants."

With Coutts & Company behind him, Payton acquired 75 percent of My Kinda Town, with the remaining 25 percent purchased by Alan Patricoff Associates, the U.S. venture capital firm. The Purveyor of Pizza was back in business, an event he toasted with a bottle of wine labeled Chateau Chicago.

Payton's third ordeal on the road to triumph was a lawsuit—very possibly the most ludicrous lawsuit in the long history of English jurisprudence. The case was *Grunts Investments Ltd.* v. *The Chicago Pizza Pie Factory;* and the trial, which was long and vicious, turned on the question of what constituted a deep-dish Chicago pizza. The background was this: Laurie Soll, Payton's old teacher in the art of pizza making, opened in Covent Garden what Payton perceived to be a Chicago Pizza Pie clone called L. S. Grunts Chicago Pizza Company. Payton sued, arguing that Grunts' pizzas were an infringement of his proprietary rights in true Chicago pizzas. He lost. After the trial, the bewigged High Court judge was quoted as saying, "I have never before heard such evidence of confusion."

"Being controversial is Bob Payton's style," says Alan Lorrimer, Soll's British partner in Bates, another Covent Garden restaurant. "An Englishman could never get away with what Bob has done in the restaurant business here. No Englishman wants to work for him. He's what you Americans call an asshole."

Payton, with a gaping grin, agrees: "There is absolutely no doubt that I can be the biggest asshole in the world. I am absolutely single-minded about my restaurants, and that single-mindedness just sets me up to be shot down."

Also admired. "Don't let Bob's bravado fool you," warns Steven Gee, formerly a managing director at Norton Warburg before joining My Kinda Town as chief financial director. "At the end of the day, he has the street smarts that others in this city wish they had." Even Lorrimer has been heard to call him other names besides asshole: "Any good restaurant owner is a bit mad, and Payton is the maddest restaurant owner in London. What he has done is absolutely impossible. That makes him an absolutely brilliant man."

Payton's brilliance plays on the wildly ambivalent attitude of Europeans, especially Britishers, toward all things American. "America is what's happening to these people," Payton cries, belting down a Diet Coke in his Knightsbridge office, "and they have a love-hate relationship with us. They watch American TV, listen to American music. America is their fantasy, and they come to my restaurants to live it out."

To keep them coming (56,000 of them a month, at an average of $8 a head at the Pizza Pie Factory and $12 a head at the Rib Shack), Payton spares nothing—neither money, nor time, nor passion, nor the feelings of his employees—to get every detail of his places exactly right.

For example, here is Payton on the opening night of Henry J. Bean's, on Kings Road. Payton is enraged. "The door is squeaking!" he bellows in the direction of a terrified-looking British bartender. "I told them to make sure that the door didn't squeak. Look! The lights that are supposed to light the front of the bar haven't been turned on. Who the hell was supposed to fix the timer!" Grabbing a small Dictaphone from his jacket pocket, Payton makes a note on the people who were responsible.

But even with the squeaking door, the Kings Road bar is a textbook example of how to transform an old pub into a fantasy American bar and grill. There are two old pinball machines in the corner and a vintage 1947 Wurlitzer spinning tunes from the fifties and sixties. The walls are covered with signs advertising fine old American products like Frostie Root Beer and 1957 Plymouths. A stuffed American bald eagle stares down at the drinkers from behind the enormous bar. At the Rib Shack and the Pizza Factories, Payton's waiters and waitresses take and serve the orders. But at Henry J. Bean's (a mythical fellow whom Payton describes as "the kinda guy David Niven always wanted to be"), the customers place all their orders for burgers, chili, and potato skins with the bartenders. The patron then receives a receipt with a number, and watches for it to appear on one of three video screens located inside as well as out in the garden. The system is the same at Hank's on Abingdon Road, except that the ready orders there are broadcast over a loudspeaker.

In the near future, Payton plans to train all staff at his own restaurant management school, above the Kings Road Hank's. Until then, staffers receive two weeks of instruction at the restaurants where they work, and are given an oral and written exam so rigorous it would be easier to get a first at King's College, Cambridge. The final exam is to serve Payton a meal. "He put me through living hell," says one graduate. "He does everything possible to make you want to shove one of his bloody pizzas in his face."

Native-born employees tend to interpret Payton's "American" management style as abrasive, uncouth, egocentric, and repulsive. No more than 47 percent of his people have ever been British; 20 percent are American students, the remainder from other European countries. He has seven Americans as key staffers. It grieves Payton that he has been able to do so little for the U.K.'s 3 million unemployed, but he can't find enough of them who want to work the way he wants them to. The service ethic seems to have vanished from the Isles.

"My staff is trained to make people happy," says Payton. "They are not waiters and waitresses. They are concessioneers. If they work hard they can make [$120] a night." Perhaps that is the problem, some observers feel. Not that Payton is rude and vulgar, but that he has introduced an uncomfortable new element into the British restaurant trade: the profit motive, pay for performance.

His own performance has made him one of the most influential men in British business. The government attends to his views. "I tell [Prime Minister Margaret] Thatcher," he says, "if British people don't want to be employed, please let us hire whoever wants to provide service. After all, our major objective is to feed the people of this country. Let us use anybody who wants to work. I can't have people in my restaurants sulking in a corner." In the meantime, until the British get used to the notion of service for profit, he can do little for unemployment.

Apart from his meticulous attention to detail, Payton's cultural invasion has been a success because he realized early what no Englishman could bear to contemplate: that the pub, Britain's most venerated institution after the monarchy, was dying.

"The majority of London pubs are awful," pronounces Payton. "They smell, they are filthy, they provide terrible service, and women do not like to go alone for fear of being hassled." He is not unique in this view. In the mid-seventies, masses of London yuppies began deserting the pubs for a variety of restaurants, upscale and down, where they could sit and be served in relative comfort. Most of the pubs in Britain are owned by the great breweries—Courage, Watney, Charrington—but the giants were slow to respond to the pub's demise. The trump card was theirs: impossibly intricate licensing laws that dictate when, where, and under what circumstances a Britisher may drink his pint. The laws have not changed much since armaments manufacturers got them passed during the Great War (on the grounds that the British workingman couldn't be relied on to drink, except at certain specified hours, and make bombs in the same day). But it still remains an expensive and chancy proposition for an independent restaurateur to obtain a license to serve liquor without also serving food.

Early in his career, Payton played the twists in the laws by cleverly locating his establishments at 'round-the-corner sites where he might obtain a license to serve people who just wanted to drink. The Chicago Rib Shack is one of only a few restaurants in greater London that can pour liquor without selling food. Payton Plaice, his 250-seat fish restaurant that will feature the Chicago version of fish-and-chips and fried clams, will open this fall with a similar license. And the great breweries are currently courting him with derelict pubs and investment capital, to see if he can bring a little American magic to their Andy Capp premises. "Never underestimate the inability of the British to pick up on a good idea, or use double negatives," says Payton. "It took the brewers seven years to figure it out, but when a restaurant with a bar goes full-tilt boogie, it means an extra [$6,700] a week. You'd think the government would realize that they would benefit from a change in the law."

To help the government realize the error of its ways, Payton has been leading a largely one-man fight to change the laws in the courts. So far he has spent some $20,000 in the effort, an enormous sum by British standards of litigation. But he is furious that what he sees as silly, anachronistic, patronizing laws make it difficult for him to help people be happy. "When people come to one of my places, it's the same as if they were coming to my own home," Payton says. His home, incidentally, is in another great English institution, an English country house, suitably modified, of course—in his stable is a horse named for a Chicago suburb. "When people arrive at my home, they are taken care of in the best possible manner. I demand the same thing at my restaurants. We provide good food, good service, and a good time. Giving good service is my life."

The sizzling question about Payton at the moment is when, or if, the man who is best at being American will take My Kinda Town public. London restaurateurs debate it, brewery executives speculate on it, and bankers massage their hands at the prospect of it. One of Payton's close associates thinks that My Kinda Town will be under public offer by the fall of 1985, but Payton denies it. "Ahhh, shit, if I go public I'll have another million assholes telling me what color my napkins should be," he moaned not long ago, slumping even further into his candy-cane chair. "I could have sold out and retired a rich man years ago. Maybe I'll flip a coin at some point—heads we go global, tails we liquidate."

And if it is heads? Is the Stock Exchange in London ready to deal with a corporate president who goes berserk if a waiter fails to hand him a hollow plastic toothpick? How will women brokers react to a stock whose major investor may be a man who calls his secretary "numbnuts" and whose girlfriend has a business card that reads "Bob Payton's Personal Bodyguard"?

"Screw 'em if they can't take a joke," crackles Payton, in his best disk-jockey voice. "Right now I've got to find a manager for Hank's in Paris, and Payton Plaice is gonna introduce London to the best mussels and frog's legs they've ever tasted."

—A. CRAIG COPETAS

PRESSURE-POINT MARKETING

It is a point of some pride to Bob Baker and Jim Watson that none of the trucks picking up and delivering air freight around the country bears their company's name. Nor do any airplanes carry the Skyway Freight Systems Inc. logo. Baker and Watson are also pleased to point out that they have never made a sales call on, sent a bill to, or even spoken with most of the nearly 16,000 businesses that ship via Skyway. In fact, Skyway has only about a hundred paying clients—and a marketing strategy that is astonishingly simple in a market that is incredibly complex.

Skyway, a young company in a low-technology business, has hitched its future to the rapidly growing but chaotic world of high-technology industries, which, for all their esoteric glamor, consume prodigious quantities of everyday goods and services like freight transportation. But selling into fast-growing markets by itself doesn't assure profits: Ask the suppliers of bankrupt Osborne Computer Corporation. Even identifying potential customers among businesses that quickly emerge (and sometimes just as quickly submerge again) in the volatile high-tech environment can drive a business to distraction. Watson and Baker, however, have evolved a marketing strategy that buffers Skyway from the ups and downs of the high-tech world. Not incidentally, the strategy also gives extraordinary leverage to Skyway's limited selling resources.

Watson, a 1969 graduate of the United States Naval Academy, and Baker, who destroyed his draft card in the sixties, met in Los Angeles in 1976 when both were consultants to an air-freight company that was reorganizing under Chapter 11. Watson knew sales, having spent several years selling IBM computers to transportation companies. Baker knew the operational side of transportation. They became mutual admirers.

"Bob," says Watson, "had a reputation for being able to price a transportation transaction and ensure that there was always something left for the bottom line."

"Jim," says Baker, "can market anything."

In 1977, as soon as the air-freight company had been turned around, they left as partners with an idea they wanted to try. Originally, the idea had nothing in particular to do with fast-growth, high-tech industries.

Frederick W. Smith's Federal Express Corporation, then only three years old, had created practically a new industry—overnight air-freight delivery—and competitors were popping up everywhere. Skyway wasn't going to be one of them, not directly anyway. Instead Skyway would offer shippers an alternative: two-, three-, or five-day service in exchange for prices as much as 75 percent lower than the overnight rates. "We figured," says Watson, "that in the majority of cases, people don't really need things overnight."

Skyway could charge less by taking advantage of changes occurring in the air-passenger business. Airlines, which experience their heaviest traffic during the daylight hours, had begun using wide-bodies—747s, L-1011s, DC-10s—with huge, and often unfilled, cargo bays beneath the passenger cabins. "Here you had all this new freight capacity flying during the daytime, and nobody wanted to use it," Baker says, "because everybody was convinced they needed overnight [freight] service. So we could go to the airlines and say, 'Hey, give us a reason to put freight on these airplanes.' They would have to give us a rate. That was our original concept."

On the strength of this idea, embodied in a 300-page business plan, Watson and Baker easily raised $100,000 from seven private investors in exchange for 35 percent of Skyway's stock. That was all the capital they thought they would need. Then they hit the road selling, and . . . nothing happened. In four months, Skyway lost $200,000—twice its capital—and survived only on trade credit.

Two things, they found, were wrong with their approach. One they figured out almost immediately.

"Customers," Watson says, "were still convinced that they needed everything overnight. We were selling a totally new concept, and I was spending all my time educating people in three-hour sales calls."

But Skyway had to sell something, soon. So the partners changed their pitch. Never mind the concept, they decided, sell price. "We'd tell a guy paying one dollar a pound that we'll do it for twenty-five cents. He had to listen to us. If he didn't, his boss would."

The shift in sales tactics worked. Within a few months, Skyway was in the black, surviving if not thriving. Still, every new shipper that signed on for the service had to be sold, and Skyway's marketing strategy consisted simply of keeping Watson on the road as much as possible.

During one two-week East Coast trip, he made cold calls in New York City's garment district, climbing the stairs to Seventh Avenue lofts. There, as he recalls, guys smoking short, unattractive cigars asked how much he would kick back to them if they put in a word for him with the apparel manufacturers who bought the buttons, collars, and laces the loft factories made. "I didn't sell anything," says Watson, "but I learned something. I learned that it was the buyer, not the guy in the loft, who made the decision. So I flew home and called on apparel manufacturers in Los Angeles, and the light bulb came on." The second problem with Skyway's sales approach had suddenly become clear. "The whole [air-freight] industry is doing it wrong," Watson concluded. "They're selling to the wrong people."

The right people were buyers, not vendors. Buyers, usually, pay the freight charges on shipments inbound to them, so buyers have a greater interest than the vendors in controlling freight costs. Consequently, Skyway discovered a receptive market among Los Angeles apparel makers. After hearing Watson's pitch, a fair number instructed their suppliers—primarily textile mills in the Northeast and in North Carolina—to call Skyway when they had a shipment ready. Business picked up modestly, and Skyway developed something of a specialty as an apparel freight service.

The discovery that it was the buyers who were the appropriate sales contacts was an important development in the evolution of Skyway's marketing strategy. But the most important changes were yet to come. First, Skyway needed a distinctive product. It was still selling the same thing—air-freight service—that everyone else was selling, just a slower and cheaper model. Second, Skyway needed another market, one that offered more growth potential than the rag trade. "We had a very bad receivables problem," Baker says, "because when things get bad in that industry, companies don't slow down, they go out of business. We knew we couldn't grow with these people, that we had to branch out." But the new market had to wait for the new product to take shape.

Now that they had found the right people to sell to, Watson and Baker began to learn that price wasn't the only thing these customers wanted to buy. "They would listen to price. If you had a lower price, you could get an appointment every time. But," says Watson, "they were also people who lived and died with delivery of product—bolts of cloth from the mill. If the material didn't get in and they couldn't do the run and make the skirt, then they didn't make the ad at Macy's or Bloomingdale's, and they didn't sell."

In short, it wasn't overnight delivery that mattered so much as the ability to schedule the delivery, to know that the material would reach the factory when it was needed. And that meant knowing when it was shipped from the mill, how it was shipped, and where it was at any given time. Because Skyway was managing *all* inbound air freight for its customers, it could easily collect and pass on this information as part of its service. A conventional air-freight carrier, which might have only one shipment for a Los Angeles manufacturer, would have no way of knowing where that manufacturer's other shipments, consigned to other carriers, might be. At Skyway, an employee kept the status of each shipment up-to-date on a clipboard, and buyers could use a toll-free line to find out where their freight was and when it would arrive. The phone line and clipboard were the first components of a now fully computerized inbound freight-management system that has finally given Skyway a distinctive service product.

One last bell had yet to ring. After nearly two years of modest revenue growth, largely from customers in the apparel industry, Watson and Baker still spent most of their time selling. Once Delta Air Lines Inc. ran a promotional special: For $369 each, two passengers could fly in one week to any city Delta served. The only stipulation was that they couldn't visit the same city twice, except to make a connection. Baker and Watson made five calls a day in five cities, and, because so many of Delta's flights originate in Atlanta, they found themselves every night in Atlanta's Hartsfield International Airport waiting to make their next connection. "I've never been that tired," Watson says. "We came home and said to each other, 'We're not doing something right.'"

Then they learned that Motorola Inc., a major maker of semiconductors and electronics products, was inviting bids on its inbound air-freight business. "Bob and I went in there and asked, 'Like, how many vendors do you buy from?' Honest to God, we didn't know. This was our first visit to an electronics business. They said, 'Well, we have about two thousand vendors.' Boy, the bells went off. If we close this sale, we get two thousand new accounts. Two thousand new companies will one day start shipping with us, and we have invested one sales effort."

They did close the Motorola sale, and finally, all the essential elements of their marketing concept had become clear: Skyway could acquire the air-freight business of tens of thousands of small but growing shippers by selling its service to a few hundred major high-tech corporations.

After the Motorola sale, Skyway grew, and grew up, quickly. From $1.5 million in 1978, the year before the Motorola contract, the company's revenues rose to $3.4 million in 1980, the first full year of the contract, and to $13 million last year. The pretax profit margin, according to Baker, is about 10 percent of sales. Aside from its $100,000 initial capitalization and a bank loan to finance the purchase of its first computer in 1979, Skyway has financed its growth internally. The nature of its business, and the hardheadedness of its founders, have kept Skyway's capital-expansion costs low.

When the partners started the company, their only corporate asset was an overcoat. "It was our East Coast coat," says Watson. "Whoever was taking the trip wore the coat." Keeping capital expenses and fixed costs at a minimum continues to be part of the business strategy. They can control costs because Skyway, unlike most transportation companies, manages only inbound, not outbound, freight. The distinction is important.

Conventional freight companies serving the national market must be prepared to pick up *and* deliver anywhere in the country, anytime. Skyway picks up only where its customers have suppliers, and it delivers only to customers' plants. And it does this, for the most part, with someone else's capital equipment. "If," says Baker, "Jim doesn't get one ounce of freight in Birmingham, Alabama, tonight, it isn't going to cost me anything. If he does, I call my contract trucker, and he picks it up. Now I've got an expense, but I've also got the revenue."

On the other end, Skyway knows that all its deliveries are going to customers easily served from one of its five leased terminals. It knows that because Watson won't sell a new customer that can't be served from an existing terminal, and Baker opens a new terminal only when a market (Denver, for example, which is now under consideration) promises to provide enough new business to support the added expense. "Bob has a sermon," Watson says, "which goes, 'Goddamn it, let's not incur costs until we've incurred revenues.'" Eventually, the company may have as many as twelve terminals, from which it can serve 80 percent of the market. The other 20 percent, Baker says, he doesn't want: too expensive. Sorry, North Dakota.

This philosophy helps to keep the company's fixed costs at a low 30 percent to 35 percent of the total, and it helps keep the business simple. "In Chicago," says Baker, "we have a trucker who started out with two trucks, and he was one of the drivers. Now he's got a big terminal and maybe fourteen trucks. . . . We were a big part of his growth, and obviously he was part of ours. . . . We've spawned quite a few successful trucking operations. We put a guy in our San Jose terminal and said, 'Go to it. We'll be your customer, your base to start out with. Go get yourself some financing.' He did, and now his customers include United Air Lines, Delta, and Skyway. . . . We did not want to make that capital investment but saw nothing wrong with providing the room for his growth, letting him live in-house with us."

"We can be creative," Baker adds, "because we're not spending management time and energy worrying about, Are the trucks ready to go? Do they have fuel? Has the driver been arrested? Did we get heisted in Manhattan?"

The operational guts of the company is Skyway Central, a twenty-four-hour-a-day control center in Santa Cruz, California, a beach resort midway between San Francisco and Monterey. When a customer's vendor has materials to ship, he calls Skyway's toll-free number. From that point on, Skyway Central personnel direct and track the shipment, building a computerized record as the material is picked up by the local trucker, held temporarily in his warehouse or delivered immediately to the airline, loaded aboard the plane, unloaded, and delivered. A truck driver, airline-freight handler, or dispatcher anywhere along the line who goes out of his way to solve a problem or meet a deadline gets a ten-pound tin of chocolate-chip cookies and a thank-you note from someone at Skyway Central within a couple of days.

Baker and Watson no longer think of the company as being in the air-freight business. Rather, they see Skyway becoming part of its customers' inventory management systems, providing just-in-time delivery of production materials.

Traffic managers at customer plants can get computer printouts each morning listing incoming material and delivery times for the day.

Later, another printout lists what has been delivered and to whom, so that "lost" shipments aren't eventually discovered on some branch-plant loading dock.

Customers can give Skyway Central standing or ad hoc instructions for handling specific materials—for example, always ship blue widgets at the five-day economy rate—thus giving the buyer, not the vendor, control over shipping mode and cost. Customers can tell Skyway when they want material, thereby preventing vendors from shipping (and billing) early. It is a flexible system that can be shaped and changed easily. Skyway is firmly imbedded in the materials-handling systems of such companies as Apple Computer, Pratt & Whitney Group, and Diablo Systems.

Cunningly included in the service is a powerful protective device for Skyway itself. Its customers' vendors have instructions to use Skyway exclusively when shipping by air. Skyway will monitor compliance with these instructions by auditing customers' freight invoices for them. Any non-Skyway bills are pulled, and a letter goes out from Skyway (but over the customer's signature) chastising the guilty vendor and informing him that his account will be debited by the difference between the freight charge he incurred on behalf of the buyer and Skyway's (usually) lower fee. "We average ninety percent compliance," says Baker. "If they don't do it, they pay, and people get tired of paying."

Skyway's next step will be the obvious one. Baker and Watson will apply the same marketing principles to surface freight that have made Skyway a success in the air. Their customers will be the same—large manufacturers with many small suppliers. "If you're buying something and you're our customer," says Baker, "we want to be the service company to see that it gets from the vendor to you. Don't tell me what mode to use. Just tell me when you want it."

Variations on the Theme

Skyway Freight Systems Inc.'s strategy is designed to find the pivotal sales points—the pressure points, if you will—in a market that offers potentially huge revenues but, because it is volatile and atomized, could easily overwhelm a company with small marketing resources. Other companies, in quite different businesses, achieve much the same result through variations on Skyway's theme.

In 1976, Barry Nathanson and Steven Garfinkle agreed that the exploding high-technology industries could be a new, lucrative market for Richards Consultants Ltd., their five-year-old, New York City–based executive search firm. But where to begin?

One obvious place would have been such easily identifiable companies as IBM, Digital Equipment, or Honeywell, all growing high-tech corporations. So, says Garfinkle, they set out to learn what competitive edge they might have in attracting business from a company like Digital that was already using a search firm. "In the course of our research," he says, "we noticed the really phenomenal growth rates of start-up companies. That led us to the thought that maybe we shouldn't go after the DECs of the world but should look, instead, at the companies that might be the DECs of the next generation."

"Keep in mind," says Garfinkle, "that at this point, I didn't know what a venture capitalist was. But Barry had a neighbor who was one. We talked to him and learned that one of the ways the DECs of the world get off the ground was through this very small industry, the venture capital industry . . . [and] we learned that venture capitalists typically prefer to put their money on individuals who have done it before, people who have already developed companies or operated in high-growth modes."

Aha.

Two ahas, actually. The first was the realization that Digital Equipment, IBM, and other large technology companies weren't Richards' market; they were, instead, its talent pool, supplying them with candidates who had the experience venture capitalists sought.

The second epiphany was that Richards could sell executive recruiting services to thousands of tiny, hard-to-find start-up companies by establishing relationships with only a hundred or so easily identified contacts. "Instead of looking ourselves for the Ferrofluidics of the world," says Nathanson, "we could find them by going first to their venture capitalists."

Ferrofluidics Corporation, one of Richards' early high-tech clients, was, in 1978, a young Nashua, New Hampshire, company in transition, looking into penetration of new markets for its magnetic-fluid technology. Annual sales amounted to just over $1 million, and the company needed marketing talent. A Ferrofluidics director, New York venture capitalist Harvey Mallement, told the company's cofounder and chairman, Ronald Moskowitz, that he had been impressed with Richards' performance of an earlier search. Since Moskowitz had no experience with other search firms, and because his venture capitalist/director had made the suggestion, Moskowitz commissioned Richards.

This experience and others like it have validated the marketing approach Nathanson and Garfinkle formulated. Going through venture capitalists not only simplifies the identification of new prospects, it also is a powerful door-opener. In addition, since young companies frequently have more than one venture capitalist sitting on their boards, successful completion of a search undertaken on one venture capitalist's recommendation frequently impresses one or two other venture capitalists. Thus a whole new set of doors is opened up.

The experience with Ferrofluidics also brought Nathanson and Garfinkle a significant but unanticipated benefit. They had, of course, expected their business to grow as their clients' businesses grew; and as Ferrofluidics' sales expanded to $10.8 million last year, Richards completed its seventh executive search (this one for a chief financial officer) for the company. But the two entrepreneurial headhunters also realized gains of more than 250 percent on the Ferrofluidics stock they had taken in 1978 as partial payment for services. Now, taking some of their fee in stock or warrants is a frequently used part of Richards' marketing and growth strategy.

Coincidentally, Ferrofluidics' own marketing strategy illustrates still another variation on the theme developed by Skyway and Richards. Among its products, Ferrofluidics makes rotary and other types of seals, which it sells to equipment manufacturers, which in turn sell their machines to end-users, semiconductor makers. Moskowitz's problem was to convince 100 equipment makers that 2,000 end-users wanted his seal in the machines they bought. Where were the pressure points? "We decided," Moskowitz says, "that out of that field of two thousand end-users, there are probably ten companies that are industry leaders, the guys who play the tune that the industry dances to. Clearly IBM is one of them, but there are others—Intel, NEC."

So Ferrofluidics capitalized on the influence of a few large end-users to persuade its OEM customers to incorporate the company's seal. Says Moskowitz, "The rationalization of the semiconductor industry—thousands of customers—for us was to identify the guys who are the thought leaders in the industry and sell them first."

Much the same tactic worked for Ferrofluidics in the computer industry, in which about a dozen manufacturers supply spindles to a hundred or more disk-drive makers. Ferrofluidics makes a seal that spindle makers can install before shipping their components to end-users—but spindle makers, Moskowitz explains, don't enjoy any of the benefits of his company's seal. "For them, it adds more handling and substantial cost. So we really had to sell the disk-drive houses, who are interested in enhanced reliability and that sort of thing."

Again, the trick was to identify the few industry leaders—IBM, Control Data, and Shugart, according to Moskowitz—and sell them. The OEMs, and eventually the other disk-drive makers, would follow. But here, because the computer market is so volatile, identifying industry leaders actually meant finding the individual design engineers who were the innovators capable of influencing their colleagues.

"It's exactly the same approach Richards is using," says Moskowitz. "They have a market that is potentially tens of thousands of customers, none of whom knows them and most of whom they don't know. Within that there are probably a thousand venture capitalists, and within that thousand there are maybe a hundred who are thought leaders, highly respected by all the others. If Richards targeted those, they'd have more business than they can handle. We've identified engineers and tracked them through three or four companies. It's almost as if we placed them there. This guy goes to a company, he designs us in. And the next thing you know, in six or nine months he's off to another company."

—Tom Richman

SPECIAL EFFECTS:
A Small Company Changes Its Image

Darkness fell, and rockets pierced the sky. Robert Pohl, the thirty-five-year-old general manager of Cincinnati's Hudepohl Brewing Company, joined the throng lining the banks of the Ohio River as more than $70,000 of his company's slim marketing budget literally went up in smoke. That is the price Hudepohl paid to sponsor its hometown Labor Day fireworks display, a lavish affair that annually draws upwards of half a million people at the height of Cincinnati's Riverfest.

Hudepohl can't afford such theatrics as a mere gesture of civic pride. The closely held, family-run beermaker spends only $1 million a year on conventional advertising, small change compared with the dollars poured into media-buying by the national breweries that dominate the industry. And for the time being at least, Pohl has declared the company will "hold the line" on its ad budget. Not so, however, with Hudepohl's rapidly growing commitment to special events. Fireworks displays, tennis tournaments, bluegrass concerts, and ski races now make up a promotional budget of $200,000 annually.

Make no mistake, Pohl intends to accomplish more than just selling some "Hudy" beer during those events. Hudepohl is one of the few small companies that have begun to use special events as marketing tools. But it is a tactic already popular with a host of larger companies—many of them such consumer-product giants as General Foods, R. J. Reynolds, and Anheuser-Busch. Lesa Ukman, publisher of *Special Events Report,* based in Chicago, estimates some 5,000 special events and festivals will be staged in North America this year, to the tune of more than $850 million in corporate sponsorships. Most sponsors see special events as a way to put their products directly before a target market. As Ukman puts it in the argot of the 1980s, "Special events reach consumers at the lifestyle level."

Hudepohl has plenty at stake in the lifestyle department. Lee Oberlag, Hudepohl's advertising director, says brand loyalty in beer "is all image." The right image, she says, is youthful and sporting. It is an image carefully nurtured by such slick and expensive advertising campaigns as the ex-jock soap operas that elevated Miller Lite to the number two brand in America. That image is fundamental to the beer business, and while Oberlag says Hudepohl cannot hope to compete with the prime-time media-buying of larger brewers, she believes the company can generate the same kind of "feeling" through the right special event. Perhaps more important, Hudepohl needs to reestablish local allegiance to its brand name in its home market. Hudepohl's image in Cincinnati in recent years has been all wrong.

"Hudepohl has come to be perceived by younger people as a local, old-fashioned beer," says Oberlag. "They see it as the beer of past generations. And we think our ads have not overcome that tendency."

But Hudepohl does think a well-chosen series of special events can help overcome that stodgy image. At $70,000, the fireworks are far and away the company's biggest single special event to date. Eight years old, the Labor Day fireworks celebration was until last year the sole property of WEBN, a top-rated local rock-music radio station, which broadcasts a simultaneous music program timed to the display. WEBN has a virtual stranglehold on Cincinnati's young adult population, a market Pohl and Oberlag believe is crucial to reversing flagging sales of their standard-bearing regular beer, Hudepohl Gold. When WEBN decided to expand the fireworks program this year, Hudepohl jumped at the chance to cosponsor.

"We want to get top-of-the-mind awareness with the youth market that listens to that station," says Oberlag. "Beyond that, we're also associating Hudepohl with the largest event in Cincinnati. We're reaching more than a half million people on site, not to mention what comes through TV coverage and the advance promotion."

The key to Hudepohl's involvement is a partnership with WEBN. This, says Oberlag, is what makes event sponsorship fundamentally different from simply buying ad time on the station. The airwaves are crowded with advertising, short messages that say, "Buy our product," Oberlag explains. The impact of an event is broader: "See who we are and what we do to have fun." It is a bit of a surprise for listeners to hear stodgy old Hudepohl linked up with youthful WEBN. In theory, at least, the effectiveness of that exposure will grow over time as the phrase "Hudy Gold/WEBN Fireworks" becomes planted in the public consciousness.

"We're not in this for a one-year deal," says Oberlag. "And we expect to get more for our money with each succeeding year." Hudepohl, in fact, has committed to at least a five-year sponsorship of the fireworks—regardless of cost.

Hudepohl has good reason to continue its marketing strategy well into the future. The beer industry has undergone major contractions in recent years, with small, independent brewers among the heaviest casualties in a war of attrition and acquisition. There are fewer than twenty-five small breweries still operating in the United States, not counting the newer "micro breweries," which produce beer for very limited, usually local, distribution. Hudepohl, with annual sales of $18 million to $22 million by *Inc.* estimate, will be one hundred years old next year and is one of only two brewers left in Cincinnati, once a major brewing center.

And competition is only going to get tougher. Although federal legislation appears certain to force the drinking age to twenty-one nationwide, many industry analysts contend such a move will mainly result in more underage drinkers. Whether they are right or not, the target market itself is shrinking. Persons between the ages of eighteen and twenty-four—just over 17 percent of the drinking-age population—consume about 25 percent of the beer sold in the United States. But the size of that age group peaked in 1981 at a little over 30 million, and will head steadily downward until the mid-1990s, when there will be just over 23 million people between those ages. The effect of the shrinkage is already being felt: In 1982 and again in 1983, growth in U.S. beer sales was essentially flat—the lowest growth rate since 1958.

Those realities only compound the endangered-species status of the independent brewer. In 1980, following the death of its general manager, Hudepohl was already suffering after a string of "very tough" years. The board turned to a young and untested Bob Pohl to run the company. The great-grandson of founder Louis Hudepohl (the name similarity is a coincidence of marriage; Hudepohl had five daughters), Pohl had his own notions about how the company ought to change, following what he saw as a period of potentially disastrous complacency.

"The company felt insulated and protected because of so many years as a dominant brewer in Cincinnati," recalls Oberlag. "There was no feeling here that we had much to worry about."

Bob Pohl's concerns, however, were largely confirmed by an internal study of the company completed that year by a group of students from Harvard University Graduate School of Business Administration. The study found that among the problems facing Hudepohl was a monumental disparity between the resources national breweries had to spend for advertising and what Hudepohl could afford. Hudepohl had, in fact, already lost one of its most important advertising venues—a longtime radio and television contract with the Cincinnati Reds baseball team—to the deep pockets of Anheuser-Busch. That left the local "King of Bowling" television show as Hudepohl's most visible media buy.

"For every dollar I have to spend on advertising, Anheuser-Busch has three hundred dollars," says Pohl. "They can literally blow us away."

Hudepohl is trying to counter by concentrating its special-events efforts in the Cincinnati area, where the company still sells 60 percent of its beer, claims to have about a 25 percent share of the local market—and is under heavy siege. Coors, the enormously popular brew from Golden, Colorado, entered the fray in Cincinnati earlier this year and is expected to make substantial inroads in the local market, as it has in expansions throughout the country. Other new competitors have arrived in the form of several cut-rate brands from major brewers looking to capture the bargain-hunter. Says Pohl, "This market is in tremendous flux right now. I don't think anybody knows how it will all shake out."

Hudepohl is also using special events—including an $11,000 sponsorship of a stop on the pro tennis tour—to introduce Bob Pohl's personal project, a new "super premium" brand on which much of the company's future may well ride. Christian Moerlein beer, named for an old and now defunct Cincinnati brewery, is a full-bodied beer with a hefty price tag intended to compete with imported beers. Tennis, says Oberlag, delivers just the right prospective customer.

"The importers are into the same kind of events," she says. "They draw an admittedly upscale crowd. These are people who want to be seen drinking Heineken or Beck's, which is exactly where we want to position Christian Moerlein."

The first American-made beer to pass Germany's 500-year-old purity standards, Christian Moerlein was brought out in Cincinnati in 1981. Hudepohl has since taken it into twenty-five states west of the Mississippi and is now looking at the eastern United States. In the first three months of distribution outside the Cincinnati area, Pohl says, Christian Moerlein was already at 80 percent of its first year's sales projection.

Pohl's gamble with a "snob appeal" brand is substantial. He says Christian Moerlein is currently "eating up about half" of Hudepohl's sales and marketing resources. And while imported beers continue to be a growing category in this country, U.S. beermakers have seen their own super premiums sagging of late. Sales of Anheuser-Busch's Michelob are off and Miller Brewing Company pulled its Special Reserve brand after a less-than-enthusiastic reception in test markets. Even so, Bob Pohl is convinced that the high end may be one of the last niches for a small, independent brewer.

"The beer analysts will tell you we don't have a chance," he says. "And if you look at the numbers, you'd have to agree. But logic tells you the big companies are more efficient than we are. In a price war, we're always going to lose. People don't know who we are. They're going to have to taste the product and form an opinion based on the product's merits. And that's a plus for us."

Lesa Ukman says special events provide just the right context for a company with a good product and a low profile. In addition, she says, "editorial mention" of the company's name in news reports of an event give the sponsor visibility that simply can't be matched dollar for dollar by conventional advertising. Ukman concedes that companies go into special events mainly on intuition. "It's still pretty much a visceral judgment," she says. But she estimates that, done correctly, an event sponsor can expect to get as much as ten times the media exposure for its money as it would buying regular ad space and time.

Clearly, however, special events may not be for everybody, just as every event is not right for a potential sponsor. The choice of events open to sponsorship is enormous, including everything from jazz concerts and rock tours to triathlons, bike races, food festivals, marathons, minimarathons, almost-marathons, and a swarm of civic-boosting celebrations taking place in virtually every burg around the country. The events range in size from such nationally televised blockbusters as the New York City Marathon to the sublime lunacies of Toad Suck Daze in Conway, Arkansas, where participants race babies as part of the program, or the Calamari Festival in Santa Cruz, California, where an orgy of squid cookery is capped by a screening of the movie *20,000 Leagues Under the Sea.*

No surprise, then, that Bob Pohl says Hudepohl has become "much more selective" in looking at sponsorship opportunities.

"Our name has to be prominent, and we have to reach beer drinkers," he says.

Even then, Oberlag adds, Hudepohl has had to look before leaping. The company was recently approached to sponsor a powerboat regatta. They demurred when they realized a likely winner among the entrants was a boat named *Miss Budweiser.*

Sold on Rock

The extravagant sums that can be spent on special-events sponsorship suggest how highly many companies value direct access to their target markets. To be sure, it takes the resources of a company like PepsiCo to put Michael and the brothers Jackson on the road. But the costs—and rewards—of a major sponsorship can be proportionally much higher for a smaller company. Consider the case of Sparkomatic Corporation of Milford, Pennsylvania, a fast-growing manufacturer of car stereos with sales of around $100 million.

Sparkomatic this year sponsored a concert tour by the British rock group Yes to 109 cities in Europe, Canada, and the United States at a cost of $1 million. Add in Sparkomatic's promotions related to the tour, and the total price tag comes to $3 million.

This was Sparkomatic's second go-round with a rock group, having sponsored a Supertramp tour in 1983. It likely won't be the last. While sales in the car-stereo industry are growing from 5 percent to 10 percent annually, Sparkomatic's revenues climbed more than 30 percent last year, a jump Edward Anchel, president of the privately held company, attributes in large part to increased visibility among young adults tuned in to rock music. Although he is skeptical that "anyone can really tell you how effective their advertising is," Anchel says that when Sparkomatic adds up the exposure it gets through a rock tour, "it's hard to believe it wouldn't cost you several times as much to do the same thing" with regular advertising.

"The fact of the matter is that you can line up a lot of car-stereo merchandise and find very little difference among products," says Anchel. "So it really becomes essential to build strong brand awareness."

Anchel, who consults with his twenty-year-old son in selecting a group to sponsor, says Sparkomatic's relatively small size works to its advantage. "The chemistry of making a deal with a rock group can be very interesting," he says. "Each side is somewhat suspect of the other. We're able to overcome some of the apprehensions they may have about corporate involvement, because we're a little less scary to them."

Sparkomatic is selective, too. Anchel says they went with Yes because it was a mature, well-managed group that appeals to a broad spectrum of the youth audience that buys car stereos. It was the group's ability to "play hardball," as Anchel puts it, that resulted in a copromotion of the summer tour by MTV, cable television's popular music-video channel. Yes negotiated concert telecasts with both MTV and Home Box Office, playing one against the other. Sparkomatic couldn't be more pleased with the outcome. Promotional mentions of Sparkomatic on MTV, Anchel says, were worth as much as $1 million.

That came on top of the exposure Sparkomatic got by having its name on tickets, programs, and T-shirts at the Yes concerts. Conversely, Sparkomatic was able to use the group's name in its broadcast and print advertising. Anchel, perhaps the only forty-five-year-old chief executive in the country to show up at a number of Yes concerts last summer, says that Sparkomatic's hefty rock 'n' roll investment has been extremely well spent.

"It would be nice to keep the money," he says. "But that doesn't build a company."

—WILLIAM SOUDE

KICKING PERRIER IN THE DERRIÈRE

When Rick Scoville began calling on Texas food brokers almost two years ago, many found him downright amusing. His plans to compete with Perrier, the French sparkling water that dominates the U.S. market, by marketing a Texas sparkling water, nc less, raised more than one eyebrow and elicited some good-natured laughs but no orders.

Undaunted, the thirty-six-year-old San Antonio entrepreneur shrugged off the laughter, loaded a few cases of his Artesia mineral water into a van, and set out for Texas's lucrative urban markets. He personally introduced his bottled water to grocery store chains and chic discos. Before long the nightclubs and supermarkets were placing large orders for the amber bottles bearing Artesia's "pure Texas spirit." Scoville wrote dozens of letters to media organizations touting his product, and stories appeared in Dallas, Houston, and San Antonio newspapers. Scoville soon found himself behind radio talk show microphones, and finally on television.

"I went out and aggressively marketed myself," says the curly-haired, bearded Texan, "and it worked."

Perrier flatly denies that Scoville's Houston-based company, Artesia Waters Inc., is chipping away at its Texas market, but Scoville has established a definite presence in the state. Gross sales for 1980, Artesia's first year, were $102,000. Revenue in 1981 jumped from $12,200 in January to $80,000 in May, and Scoville predicts Artesia will post total 1981 sales of $1.5 million. And he contends Artesia has already taken up to 30 percent of Perrier's sales in Texas and will overtake the French bottler in the state this year. *"Au revoir, Perrier,"* his advertising slogan bids his competitor, but he's fond of putting it another way. "I'm out to kick Perrier in the derrière," Scoville says.

His success rests largely on his marketing strategy. He has combined self-promotion with a classy ad campaign and a healthy dose of confidence in his product. He has focused his campaign by taking direct aim at the French company, whose groundbreaking efforts several years ago virtually created the U.S. market for sparkling water. "When I started I was riding Perrier's coattails," Scoville admits. "Now, in Texas, I'm halfway up their back."

Scoville had his marketing ideas but little money when he launched the venture in early 1980 with a $25,000 loan and a small aging bottling facility in San Antonio. Without a nickel for advertising, he created his own crafty public relations assault that snatched headlines for "Texas Hill Country" spring water.

One of the first and most valuable bits of exposure for the young entrepreneur came from a business writer at a Houston newspaper, who wrote a success story about Artesia when it was still too early to determine the company's future. Scoville made copies of the clipping and sent it to other publications. It was the best press release anyone could write—and it was free.

He wrote letters to major magazines and newspapers touting his product. Follow-up calls produced a one-paragraph front page story in the *Wall Street Journal* and a new product feature in *Texas Monthly* magazine. The *Texas Monthly* piece, in turn, earned him an invitation to compete in a locally sponsored bottled water taste test. The taste test, which Artesia won, was filmed by a Dallas TV station, and suddenly Scoville was on the air, reaching thousands of Texans. Artesia sales in the Dallas area tripled one day after the broadcast.

The regional character of Scoville's public relations efforts is deliberate. He emphasizes that Artesia is a Texas product ("Texans are very loyal," he says) and plays up Artesia as an American product made by a small company that's taking on a big foreign company. "We tell Perrier drinkers, 'We're chic. We're American. We're Texan. We're good. *And* we cost less.' "

Scoville says the amber seven-ounce and quart bottles help, too. Looking like beer bottles, they stand out on the tight shelf space in convenience and grocery stores, where 70 percent of his water is sold. The fancy Artesia label adds to its sales appeal; Scoville spent three months on the label design alone.

All the media coverage sent the young company into a spin. "My PR was taking off faster than my distribution," says Scoville. Bottling his brew was slow as well, because the intricate Artesia label had to be applied by hand. Last fall he finally mechanized the labeling process and set up a distribution system. That, with a shot of venture capital, enabled Scoville to begin direct mail, outdoor, and print advertising.

His print ads feature a sexy cowgirl reclining on a saddle, with a saddlebag containing two iced-down bottles of Artesia. "It's a Texas theme," says Scoville, "and the campaign has generated a lot of favorable response." It has been costly, though. He has already spent $200,000 of the $270,000 budgeted for advertising this year. "Our sales are better than we expected," he says, "so the cost hasn't been a problem, yet."

Even with his big ad budget, Scoville still considers himself a master of free PR. Even Ron Davis, the president of Perrier's American distributorship, has to agree: "He's a good promoter. He's getting a lot of good, free publicity in a tough category."

How Scoville Did It

Rick Scoville got his business off the ground by generating mounds of free publicity. “Basically, I wouldn’t pay for anything if I didn’t have to,” he admits candidly. The methods below have worked for Scoville—other entrepreneurs can modify them for their own success.

- First, take your story straight to those who can give you free exposure to thousands of people—newspapers, trade magazines, radio and television stations. Keep in mind local radio and television talk shows looking for “people” stories. Find out the names of editors and program directors in your area so you can send letters directly to them. Write short letters, getting to the point very quickly without being pushy. Include any supplementary information that could be useful. Scoville, for instance, tested the mineral content of his water and published his findings in a series of press releases.
- Once you have the free press, use it. Make quality reproductions of any newspaper clippings, even if you have just one, and include the copies in future mailings to news organizations. The *Wall Street Journal* wrote only a paragraph about Artesia, but it was on the front page. When someone opens Scoville’s press packet, he sees the familiar logo of one of the most prestigious newspapers in the world.
- Create a business or feature angle for telling your story. Scoville emphasized the small company versus big company and the American versus the foreigner aspects of his company’s competition with Perrier. If you emphasize unique qualities, however, you should steer clear of gimmicks.
- Design packaging for maximum consumer appeal. Scoville conducted intensive market research to determine what graphics to use. He concluded that mineral water consumers want to drink out of elegant bottles, so a sparkling waterfall is pictured on his logo and on the amber bottles containing Artesia.
- Be patient but persistent and flexible. Don’t worry if someone says no. If your story is worth telling, someone will take an interest in it sooner or later.

—John Sharkley

NAME YOUR PRICE

Lenny Mattioli knows a chump when he sees one. He bumped into a mess of them during his years as a mechanical engineer for Eastman Kodak Company. Every so often, he recalls, the giant company sized up the work of every engineer in Mattioli's shop in the Rochester, New York, headquarters and then gave each of them pretty much the same raise. To Mattioli, only a bunch of chumps would press a one-size-fits-all salary policy.

"There were lots better engineers than I was, but they didn't get a nickel more than I got," says Mattioli. "Kodak never gave me a hard reason to try to do a better job. What a way to run a company, huh?"

Of course, Mattioli muttered the obligatory vow, "If *I* ever run a business . . .," only to be jolted in 1969 by the chance to make good on it. His older brother, the owner of a small and struggling storefront television sales-and-service shop in Madison, Wisconsin, died. It fell to Lenny Mattioli to try to liquidate the business for whatever he could get and pay off some of his brother's six-figure debt. To his surprise, he found that he liked to hustle TV sets. So he quit Kodak and quickly put the shop into the black. Then he began to build a business, American TV & Appliance of Madison Inc.

Today the Madison flagship store is the size of several football fields, and American has opened equally vast stores in Appleton and Milwaukee, as well as in the Michigan mining town of Marquette. Its original product, TV sets, has evolved into the broader line of video components, and Mattioli has added such products as cameras, computers, stereo gear, appliances, and furniture. The company's workforce has reached some 850 people. Sales for 1984 hit $160 million.

Mattioli, chairman of the board and owner of 55 percent of American's stock, credits its success to an aggressive marketing strategy that rests chiefly on the ability of his salespeople to fix their pay and his profits through their performance on the floor—the exact opposite of the system that Mattioli saw at Kodak. "We've taken the bottom line and planted it between every salesman's ears."

The powerful commission system also gives American TV the appeal of an electronics bazaar, where the attraction is the bargaining as much as the bargains. Except on sale items, American has no fixed prices. Its advertising loudly exhorts people to "C'mon in *now* and negotiate your own price."

That breaks with the consumer electronics industry's standard method for setting prices. "The rule of thumb says you tie your prices to your costs," says Mattioli. "But we try to tie ours as close as we can to just how much the customers are willing to pop. We don't ask ourselves, 'Gee, what did this product cost us?' We ask, 'What will this particular customer be willing to pay for this particular product at this particular moment?' How do you establish that? Well, we give every customer a shot at setting their own price."

Consumers seem to like the challenge. Buyers pore over American's merchandise and then go nose-to-nose with the company's sales force.

No chump, Mattioli gives his sales force hard reasons to do hard bargaining: a commission system that is common in big-ticket industrial sales but a rarity at this level of retail marketing. Salespeople are paid on a straight commission basis. The commission is a percentage of Mattioli's markup on each item. The higher the markup, the larger the commission. It is a sliding scale, from 15 percent to 22 percent, with higher commission rates for sales staffers with higher sales volume.

That leaves it up to each salesperson to strike a balance between making fewer sales at higher prices or more sales at lower prices. So two different salespeople can sell precisely the same product in the same store at the same time to two different customers, charging two different prices, and reap vastly different commissions.

"Our salespeople are individual entrepreneurs drawing on our inventory and taking advantage of floor traffic," says Mattioli. "I try to give them as much power as possible to control their incomes. So it comes down to the salesman's ability to turn every looker into a buyer."

The approach can sometimes backfire, however. In the Madison store, for example, shoppers complain of a seller's market, particularly on weekends, squeezing out the opportunity to haggle. In some departments, these shoppers say, customers must suffer through a long wait only to get a sell as hard as carbon steel. "If you aren't ready to buy in the first minute at their first price, then the salespeople will just break off and go wait on someone else," claims a disaffected American TV shopper. In those cases, the company's incentive structure may actually do long-term damage to its standing in the market.

Then again, some customers think that they have come up with a three-step polka to make American TV dance to their tune: First they go to a small store where there is plenty of personal service and they get fully versed in the product they want to buy. Next, they price the product at several discount stores to find the lowest price. Then they walk into American and ask for a price below the competition's. This way, customers translate free product information and free price savings into cash savings. Mattioli and his salespeople aren't the only entrepreneurs in this game.

—RALPH WHITEHEAD, JR.

STRANGE BREW: Distributors Can Make All the Difference

About three and a half years ago, two young men from California's dusty Central Valley started delivering a new, low-alcohol beverage to local liquor stores in a 1953 GMC truck. Today their lightly carbonated, tangy concoction of cheap white wine and fruit juices, called California Cooler, is distributed in forty-nine states and has become a shining star in the wine industry.

In this short time, California Cooler Inc. has developed into the state's fourth-largest wine shipper, with 1984 sales through August totaling $72 million, according to Jon A. Fredrikson, a San Francisco wine-industry consultant, who calls the company "the Apple Computer of the wine industry." And California Cooler pioneers Michael Crete and Stuart Bewley, both thirty-one, think they have only begun to tap the market of consumers who are ready for something different than wine, beer, or soft drinks.

The drink may not suit everyone's taste. The lemon-line, grapefruit, and pineapple-flavored drink has all the oenological complexity of Ripple. But all-natural California Cooler is a winner with Americans who like their beverages cold, sweet, and, presumably, healthy. Retailers and beverage analysts say it tastes far better than the forty-odd cooler clones that have sprung up.

Taste alone, however, has not been the secret to California Cooler's success. Crete and Bewley didn't even invent the drink. Homemade coolers have been around for years—so long that Crete's parents called them "Okie cocktails," a reference to the poor migrant workers of the Depression. Crete created his first batch of cooler at a beach party during his college days in the early 1970s, and for years he made up small batches just for parties. He finally gave in to friends' suggestions and decided to offer the potion for sale, scraping together $5,000 and teaming up with Bewley, an old high school chum, to get the company going. The marketing strategy they worked out—perhaps the crucial element in California Cooler's success—was to package the drink like beer and sell it through beer distributors.

Although other pop-wine drinks, such as Boone's Farm Apple Wine, had appeared before, they were always packaged and distributed like wine. But California Cooler, sold in a twelve-ounce green bottle and sheathed at the neck with gold foil, is a dead ringer for an imported beer. It is aimed not at the snobbish market of wine sippers, but at the broader market of beer and soda gulpers. Crete, who had been a wholesale beer and wine salesman, decided that beer distributors could provide the means to reach that mass market. By selling through beer distributors that call on every outlet from mom-and-pop stores and bait shops to Safeway Stores, California Cooler was presented to a universe of parched throats that no other wine product, save the ubiquitous Gallo, could find.

"This is a thirst-quencher you consume just like a soft drink, versus something you swirl with a steak or lobster," says Crete, sitting in his office adjoining the company's stainless-steel storage tanks in a Stockton, California, industrial park. Crete and his partner make no attempt to veil their disdain for the aura of snootiness surrounding the wine industry. "We don't want any of this 'gold medal, silver medal, we will sell no cooler before its time' stuff," snorts Bewley.

Besides providing access to the mass market, beer distributors offered the young company several other advantages over wine wholesalers. Beer salesmen carry fewer items, for example, so a new brand like California Cooler was less apt to get lost in a blizzard of competing labels.

Moreover, Crete and Bewley felt strongly that the cooler would often be an impulse buy, particularly in the summer heat. That meant it had to be well stocked in retailers' refrigerated sections, a beer route salesman's home turf. And, finally, they thought the beer salesmen had more in common with the retailers to whom they wanted to pitch the product.

"A beer route salesman is a down-home good ol' boy," explains Crete, who once sold Coors beer. "They're very good at relating, and that's very important."

California Cooler's founders showed that they could be good ol' boy salesmen, too. After selling just 700 cases in five months off the GMC truck in 1982, Crete used his beer contacts early to sound out Adolph Coors Company distributors in the San Francisco Bay area.

While passing out taste samples, he and Bewley talked up the California Cooler's solid, if short-lived, sales history, especially a spurt of ten-case-a-week sales to each of the company's accounts during the 100-degree summer days in Central Valley. They also told the beer distributors that their product's classy packaging would help support retail prices—and hefty distributor markups—in line with those for imported beer. This was a powerful lure to the wholesalers, since profits on domestic brews, their mainstay, were withering in the heat of the market-share war among major breweries.

Crete stressed California Cooler's simplicity. "It is packaged just like beer; it can be warehoused and handled on the trucks just like beer," he says. "There was nothing they had to do differently." Still, they got quite a few turndowns, Bewley recalls. Wholesalers wanted to know about advertising support and production capacity, two subjects to which the partners had given little thought. They quickly learned to promise point-of-sale displays and to talk about their plans to expand their bottling capabilities.

One of the first distributors they signed up was in the Napa Valley, California's premier wine-making region. "To be in Napa Valley and carry a wine that doesn't have a Napa label is kind of ridiculous," says Clark Miller, a former defensive end for the San Francisco '49ers who is now a Coors wholesaler in the Napa Valley. "But I liked the product for being all-natural and [having] no additives or preservatives, and I liked [the company]."

Miller also liked the aura of an imported beer conveyed by California Cooler's packaging. "This was the time the super premium beers were super popular," he recalls, "and this tied in with that image." But he had reservations about whether the product would sell, so he ordered only 150 cases in May 1982 and put them into just forty accounts.

It took nearly a year, he recalls, before California Cooler sales really rocketed. Here again, though, Crete and Bewley's decision to use beer distributors paid off. Before long, Miller and a few other distributors in northern California were spreading the word about their hot new product throughout the tightly knit network of Coors distributors. "When they get something that works," says Bewley with a satisfied smile, "they call their buddies." Soon California Cooler had penetrated major southern California markets; by spring 1983, it was in Texas and Arizona. Now it is available through 500 beer distributors in every state but Oklahoma, where state liquor laws keep it out.

That national distribution has become particularly important in light of the way competitors are plunging into the market. So far, California Cooler is thought to control about two-thirds of the market. According to Crete, half the company's competitors, including some established wineries, are using beer distributors. Heublein Inc. introduced a cooler about a year ago, and Joseph E. Seagram & Sons introduced its own version last fall. There is even talk that three major brewers have plans for citrus-flavored coolers made with beer instead of wine.

What has drawn that competition is the heady pace of California Cooler's sales increases: From a paltry 700 cases in 1981 to 80,000 in 1982, sales grew to 6.7 million in the first eight months of 1984.

Most of that growth has come from expansion into new markets. But even in California, sales for the first eight months of 1984 were up 136 percent, according to analyst Fredrikson. "It just continues to grow and grow for us," said Michael Haarstad, merchandising manager for Liquor Barn stores, a Safeway Stores Inc. unit that operates in California and Arizona. "Coolers are a natural to tap the person who doesn't drink wine, from construction workers to housewives."

That natural connection, bolstered by their beer-distributor network, has paid off for Crete and Bewley. Until 1984, when the company budgeted some $9 million for television, radio, and print ads, California Cooler barely got around to advertising.

—PETER DWORKIN

PART

II

SALES MANAGEMENT

Sales make a company grow. And a strong sales force is an essential ingredient for success. But even the experts need advice on training and motivating salespeople. "Sales Management," Part II of this marketing and selling guide, will help you find, develop, and keep a sales force that will make the difference between success and failure. "Sales Management" will provide you with cost-effective ways to secure, train, and motivate top salespeople. The articles also discuss various sales strategies. This collection is an excellent source of quality information on every angle of sales management.

We begin with a look at William Kelly, founder, chairman, CEO, and top salesman for Semi-Specialists of America Inc. (SAI). In "You Can't Turn Your Back on Selling," Kelly explains why selling is SAI's crucial focal point. As he insists, "Anybody who runs a company has to have the capacity to sell, and sell well. You may be trying to sell the image of your company or selling employees on the idea of working hard, but it's all salesmanship. You can't turn your back on that part of your job." Together, Kelly and his salespeople have made SAI a flourishing business.

"Recruiting, training, motivating, supporting, evaluating. These are the disciplines of the sales manager," says Jack Falvey, management consultant and author of the second article, "A Cheerleader, Not a Quarterback." He analyzes the role of the sales manager and compares the skills needed to manage with those used to sell. This article provides a solid background for the articles that follow.

In the third article, "A Low-Cost Way to Find Top Salespeople," Gary Seidel tells his story of how and where he found some terrific sales reps. Some of the reps he reached through trade journals and catalogs were interested in selling his product along with their other lines. Eventually Seidel developed three new western markets for his New Jersey–based company without having spent more than the cost of flying out to meet his new reps and their clients.

How can you know whether a salesperson will be effective? You might want to consider personality testing. Many employers use tests to evaluate potential salesmanship, but others argue that the tests can overlook good candidates. "Improving the Odds for Success" examines the pros and cons of a reasonably priced but not completely foolproof tool for predicting success.

Two articles in this section examine the topic of training, beginning with "He Found a Cheaper Way to Train Salesmen." Here, Arthur Sells, president of National Merchandising Corporation, shares his low-cost training plan. To avoid high turnover, employee dissatisfaction, and low productivity, Sells designed his own training program, which incorporates special commission rates, specific field training, and follow-up instruction. The result is a program that almost pays for itself and prepares the sales force better than more generalized (and expensive) outside training could.

David Bentley, publisher and executive vice-president of Marketing & Media Decisions, taught his staff to write a formal proposal for each sales call, believing that a well-researched, written proposal demonstrates thoroughness and professionalism. "Putting Your Pitch in Writing" describes how articulating a pitch in writing helped focus presentations and promote sales. While challenging his staff to become more professional, Bentley increased several large accounts from 10 to 50 percent. The article concludes with consultant Deborah Dumaine's five steps for "Writing for Results."

If your sales force fits the 80/20 rule (80 percent of sales by 20 percent of your sales force), you should consider new methods of motivation. "Money Isn't Everything: Just Ask Your Salesmen" provides solutions to the problem of incentive. Money is one kind of incentive, but another way to motivate salespeople and simultaneously improve the work environment is to support personal interests and hobbies with incentives. Tips from this article will help you find out what motivates your staff.

Food Dynamics Inc. recognizes the importance of retaining valuable salespeople. "Making Salespeople into Entrepreneurs" describes how three star salespeople who started their own company installed methods of motivation that had been missing in their previous workplaces. Receiving a percentage of the company's profits instead of a straight commission keeps Food Dynamics' salespeople actively motivated and loyal to the company.

Tracking sales provides a monitor of growth and productivity. It also provides solid and easily accessible data for projections and budgets. Two articles examine the significance of tracking sales stats. In "They Showed Salesmen That Time Is Money," we learn that Acme Manufacturing Company's increased productivity and successful product launches stemmed directly from their careful monitoring of sales calls. "Track Sales to Control Company Growth" explores how Dranetz Engineering Laboratories pinpointed ineffective reps, identified their seasonal sales cycle, and doubled sales through a sales charting and forecasting system.

An increasingly favored alternative to field calls, telephone sales are an important way to keep business booming. Two articles look at ways to improve and forecast growth with telephone sales. "Turning Sales Inside Out" describes the transition at Beaver Industrial Supply from face-to-face sales calls to telephone or telephone-field combination calls. While top field salesman Earl Jamison was skeptical at first about the effectiveness of telephone sales, he soon discovered that sales increased while costs decreased. "Techniques for Ringing Up Orders" describes Stephen Perchick's use of super teleselling to exploit Amekor Industries Inc.'s sales potential.

Trade shows give you the opportunity to sell, but how do you take advantage of them without wasting your time? The last article, "Getting Ready for Show Time," provides advice on making trade shows work for you.

Finding and hiring, training and developing, motivating and securing. Building a sales force takes time, skill, and knowledge. "Sales Management," Part II of this *Best of* Inc. *Guide to Marketing and Selling,* brings you *Inc.*'s best advice on every step of this challenging job.

"YOU CAN'T TURN YOUR BACK ON SELLING"

William Kelly, in the backseat of a twenty-seven-foot chauffeur-driven Silver Hawk limousine, is on his way to take a major customer to lunch. The ten-speaker stereo system plays soft music while Kelly uses his car's mobile computer terminal to call up an inventory report for the thumbnail-size integrated circuits his company sells. Today Kelly expects to clinch a deal for at least 10,000 units with a company that makes electronic games and pocket-size calculators.

Kelly is by far the most effective salesman of the twenty-four currently on the road for Semi-Specialists of America Inc., a $30-million electronics distributor based in Farmingdale, New York. Last year Kelly landed $4.5 million in orders, and his hefty salary—a well-publicized $764,000—is a direct reflection of Kelly's skills as a salesman for SAI.

But Kelly is more than SAI's top salesman: He is also chairman of the company, its founder, and its chief executive officer. Seven years ago, in the midst of a recession, Kelly launched SAI with 4 employees, 10 customers, and a minimal inventory of electronics components. The company has grown spectacularly ever since. It now has 2 million circuits on its warehouse shelves, 107 employees, and 4,500 accounts—and Kelly insists the major reason for SAI's success is that he has always taken the job of selling more seriously than do most company heads.

"Anybody who runs a company has to have the capacity to sell, and sell well," he insists. "You may be trying to sell the image of your company or selling employees on the idea of working hard, but it's all salesmanship. You can't turn your back on that part of your job."

At first, SAI's chairman hit the road with his sample case simply because the company was so small that it couldn't afford the luxury of a full-time chief executive. Kelly had spent nine years as an electronics components salesman—"always the top performer wherever I worked," he says—and he was willing to make the extra effort that got him a foot in the door with buyers from companies like IBM. "Not many salesmen on commission will go out of their way to make a twenty-dollar sale for a difficult-to-find item," he recalls, "but this kind of service led to some very lucrative accounts for us." For five years, Kelly opened account after account, working long hours for hardly any salary and with no time off. As the business grew, Kelly hired his brother Mike to handle administrative matters and promoted him to president and chief financial officer; Kelly himself took a desk in the sales office, surrounded by ringing telephones and piles of catalogs and order forms.

By 1977, the effort began to pay off. SAI was doing $10 million in business and had eight other salesmen in the field besides Kelly. SAI's super-salesman chairman found he had a new job—managing and motivating SAI's sales force.

"I try to set an example for everyone else in the company," Kelly says. "I know I can't get every sale, and I don't take it personally when something falls through. But I'm still willing to lay my ego on the line all the time for the company. I'm not embarrassed to make the same kind of demands on my other salespeople.

"At the same time, though, the people at SAI know I don't make unreasonable demands. I know what they're up against in the market, because I talk to the same kind of customers as they do every day. I know when a slump is industrywide and when someone is just not living up to his potential. And I think the fact that I take pride in being good at selling is a lesson that gets across to everyone else in the company."

As SAI prospered, Kelly found his selling skills were needed for still another area—expanding the franchised lines his distributorship carried. To take on new lines, Kelly beefed up his staff by adding fifteen top salespeople, all of whom had at least ten years of experience in electronics distribution and plenty of useful customer contacts. But that wasn't always enough to persuade manufacturers to give SAI the distribution franchises Kelly wanted. SAI had grown so fast that manufacturers were often concerned about the company's financial stability. Proving that SAI was solvent turned out to be a surprisingly difficult task, despite the fact that its financial resources were in enviably good shape.

"A manufacturer wants to see a financial statement to make sure you can pay for his products on delivery, which is how this business works," Kelly explains. "But our sales were increasing so fast that we had a hard time simply making ourselves credible. In just a few years, we'd gone from nothing to being the nineteenth biggest distributor in the nation, and we'd done this without borrowing any money.

"We finally decided about a year and a half ago that we had to establish a good-size bank credit line to show manufacturers we were a healthy outfit. And that's where we ran into trouble. Quite frankly, even the banks didn't believe our financial statements until we went out and had a certified audit done."

The audit helped SAI land a $5-million line of credit, but the experience also taught Kelly that he had to do a better job of selling

SAI's image as a successful company. A touch of razzle-dazzle was called for.

"The reason I bought the Silver Hawk, which cost over one hundred thousand dollars, was to attract attention to the fact that we're doing so well," he concedes. "That's also the reason we make a big deal about the size of my salary. It might seem flamboyant to some people. But in this business—like any other—recognition is the name of the game."

That same kind of recognition also proves helpful for Kelly in dealing with major customers. Kelly still personally handles SAI's ten largest accounts, many of which he developed over the years himself. "If I'm calling buyers," he says, "they're rather impressed that I'm taking the time to see what their needs are. They like talking to the guy in charge. They tend to feel they're going to get the best possible price and terms on their orders."

Moreover, says Kelly, it's important for him to take a personal interest in these accounts, because they may have a major impact on SAI's development. "A salesman on commission is bound to have a narrower point of view than I will as chief executive. I may have different priorities for some customers. By handling these customers myself, I make sure our long-range goals get carried out."

The kind of selling a chief executive does, Kelly maintains, is often nothing more than image-building and leadership—but to be done well, selling also takes hard work. The customers who get Bill Kelly's personal attention may be flattered by a chance to talk to the boss; they also know Kelly will take the time to call and ask whether their orders arrive on time, will get quotes in the mail to them promptly, and will track down the answers to difficult questions.

"My company exists because we do things our consumers want," says Kelly. "If the time ever comes that I'm too busy administering this place to take care of a customer, I'll know we're in trouble."

—Carol Rose

A CHEERLEADER, NOT A QUARTERBACK

Perhaps the most misunderstood job in small companies is that of the sales manager. It is so misunderstood, in fact, that it is often the last management slot to be filled. As a company grows, specialists are hired to handle research and development, engineering, accounting, and so on, but sales stay in the president's office, especially if big contracts or big customers are involved.

There is, of course, a reason for this reluctance to delegate responsibility for sales—namely, the critical importance of the top line on the income statement. Unlike industry giants, smaller companies seldom have a base of "automatic" sales that just seem to flow month in and month out. For that same reason, a sales manager, once hired, is often expected to handle key accounts personally, while trying to manage the sales operation at the same time. The paradox is that no company can grow to its potential until sales becomes a managed function instead of a manager's duty.

Sales managers should never manage sales. They should manage the people that produce the sales. The distinction is a critical one because, in order to build sales, a company has to invest in salespeople. *Invest* is the key word here. Selling costs are indeed investments, just like money spent on research and development or equipment, and they should be evaluated in that light. If, say, you invest $60,000 for a sales representative in one area, you should have some idea of the business that you expect to generate and the amount of time the process will take. Similarly, if another area is very profitable, the question is, should you be reinvesting that profit by opening new territories?

The same logic applies whether you go with independent sales representatives or a direct sales force. With reps, your sales costs will be a constant percentage of sales, and so budgeting and cash flow may be easier to manage. On the other hand, a direct sales force gives you more control. But either way, you need to invest in the people who are selling. Those people, in turn, must be managed. And just as there is more to selling than a shoeshine and a smile, there is more to sales management than being a super salesperson.

The most important element of the sales manager's job is the selection of salespeople. There is simply no substitute for high-quality raw material. Forget about budget or time constraints: Economies in this area will almost always come back to haunt you. An organization forced to hire the "best available" talent is an organization headed for disaster.

The alternative is for the sales manager to undertake an unending talent search. Patience and persistence are the watchwords. When a superior candidate shows up, that's the time to hire, regardless of vacancies. This does not mean that decisions need be made hastily. Even the most valuable candidate can be kept on ice for thirty days while the first flash of enthusiasm fades. Indeed, it is not unusual, or excessive, to take sixty days and four interviews to confirm that a candidate is right for the job.

So how is it possible for a sales manager to do a thorough, disciplined job of recruiting if he or she is expected to be out selling the company's products? Clearly, it is not possible.

The sales manager is also responsible for training, something that many smaller companies think they can't afford. Instead, they try to "buy experience," hiring "Xeroids" or veterans of IBM or Procter & Gamble. But big-company salespeople are not necessarily the best recruits for small companies. Besides, sales training is far less time-consuming and costly than you may think.

The secret is to train salespeople the way surgeons are trained: See one, do one, teach one. Shrewd sales managers often team up recruits with middle producers in the sales force—not the top producers, who often take a lot of shortcuts that work well for them but are not transferable. Customers will also help train new salespeople by letting them observe their businesses for a few days.

As for training materials, there is absolutely no reason that a company can't generate its own. To create an orientation manual, the sales manager can simply have some recruits keep daily journals of impressions and facts, in prose, for their first month on the job. Similarly, field salespeople can write the training manuals by putting together case studies of actual accounts.

Using such methods, recruits can be brought up to solo speed in a few weeks, or even days, no matter how technical the company's business may be. But this will happen only if the sales manager puts in the time and effort required to guide the training process.

On the other hand, sales management does *not* include developing people. They must develop themselves. A sales manager is paid for cheerleading, not quarterbacking. Granted, new salespeople may require a limited amount of coaching—less so if the level of incoming talent is high. But even recruits with zero experience—for example, those directly out of college—can become productive in a few weeks with a well-managed program that rewards early success with high recognition.

Bear in mind that almost all successful salespeople have one thing in common: high ego drive, coupled with a positive mental attitude. The sales manager's job, therefore, is to feed those insatiable egos and promote those positive thoughts. For junior people, that means treating minor contributions as if they were major accomplishments. The truth is that new recruits often need an *inordinate* amount of encouragement, so much so that some managers may feel foolish giving it out. Nevertheless, that's what it takes to put together an effective sales force and build sales.

For senior people, of course, you and your sales manager have to be more creative in recognizing accomplishment. The strategy is fairly straightforward, based on a simple fact: Salespeople, like most of us, work for love and money, and they seldom get enough of either. Accordingly, the way to get the most out of them is to shower top producers with affection, perks, cash, and "recognition gifts"—the custom-made awards (rings, trophies, framed letters) that acknowledge their special contributions to the company.

In this regard, one effective, and underutilized, sales builder is the company car. The car has long since outgrown its function as transportation. Today, the salesperson looks out at the hood ornament and sees his or her image. What's wrong with letting your top people drive Lincoln Town Cars? If Mary Kay can put powder-and-paint sales reps into pink Cadillacs, why can't you put the people who guarantee your company's income into something that reflects their contributions?

The point is that sales management demands a rewards system designed with the needs of salespeople in mind. You and your sales manager should not make the mistake of building a system around your own needs. Someone may be a great shot with a rifle, but—when hunting ducks—the duck dictates that a shotgun be used.

It makes no sense, for example, to have salespeople performing administrative chores, a popular pastime at big companies. How many *Fortune* 500 salespeople say that they take Friday to do their paperwork? Businesses operate on Friday. Why turn salespeople into clerical workers one day a week? When that happens, a company succeeds only in cutting productivity by 20 percent. Let your sales manager do whatever must be done, but don't have salespeople working four-day weeks.

By the same token, it is wise to avoid the big-company practice of equipping salespeople with personal computers, thereby reducing them to "scope dopes." These highly labor-intensive machines are not selling tools. If you want to invest in technology, your sales manager can always get car phones for salespeople and let them make appointments, telephone in orders, and impress their customers while on the road. Again, the important consideration is return on investment, not cost.

The care and feeding of salespeople aside, the sales manager must also look after the staff that provides sales support and customer service. That staff is like the ground crew for a fighter squadron. A company simply cannot afford low skill or high turnover in this area. The challenge for the sales manager is to build this group of employees into a team. Inside people have to spend time on the road, and salespeople have to learn to depend on the support people.

In addition, the sales manager has to watch out for the mistakes that can undermine the sales effort—for example, poor handling of telephone calls. Anyone who answers your company's phone has the power to screw up your biggest account. No call should ever be answered with the company's name and a quick "please hold." The solution is to establish rigid telephone procedures, getting whatever hardware or backup staff may be needed to ensure that callers are treated well.

Last but not least, a sales manager must be a field person, visiting salespeople regularly, spending time with them, walking the ground to see how things are going. In sales management, there is no substitute for field time. Written reports are valuable only to those who write them. They seldom benefit the reader.

Sales analysis, on the other hand, is a matter of simple arithmetic. You add up the numbers and look at the results. No computer program is necessary for that. If you want a pie chart, draw a circle with a crayon and a paper plate, and then fill it in. When the numbers are good, the sales manager should so inform the people who produced them. When the numbers are not good, he or she must act swiftly to revive the sales effort with new blood. People seldom change dramatically. An organization is improved over the interview table, not by spoon-feeding and coaching.

These, then, are the disciplines of the sales manager—recruiting, training, motivating, supporting, evaluating. It is a demanding job, and one that can't be done part-time. Is it any wonder that sales managers who sell generally do a poor job of managing? Or that companies without sales managers soon rub up against the limits of their growth?

True, the founder, president, or chief executive officer may have a fair level of personal selling skills. That's because the CEO has often had to sell the company's concept, whether to attract customers, investors, or key employees. But even a chief executive with exceptional selling skills seldom has the time or inclination to manage a sales force. Besides, sales-management skills are very different from selling skills, and talent in one area does not necessarily indicate talent in the other.

This is not to suggest that it isn't important for a sales manager to have some sales ability—but only to understand the function, not to dazzle the troops or to knock off big orders. Top salespeople tend to be a breed all their own. They should be left to do what they do best and should be rewarded appropriately—with perks, cash, and inordinate amounts of praise and visibility. The best sales managers, on the other hand, often come from the middle group of salespeople. What they do best is what all managers must do well: They know how to manage people.

That, moreover, is how they should spend their time.

—JACK FALVEY

A LOW-COST WAY TO FIND TOP SALESPEOPLE

Three years ago, Gary Seidel, vice-president of Utility Chemical Company in Paterson, New Jersey, decided to expand his family's business west of the Mississippi.

"The ideal situation would have been to hire two super salespeople and give them each a mobile home, a map of the United States, and a list of the largest retailers in the country," says Seidel, whose company manufactures swimming pool chemicals and accessories and institutional cleaners.

Since that route was too expensive, "we had to find a low-cost way of opening up these new markets," Seidel remembers.

He resisted hiring a firm to match his company with sales representatives in his targeted expansion area. Instead, Seidel began to search through trade journals and catalogs sent out to mass merchandisers, his prime market. He hit it rich when he found an article in *The Discount Merchandiser* magazine that listed representatives and distributors with contacts in the appropriate outlets. From that list, Seidel contacted a salesman who would end up being one of his top representatives in the state of Arizona.

"The magazine had an ad for a new cosmetic line by a major cosmetics company," recalls Seidel. "They printed a list of all their distributors and reps in fifty states, with addresses and phone numbers in the ad."

Seidel reasoned that it wouldn't be hard for a rep who's selling cosmetics in a drug or department store or a supermarket to walk a few aisles farther and place swimming pool chemicals on a shelf. So he sent a form letter to each rep on the list, saying why he felt it would be profitable and convenient for the salespeople to represent his product. The total expense for typing the letter and for postage was about $150.

About four days later, Seidel got a telephone call from Shelly Klein, an independent rep working out of Phoenix. Seidel asked about his background, the lines that he represented, and the stores he sold to.

"I was impressed by his accounts and the stores he was selling to," recalls Seidel. "They were the same markets we were after. And the size of Klein's organization was also right. He had about ten people—

two or three assistants, a secretary, and service personnel—working for him. At least twice a month, he was able to service customers to make sure displays were attractive and shelves well stocked."

Just as the rep needed to sell himself to Seidel, Seidel knew he had to convince Klein that taking on his company's line of swimming pool chemicals would be profitable to him.

During their initial conversation, Seidel explained to Klein that Utility Chemical prefers to work with reps without contracts. "If you find you can't sell our line, it's not worth your time or ours to keep you on," Seidel said. "And if you are selling it, you won't want to leave, and we won't want you to leave." Seidel also explained the company's commission structure: Utility has two price sheets; the higher offers customers discounts and free merchandise, the lower doesn't. The company pays a 7.5 percent commission for sales on the higher price sheet, and a 5 percent commission for the other. The rep decides which sheet he'll show customers.

Seidel also told Klein that the company had done preliminary work in the Arizona market, sending out detailed proposals to outlets there. The proposals described the company's background and prices and told why the products were profitable and desirable. "If you can do preliminary footwork in the market area before contacting the rep, you'll be ahead of the game," says Seidel.

The information, and the fact that Utility Chemical had been in business since the 1920s and had some of the top mass merchandisers and chain stores as customers, apparently impressed Klein. Seidel followed up the phone call with samples and literature. Within a few weeks, Klein had made appointments with six buyers, distributors, vice-presidents, and merchandise managers.

Seidel flew to Arizona to accompany Klein to the initial interviews. "I wanted to acquaint him with our products, so the trip was a kind of training program," Seidel explains. "I wanted to be there in case a prospect asked the rep a question he couldn't answer, and I wanted the potential customers to feel they'd always get support from the factory. Having a factory rep at these initial interviews lent credibility to the product as well as to the rep."

Five of the six people Seidel and Klein saw in those days became customers, and Klein has lined up business with two distributors. Between March and December of last year, Klein had brought in $600,000 worth of new business.

"Arizona has been our most lucrative new market west of the Mississippi," says Seidel. "We followed similar procedures—beginning with contacts we made through trade journal information—to build up our second and third most profitable western markets in California and Texas.

"Once you've established a relationship with a rep," adds Seidel, "it's important to maintain constant contact. The more follow-up you have, the better selling job the rep will do for you." For example, Seidel regularly sends his reps industry surveys and profitability studies and keeps them up-to-date about customer services the company offers—anything that might help them do a more effective selling job.

Where to Hunt for Reps

Reading trade journals and company catalogs has enabled Gary Seidel to build up Utility Chemical's West Coast market at a low initial cost. Here's what to review:

- ***Advertisements*** are the best source for lists of reps and distributors, says Seidel. "When companies launch a new product, they'll often include a list of their reps and distributors in the ads. Most likely, these will be some of the best in the business."
- ***Annual directories*** published by industry trade journals provide information on how businesses or consumer outlets have done in the past year. They also contain sections where manufacturers' reps advertise. Seidel's Texas rep, for example, had listed himself as president of the Southwestern Toy & Hobby Association, which told Seidel that he was experienced and had good contacts.
- ***Catalogs*** of companies manufacturing similar products often list their reps and distributors.
- ***Feature articles*** give another valuable source of information. "I might read that a chain has opened a new house-and-garden section," says Seidel. "It's a perfect opportunity for us to introduce our swimming pool chemicals." The information Seidel gets for the price of a magazine subscription is available elsewhere, at a greater price. Matching services will match companies with sales reps, but they'll charge a percentage of the first year's volume you do with that rep, Seidel points out. Books that contain lists of manufacturers' reps can cost anywhere from $50 to $200, and mailing lists might run from $250 to $1,000. "With all of these other options, you're still taking a chance," says Seidel. "So why not take a chance in the least costly way?"

—Carol Rose Carey

IMPROVING THE ODDS FOR HIRING SUCCESS

If performing the following activities paid the same compensation and carried equal status, which would you choose: (a) representing clients in court; (b) performing as a concert pianist; (c) commanding a ship, (d) advising on electronics problems?

Among these statements, which best describes you: (a) I don't need to be the focus of attention at parties; (b) I have a better understanding of what politicians are up to than most of my associates do; (c) I don't delay making decisions that are unpleasant?

Your answers, when evaluated along with the responses to more than 170 other questions, could say something about your potential as a salesperson, says Herbert Greenberg, president of Personality Dynamics Inc. (PDI), a Princeton, New Jersey, management consulting and testing company.

Although many people regard personality tests with distaste and skepticism, others report that they are a cost-effective way to make wiser hiring decisions. One example is L. "Fritz" Covillo, senior vice-president and general manager for United Foods Inc. in Denver. "People razzle-dazzle me in an interview," admits Covillo, who heads up a sales force of more than fifty people, "but how do I know if they have drive, if they can handle rejection, or if they can be self-disciplined enough to go out and sell in the boonies? Good vibes are okay, but how do I get inside a guy's head?"

Covillo began using personality testing more than five years ago. It has, he reports, not only helped confirm his hunches but has also challenged his first impressions about people.

To those who question testing's validity, Covillo argues that subjective feelings after interviews and reference checks are even less valid as predictors of sales success. "The interview is the greatest lying tool in the world," says Greenberg of PDI. "It's a sophisticated world. People know how to handle themselves; they know how to dress and what to say. They have résumés professionally prepared and give reference checks that are going to look good. Everything is beautifully designed to put up a very nice facade." Conversely, he notes, people with no track record in sales may present an unpolished appearance that belies their sales ability.

For more than twenty years, Herbert Greenberg and his wife, Jeanne, have studied salespeople to try to understand what makes them successful. During the 1960s they surveyed 18,000 salespeople in fourteen different industries and found that success was not related to experience, sex, age, or education—the criteria upon which many people base their hiring decisions. A recent study conducted by Xerox Learning Systems in Stamford, Connecticut, which analyzed more than 500 sales calls in more than twenty companies, also found that age, college education, sex, or years of experience had no correlation with success. Instead, a person's behavior during the sales call—including how well he or she listened to the client, handled objections, and closed the interview—was what determined success.

While the Greenbergs agree with Xerox's conclusion that sales skills can be learned, they argue that companies should start out with the best raw material possible. Their research has shown that certain basic characteristics—which can be partly revealed, they say, through testing—are found in nearly all successful salespeople. For example, most top performers display strong drive marked by an intense desire to persuade others, not so much because of money but because of a feeling that they *have* to make a sale. These people also have "empathy"—they listen well and can tailor an interview to suit a customer. Finally, the best performers are resilient, even when they repeatedly lose sales.

But the Greenbergs also emphasize that each sales job requires a different balance of strengths and that the most difficult part of the hiring process, understanding the job well enough to match the right person with it, always precedes recruiting. For example, Harvey Kimmel of Edward Don & Company of New Jersey, a Mt. Laurel restaurant supply distributorship, points out that independence, aggressiveness, and the ability to take rejection are a lot more important to job success at his company than a college degree. "We're selling pots and pans out of thirty-pound bags," explains Kimmel. "This isn't high tech."

PDI's test consists of 181 questions. "To a certain extent, we know people are going to put up a facade—just as when they interview or when they prepare a résumé," says Herbert Greenberg. "They're going to at least put their best foot forward. If we ask them, 'Do you want to be a salesperson or a forest ranger?' do you really think they're going to tell us they want to be a forest ranger? Or if they blush easily, are they going to admit it? We analyze the perfect person they tell us they are, and that gives us clues to the person they really are."

Companies that use PDI's test pay $125 to have the results evaluated. A PDI account executive calls the client with an evaluation within twenty-four hours of receiving the test. The call is followed by a written report. Once the fee is paid, PDI will review the results as often as the client wishes. For example, when Lumberman's Underwriting Alliance in Boca Raton, Florida, considers promoting a salesperson to a management position, the company asks for a reevaluation of the test results in light of the new position. "We know we've got a chocolate cookie," says Bill Weston, assistant vice-president of Lumberman's. "But can we make angel food cake out of the same ingredients?"

"So often," says Herbert Greenberg, "companies take their best salesperson and 'reward' him by making him or her a manager. They've taken their best producer—who's a doer not a delegater—and ended up with a mediocre or worse manager. When he fails, he often takes a sales job with a competitor and beats their brains out." Reevaluations often result in PDI's recommending a better compensation or bonus package rather than a promotion.

Sometimes, however, recommendations encourage promotions and job shifts that go against the company's wishes. For example, an insurance company called PDI when it was wrestling with a junior accountant about a promotion. The accountant, who had been with the company more than fifteen years, wanted to sell, and the company asked PDI to give him the test in hopes that it would convince the accountant that sales wasn't his forte.

"The test came in as one of the most classic sales patterns we've ever seen for life insurance," recalls Herbert Greenberg. "He had empathy, drive, and the ability to take rejection. In fact, we sat around laughing, wondering how this person could have been an accountant and sat still for two minutes without cutting his throat." PDI told the company the bad news: The junior accountant, they believed, should not continue as an accountant but should be transferred into sales. Reluctantly the company followed their advice, licensed the individual, and he became a top producer.

Personality tests are just one brand of testing available to businesses. Many of the large test publishers, such as Psychological Corporation, a subsidiary of Harcourt Brace Jovanovich, distribute hundreds of tests.

One of the tests most popular among companies hiring for field sales positions is the Wesman Personnel Classification Test, a twenty-eight-minute test for verbal and numerical ability. Although Psychological Corporation will sell the self-scoring Wesman test directly to a businessperson at $9 for twenty-five copies, other tests, particularly personality tests, are often available only to psychologists or consultants who know how to interpret the results. While most industrial psychologists believe that testing can be useful, they emphasize that it should be approached with healthy skepticism. "Testing should not be the instrument of decision," says Robert Guion, a professor at Bowling Green State University and author of *Personnel Testing* (McGraw-Hill, 1965). "It should be used as a flag that either agrees with or contradicts your impressions about a person." Testing works only when it is accompanied by thorough interviewing and reference checks. In fact, one advantage of testing may be that, if used correctly, it adds another dimension to and helps organize the selection process.

Before trying out any test on applicants, says Harvey Kimmel, try it on yourself and on current employees, and find out if what it measures really relates to success on the job. Kimmel, for example, tried

PDI's test on twenty salespeople—top performers who had been with the company as long as twenty-five years as well as on a couple of people Kimmel said he was planning to fire the next week. "Without knowing any background on the people," says Kimmel, "the test hit them right on the nose."

Like any aspect of the hiring process, testing is illegal if it discriminates against groups, such as women, blacks, or the handicapped—unless it can be proven that certain skills being tested are related to job success. For example, an eye test might discriminate against the elderly, but the court might allow such discrimination if the company could prove that driving was essential to the job. Before using any test, a company should make sure that what the test measures is related to the job and that there is statistical evidence that the test is nondiscriminatory. Does a woman, for instance, stand the same chance as a man of passing the test?

Businesses interested in using tests can write for a guide published by the Division of Industrial-Organizational Psychology of the American Psychology Association called *Principles for the Validation and Use of Personnel Selection* ($4; Assessment & Development Associates, 12900 Lake Ave., Suite 824, Lakewood, OH 44107). For a list of about fifty tests that can be used to evaluate salespeople, write for *Measures for the Selection and Evaluation of Salespersons* ($3; ETS Test Collection, Educational Testing Service, Princeton, NJ 08541).

—Sara Delano

HE FOUND A CHEAPER WAY TO TRAIN SALESMEN

Sales training that costs nothing, that actually pays for itself? Arthur Sell doesn't think that goal is unrealistic.

His company, the $6-million National Merchandising Corporation of Natick, Massachusetts, sells advertising space on telephone book covers to local merchants. It's a simple product, a simple concept. The management thinking behind NMC's training program, however, isn't simple. It's effective sales management: deciding what skills and knowledge your sales force needs to sell your product and training them to use those skills to get the sales results you want. In NMC's case, Sells has built the company by finding a way to recruit and train a large sales force at the lowest possible cost.

Like most small companies, Sells' doesn't have the cash to invest in elaborate training programs. But training is important to companies like NMC. "If you don't have a training program, you pay for it in high turnover, employee dissatisfaction, and lower productivity," Sells says.

NMC's training center is paid for and run by the company; it provides four days of instruction and eight weeks of field training. Last year, the company claims, the sales training program actually paid for about two-thirds of the company's budgeted costs. NMC budgeted $155,000 for recruiting and training, but the 280 trainees generated $973,000 in sales during the eight weeks of field training. The result was a cost of about $242 for each person who entered the four-day training center, NMC claims.

The sales training program was developed by Sells and former NMC president William Zollo. (Zollo left NMC recently, after nine years, and is pursuing other business opportunities.) NMC keeps its training costs low by reducing the commissions it pays during the field training period. The trainee's commission is 20 percent rather than the 25 percent paid a regular salesperson. Trainees are supervised by regional sales representatives who are paid 5 percent commissions instead of the 10 percent they usually receive. NMC contends that this net 10 percent reduction in commission substantially reduces training costs.

On the other hand, attrition in the training program is high; only 55 of the 270 people who entered the training center in 1979 remained with the company after a year. While he's unhappy with the high turnover, Zollo points out that the 55 new salespeople helped NMC grow from $4 million to $6 million last year.

NMC's low-cost sales training, Sells says, is a great improvement on the training system he found when he joined the firm in 1971. "Their idea of training," Sells says, "was to send new trainees out in the field with an old pro, and pay them one hundred fifty dollars in salary each week until they got the hang of it." But in that system, turnover was running about 90 percent a year and sales had stagnated at about $900,000. Sells set two goals for the company: a 20 percent annual sales increase, and geographical expansion well beyond the ten states where NMC then sold advertising.

He stopped paying "wasteful" salaries to trainees and put them on a commission-only basis. But this created a problem: Why would recruits slave for NMC when they could get $10,000 plus commissions from a large insurance company? Sells knew he needed to offer other inducements: strong potential of good first-year income, bonuses, financial incentives, opportunities for rapid advancement, and solid training.

But outside training programs were expensive—sales training manuals typically cost $100 each and outside training centers $500 a person—and too generalized. "They couldn't give our people the specific information and training they needed to sell our product," Sells says.

Sells didn't know anything about the mechanics of putting together an in-house training program, so he hired William Zollo, a sales training expert and vice-president of Fidelity Corporation. Zollo thought that big-company sales training techniques could be adapted to the small firm if NMC could find a way to "prove" its trainees quickly in order to cut the large initial costs.

Zollo's idea was to link the recruiting and training process in a nine-week make-or-break period. If a trainee didn't ring up a minimum amount of sales, he would be dropped from the program.

Such a survival-of-the-fittest approach is necessary, Zollo and Sells say, because NMC can't afford to carry the cost of failures, and there's no way NMC can determine in advance whether a prospective trainee will be a successful salesperson. "We give trainees all the technical training and support necessary," Sells says. "After that, it's an acid test in the field."

But NMC also faces the challenge of helping promising recruits survive the acid test. The more trainees NMC can retain, the lower its costs will be. So motivating people to succeed starts during recruiting. "My job is to sell people on the opportunities of being a salesperson at National Merchandising," says Rick Mayo, a divisional sales representative in NMC's Washington, D.C., region, one of eleven regions covering thirty-five states.

"To be successful," Mayo says, "I have to make some pretty intelligent guesses about who can become a good salesperson." (Fewer than 10 percent of the people who enter NMC's training center have previous sales experience.) Mayo says he's tough during the initial interview, pointing out the drawbacks as well as the rewards of the training program. "I ask them if they're willing to go several weeks without making any money. I want to make sure they're willing to gamble for a new career."

One such gambler was Mark Zelinger, who had grown tired of his job as a rehabilitation counselor and saw sales as a possible new career. Mayo felt that Zelinger was ambitious and aggressive enough to be pushed into succeeding. "I also knew it was tough for him to leave a field in which he had a master's degree and a lot of experience," Mayo adds.

Mayo pointed out to Zelinger that average earnings in the first two years at NMC were between $17,000 and $24,000, and that there were performance bonuses and sales contests, one of which sent ten salespersons to the Super Bowl. If Zelinger eventually became a manager, Mayo told him, he could earn $35,000 to $70,000 a year.

Mayo's pitch worked. In January 1979, Zelinger turned down a job offer at an insurance company that offered a $16,000 salary plus commissions. He joined NMC, he says, because "the fact that they really wanted me gave me a lot of gratification. I was ready for a gamble, and they made me feel like I would be part of the team."

But the four-day training center was "like being taught to swim by being thrown in the water." At least the training center had NMC managers there to help him out. When he got out in the field he found the situation was worse than he had anticipated. The first two weeks Zelinger didn't make a single sale. "I told Rick that this wasn't for me. I said I would give it one more week before I quit."

Mayo knew he had to move quickly to save his investment in Zelinger. About 50 percent of his income comes from personal selling; the time Mayo puts into recruiting, working at the training center, and providing field support for trainees like Zelinger cuts down on the time he could be out in the field earning a commission. He also had to meet an NMC goal of building his sales force to increase market penetration in his area from 25 percent to 80 percent. To do that, Mayo says, "I had to get Mark and others like him to succeed."

Mayo and regional representative Ron Szpatura decided to spend a day in the field with Zelinger, working on Zelinger's two major problems: calling on the right prospects and giving a better, more effective sales presentation. The effort paid off. Zelinger made his first sale in his third week of field training. He made nine sales in the seventh week and total sales for the training period went over $10,000. Sales in his first year were $89,000; he has since won a Super Bowl trip and is slated for a promotion to divisional representative.

William Zollo maintains that the figures speak for themselves. The cost of making Mark Zelinger—and the fifty-five others who stayed with the company for a year—successful was about $1,231 each, Zollo claims. He figures that's a good investment for someone who added $89,000 in sales in his first year.

MAY THE SALES FORCE BE WITH YOU

"What skills and knowledge do my salespeople need to sell my product, and what can I do to make them succeed?"

Those are the key questions any smaller company manager should ask about his sales force, experts say. Effective sales force management means controlling the way your sales force operates in order to get the results you want.

National Merchandising Corporation has defined, more clearly than most small companies, what it needs to do to make its sales force achieve company objectives, says Robert P. Currie of Neville & Currie Associates Inc., a Wellesley, Massachusetts, consulting firm. NMC's approach certainly isn't sophisticated, he adds, but the company has analyzed what Currie considers the three major aspects of effective sales management:

1. *Coverage.* Are enough sales calls being made to cover the territory and meet company marketing objectives? Are salespeople being added quickly enough to keep the rate of sales growth constant?
2. *Salesmanship.* How sophisticated does the sales force have to be to sell the product or service? How much training is necessary?
3. *Qualified prospects.* Are salespeople calling on only those people who can make purchasing decisions?

A small firm must decide which areas are most critical in marketing its product or service, Currie says. Deciding how significant salesmanship is becomes particularly important. "The degree of salesmanship necessary," he says, "depends on how difficult and how sophisticated or complex the sell is. The higher the degree of salesmanship necessary, the more money has to be allocated for training and sales force development."

Selling computer software or construction equipment, for example, requires sophisticated sales training. The salesperson must have a thorough understanding of customer needs and concerns. He must be able to meet many different objections and to make a customer prefer his product to a competitor's product.

Selling advertising on telephone directory covers to local retail merchants, as NMC does, is relatively simple, Currie says. It's a product that can be sold by knocking on doors. NMC has recognized that contacting retail merchants and making them aware of the product and its advantages are the most important aspects of its sales approach. So the company asks two basic questions: Are salespeople making enough calls, and are they calling on the right prospects?

NMC decided that it could teach trainees the basics of selling telephone directory cover advertising in four days of intensive, in-house training. But one consultant questions whether the four-day introductory session prepares a trainee for the rigorous eight-week field training.

NMC trainee Mark Zelinger was actually a training center failure, says Robert Whyte of Porter, Henry & Company, a New York consulting firm specializing in sales management. When Zelinger entered the field, Whyte points out, he felt like he had been thrown in the water to learn how to swim. "A good sales training program," Whyte says, "should teach him how to swim. It should stimulate what's going to happen in the real world."

Yet, Whyte says, Zelinger was "saved" with the help of NMC field managers and became a successful salesperson. NMC's strength, Whyte adds, probably isn't its classroom training, but its field sales management.

"Field coaching is the most important aspect in influencing the performance and potential of trainees," Whyte says. It's a cliché in the sales management business that only 20 percent of a salesperson's knowledge comes from formal training; the remaining 80 percent comes from field training.

A good relationship between field manager and trainee is important whether a small company hires 2 or 200 new salespeople in a year, consultant Currie says. "A field manager should virtually live with the trainee for two weeks," he says. "He should go on calls with trainees, interact with them, role play, and do everything possible to encourage them." If companies force trainees to develop on their own, Currie adds, they will flounder about, become frustrated, and quit.

—BILL HENDRICKSON

MONEY ISN'T EVERYTHING: Just Ask Your Salesmen

Take a couple of minutes to look at your recent sales records. Examine how each of your salesmen has performed.

You may notice a pattern often referred to in sales management as the 80/20 rule. It simply describes the fact that in most companies, a small group of salesmen—20 percent—account for the bulk of the sales—80 percent. You will probably also notice that the performance rankings among your salesmen hardly ever change; the top salesman is consistently the top salesman, and there is little variation in the order of finish. Finally, you will probably find that much of the turnover in your sales force occurs in the 80 percent who contribute only 20 percent of the business.

These are all symptoms of sales management that is in a rut. Quite often, this rut is caused by the mistaken assumption that all salesmen are motivated by the same rewards. One way to improve a sales force's peformance is to make sure that the rewards and incentives you offer each salesman are tailored to his needs.

Want to try a little experiment to check the claim that each salesman responds to a particular motivation? Casually ask each member of your sales staff what sports he likes to compete in. Probably the majority prefer individual sports like running, tennis, and golf. They may like to watch team sports, but they prefer to compete either alone or against one other person. Salesmen are alike in that they want to be recognized for their individual abilities. It follows, then, that each demands a different kind of recognition.

Sales managers spend countless hours in sales training sessions emphasizing that the key to selling is to find out what motivates each customer to buy. Yet, when it comes to motivating their own salesmen, managers tend to forget their own advice. They treat their sales force as a group, and they apply solutions that fit a group, not making an effort to find out what motivates each salesman.

In fact, most sales managers rely on cash alone to motivate: "Let's just give him another quarter percent on anything over $300,000." Often, that works. We used to have a salesman who knew to the penny what his commissions were on every sale. If we wanted him to sell more, all we had to do was offer him a higher commission. He would be a top performer in almost any company, probably always finishing in the top three. The reason, however, has little to do with his overall sales ability. He would always rank high because he was motivated by the incentive most commonly offered, money.

Now, you do have to reward salesmen with cash. But each salesman has a threshold of "enough money." Once he reaches that level, the extra commission will have little effect. That's the prime reason why the salesmen's performance rankings stay the same.

If you can get the rankings to change frequently, however, you will find your total sales consistently reach higher levels. But how do you get this competition going strong among the members of your sales staff? How do you get a salesman to double his billings in one year? Basically, by motivating the individual and not the group.

For example, one salesman, who we believed had all the attributes to be a top performer, was consistently at the bottom of our rankings. He never won a contest, and more importantly, he rarely met his goals. We finally discovered that his particular motivation was attention. All it took for him to move up was for his sales manager to call on him at least three times a week. In a year, with no other changes, he began to meet his quotas and move up fast.

Vintage wine was the key to getting the best out of another salesman. After probing to find what recognition this salesman required, we discovered that his hobby was cooking. A case of vintage wine, time off for a cooking class, or even an unusual cookbook meant more to him than any other monetary bonus or vacation contest. Our use of these incentives also showed the salesman we were interested in him as an individual.

Sometimes the salesman himself will give you the key. "I want to get into sales management," one of our salesmen told us. The only reason he sold was to get promoted.

It isn't always easy to determine the motivating element for a salesman. However, there are proven areas to investigate. You will find clues in their lifestyles, the kinds of cars they drive, the way they spend leisure time, and the nonbusiness subjects they talk about in the office.

Watching a salesman work in the field may also give you clues. Take the time to look at what sales techniques the salesman uses. There are hard-sell and soft-sell salesmen. You'll probably have a tough time motivating a hard-sell salesman with a soft-sell approach. And it took us a long time to learn that some of the soft sellers just couldn't be motivated with a "kick in the pants." In fact, we got the reverse reaction—they sold less rather than more.

How you apply what you learn is also a result of what you know about the individual. In one case, a salesman was a strong family man, and his ambition was to win the exotic vacation contest so that he could take his wife along to share the prize. For him, talking about the vacation site and the standings in the contest were strong propellants.

Some salesmen are self-motivators who will not work under pressure or outside motivation. All you need to do with such individuals is give them the ball and point the way.

Other salespeople need help setting short-term goals that will keep their sense of accomplishment high. These salesmen may appreciate being told exactly what they're doing right and what they're failing to do.

Andrew Carnegie said it best: "You cannot push anyone up the ladder unless he is willing to climb himself." When appropriate motivation is applied, each person is getting what he wants and giving you what you want. Everybody wins.

—GEORGE DEBENEDETTO

MAKING SALESPEOPLE INTO ENTREPRENEURS

Food Dynamics Inc. was born in 1976 when Bob Galvin, Bob Beaudry, and Florence Busch decided to strike out on their own, leaving a large New England food brokerage firm where they had been star salespeople. Within thirty days, they'd signed on seven product lines—which meant a total of $8,000 a month in commissions.

Their move, though, presented them with an important question: How could they keep top salespeople from eventually leaving their new company? If Food Dynamics was going to grow, the three partners knew they'd have to give their salespeople a reason to stay with the company.

At first, there were no employees to worry about losing. Galvin, Beaudry, and Busch, representing their manufacturers' food lines, traveled around New England with their sample cases; they called mainly on buyers from hospitals, restaurants, schools, and food distribution companies. Since they put any profits into building up Food Dynamics' image, they ran a lean operation.

"I remember when Beaudry and I first began going down to Connecticut for overnight stays," Galvin recalls. "One of us would check into a motel room and the other would sneak up later. It worked out fine until one night we got to the room only to find a single bed." Then, he remembers with a laugh, "we learned just how close a partnership we had."

After two years, the partners decided they were ready to expand. They wanted to hire individuals who were not just good salespeople but would also become almost as loyal to the company as they themselves were. All three believed that the best salespeople were entrepreneurs at heart who wanted a sense of participation in the business as well as a paycheck. One way to inspire loyalty, they felt, was to give the people they hired a stake in the company by tying commissions to the salesperson's contribution to overall profits.

According to Michael King, a vice-president of the National Food Brokers Association, most food brokers pay their salespeople on a salary basis, with a bonus arrangement. The problem then, says Galvin, "is that there is really no accountability. Salespeople may know how much they do in sales, but they have no idea what their contribution is to the profitability of the company."

So when Galvin, Beaudry, and Busch hired their first seasoned professional, John Vaillancourt, they decided to offer a compensation plan that would give him a stake in the company's growth and to use this plan as a prototype when it came to compensating future employees.

Under the system set up by Food Dynamics' owners, a salesperson would not only develop sales in a territory but would also take charge of maximizing the territory's profitability for the firm, in return for a portion of the profits earned. Vaillancourt, for example, took total responsibility for the North Country market of Maine, New Hampshire, and Vermont. Food Dynamics, which specializes in providing food for restaurants, hospitals, and schools, among other institutions, had barely penetrated the three northern states and hoped Vaillancourt could increase its sales there to distributors and large-scale consumers.

Vaillancourt received a salary, plus a quarterly bonus based on a careful calculation of the profits he brought in from his area. The owners issued regular reports, advising Vaillancourt of the direct expenses that Food Dynamics had paid out for his salary and expenses. They also added in indirect expenses, figured as a percentage of the cost of maintaining the company's Wellesley, Massachusetts, headquarters and its sales and service staff. After all expenses were subtracted from total sales for the territory, Vaillancourt then received an agreed-upon percentage of the profit.

Vaillancourt found the system gave him incentive to develop his territory—and an equally strong incentive to stay with Food Dynamics once he had developed it. "They treat my territory like another branch of the company," he says. "I've been given a great deal of autonomy, but when I need help the company is right there beside me."

"By making our salespeople responsible for their costs," says Galvin, "we make them more conscious of what's involved in the day-to-day running of our operation. People tend to think that items such as typewriter ribbons don't cost anything. Our financial reports also show the cyclical nature of the business—that we rely on the third and fourth quarters to carry us through the slower half." Moreover, tying bonuses directly to profits conserves Food Dynamics' cash flow in unprofitable periods.

Food Dynamics now has three key salespeople—out of a total staff of nineteen—managing portions of New England. The share of the firm's overhead and sales-support costs that each salesperson must cover varies, depending on the owners' assessment of his territory's potential. Once a year, each of these salespeople meets with the owners to discuss the projected revenues the company can expect from his territory. Expenses are also estimated for the coming year, and the difference represents the profit likely to be shared with the salesperson.

The company had to work closely with its salespeople in adjusting the profit-based compensation system to the firm's changing needs. Occasionally the company decides to invest in expanding its influence in a given territory; initially there may be no profits for the salesperson to share. That happened when Food Dynamics first hired Vaillancourt to develop the North Country. The solution: an agreement that for the first few pay periods, Food Dynamics' headquarters' budget would absorb some of the expenses that would normally have been charged against Vaillancourt's territory.

Finding a compensation system that gave salespeople a stake in the company was a major step for the three partners, but they also recognized that they needed to go beyond dollars and cents if they were going to hang on to their top performers. "At some point," says Galvin, "salary becomes a moot question. More money is not always the way to secure a salesperson's loyalty."

Thus the partners structured the company so that salespeople in the field could count on a maximum of support and personal attention from the three owners. As additional salespeople were hired, each was assigned to the partner who knew the territory best and who could offer the most expert help whenever it was needed. Several times a year, for example, Beaudry visits Vaillancourt's territory to make special presentations to local distributors. And at trade shows at least one partner always works side by side with Food Dynamics' salespeople.

Constant telephone contact is the rule. "When we talk with our salespeople by phone, often three to four times a day, they don't feel that we're checking up on them," Galvin says. "Usually we discuss things like 'How can we increase distribution here?' or 'What's the quickest way to ship a product?' There are no mandates sent down from a central office."

The three partners have placed a great deal of emphasis on developing the skills and knowledge of their salespeople. They send them on trips to manufacturing plants to get a firsthand view of how products are made, and encourage direct contacts between salespeople and the manufacturers whose lines they represent—considered a risky tactic in the food brokerage business, since good salespeople often use their connections with manufacturers to launch their own firms. "We have faith in our ability to pick the right people," says Galvin. "In six years, we've lost only one line through a salesperson's leaving the company—and that salesperson came into our company with three lines."

The results of Food Dynamics' approach to managing salespeople have been financial success and team spirit. Only one salesperson has resigned in the company's history. Today annual sales are $30 million, and twenty-two top food manufacturers are represented.

"I guess the possibility that we could lose a key salesperson always exists, but I don't lose any sleep over it," Galvin says. "We feel pretty confident that our salespeople enjoy their work, are motivated, and have little reason to move someplace else."

THEY SHOWED SALESMEN THAT TIME IS MONEY

The Acme Manufacturing Company manufactures a line of industrial specialty products that it markets both directly and through distributors. Four years ago, the company became concerned about its development of new products and markets. Business was generally satisfactory—sales were increasing by 8 percent to 10 percent a year—but the company's efforts to expand its line and enter new markets were disappointing.

Acme had been introducing four or five new products a year, and it expected its fifty-man sales force to develop two or three new markets in the same twelve-month period. The results were mediocre at best, and no one quite knew why.

Management decided to take a closer look at sales call patterns and costs per call. It sought answers to three key questions: (1) How much does a sales call cost us? (2) How many accounts of different types can our sales force serve properly? (3) How many new products and markets can we develop in the year ahead?

The analysis that followed led to establishment of a realistic annual budget of field sales calls. The budget enabled the company to allocate and control the amount of time devoted to specific products and markets. Management also made some interesting discoveries along the way, not the least of which was that its cost of $32 per sales call would almost double between 1976 and 1979.

Acme's sales call budget was developed by cooperative effort between individual field men, district managers, and sales management. The budget's primary purpose was not to regiment salesmen but to provide the increments of time needed to do a professional selling job. It focused solely on the salesmen's movements, week by week and month by month, during the year.

To establish its call budget, Acme started with the basic account-servicing function. That meant classifying its accounts. Tops on the list were 300 "key accounts"—major customers who as a group generated about 75 percent of total sales volume. The initial plan was to call on these accounts every week. But several salesmen suggested that there was danger of wearing out the welcome mat. It was agreed that calling on each key account every two weeks would be sufficient.

Acme's next customer category included 2,500 small accounts. These could not be neglected—each year some developed into key accounts. Yet, with sales costs rising and with distributors serving these accounts, how much time did they deserve? Acme adopted a call pattern of once every six weeks.

The company had 150 distributors who served some key accounts but generally called on small accounts that required prompt deliveries from local stocks. Careful consideration of the distributors' needs by Acme's sales force, sales management, and the distributors themselves indicated that calls on distributors should be scheduled every other week. However, *double* call time was assigned to the distributor calls. This would enable Acme's salesmen to hold distributor meetings when required, to cultivate individual distributor salesmen, and to accompany distributor salesmen on occasional customer calls when necessary.

Classifying the three types of accounts seemed to take care of the company's basic call needs on its established product line, until one field salesman pointed out the need for "crisis" calls. "What do we do when a customer or distributor suddenly has a service problem, or headquarters raises a question about a customer's credit, or the individual I must see is called out of town?" he asked. Acme's answer: Budget an extra allowance of four "crisis" calls per salesman each month.

This brought the company's total call requirements for "staying in business"—i.e., calling on key accounts, small accounts, distributors, and handling occasional sales crises—to 3,666 calls per month for its fifty-man sales staff. With each salesman averaging 25 calls a week, for an effective forty-eight weeks of the year, Acme's sales organization could make 5,000 calls a month, or 60,000 a year. In short, there was capacity for only 1,334 additional calls a month.

Enter the problem of expanding business. Management had carefully studied new markets and had forwarded full information to each salesman. New product introductions had been backed by thorough briefings of the sales force, excellent literature, and creative advertising. But the product developments, so important to the company's growth, had never quite paid off. The new markets seemed interested, but they bought sparingly. Sales of the new products generally remained sluggish.

It became obvious, during the analysis of sales calls, that the problem was threefold:

1. The calls actually required to serve Acme's existing customers and distributors (3,666 of the 5,000 calls available per month) hadn't left the field men time to tackle ambitious new product and new market

ACME'S ANNUAL SALES CALL BUDGET

	Jan	Feb	Mar	Apr	May	June	July	Aug	Sept	Oct	Nov	Dec*	Total
Key account calls	1,200	1,200	1,200	1,200	1,200	1,200	1,200	1,200	1,200	1,200	1,200	1,200	14,400
Small account calls	1,666	1,666	1,666	1,666	1,666	1,666	1,666	1,666	1,666	1,666	1,666	1,666	19,992
Distributor calls	600	600	600	600	600	600	600	600	600	600	600	600	7,200
Unplannable "crisis" calls	200	200	200	200	200	200	200	200	200	200	200	200	2,400
Sub-totals	3,666	3,666	3,666	3,666	3,666	3,666	3,666	3,666	3,666	3,666	3,666	3,666	43,992
New program A introduced 1/15	1,334	1,334	1,334	434			434	434					5,304
New program B introduced 4/15				900	1,334	1,334	900	900					5,368
New program C introduced 9/1									1,334	434			1,768
New program D introduced 10/15										900	1,334	1,334	3,568
Total calls per month	5,000	5,000	5,000	5,000	5,000	5,000	5,000	5,000	5,000	5,000	5,000	5,000	60,000

*Despite seasonal holidays, it is assumed normal calls will be made during December.

Here's a sample of the sales call budget devised by a manufacturer of industrial specialty products. Budgeting the calls of the company's fifty-person sales force was designed to accommodate existing accounts and business development. It establishes the following call plan, based on an average of five calls per salesman: 300 key accounts (once every two weeks), 2,500 small accounts (once every six weeks), 150 distributors (once every two weeks, but double time allowed for each call), and four calls per month per salesman for emergencies. Remaining calls are scheduled to introduce four new product or market programs in the calendar year.

jobs the company had asked of them. Where a good selling job had been done, existing customers had been neglected.
2. Since only 1,334 calls a month were available for introducing new products and tapping new markets, Acme had to choose between greatly expanding its sales force and slowing new product and market development. The company chose the latter. "It takes us two years to train a competent salesman," stressed management.
3. The development efforts lacked coordination. The advertising was effective, the literature was powerful, the salesmen (when they had time) could sell intelligently, but no one had coordinated the effort so that each program was launched on a scheduled "D day" during the year.

With only 1,334 calls available per month (at a cost of $32 per call, an investment of over $42,000 a month) to support all its development work, Acme scaled down its plans to four new product programs for the year ahead.

Programs A and B were worth over 5,000 calls each; C could be handled with fewer than 2,000; and D required about 3,600. Four program launch dates were established: January 15, April 15, September 1, and October 15. Each date was based on the availability of field men to make adequate calls in support of the new efforts. "There's no use launching an ad campaign unless we have the field sales force to go in and follow it up," insisted Acme's sales manager.

Advertising and sales promotion staffers cheered. For the first time, they had dates to work toward and could plan with the certain knowledge that there would be at least 1,334 calls available per month to follow up inquiries. The salesmen were happy, too. They now had time to devote to the new efforts without skimping on regular customers or distributors or neglecting their small accounts. Even the production department was pleased—enough new product could be inventoried so they wouldn't run out of stock just when everyone wanted the product.

The strategy worked. New product A got off to a flying start, with support from magazine advertising in year-end issues. Inquiries were piling in by early January, and the field men had over 4,000 calls available in January, February, March, and April to follow them up. The remaining calls scheduled for July and August were used for "mopping up," and new product A took a firm place in Acme's line—and on its sales charts.

The enthusiasm carried over into Program B, another new product launching, in April. Again, advertising prepared the way, literature was ready, production built a ninety-day inventory, and—most important—over 5,000 sales calls were made to sell the new product to distributors and customers from mid-April through August.

The two new products added 12 percent to the company's gross sales in the first year—1977—and they have contributed even more in the two years since.

Program C worked well, too. It established the company in a new, specialized market that, although national, was concentrated in New England and California. As a result, Acme has since added two new salesmen in these territories to provide specialized service. But the original 1,800 calls laid the groundwork for success.

Program D—another new market development effort—surprised everyone. As early sales calls were made in October, Acme learned that this market required a different approach than had been planned. Instead of heavy cultivation of key accounts and distributors, it needed a heavy call pattern among widely distributed end-users in the market. So the remaining 2,700 calls planned for November and December were devoted to this job, with excellent results. By early the following year, Acme was enjoying an important new share of this market.

In the end, Acme's salesmen didn't make the exact number of calls budgeted. The year's calls on key accounts didn't total exactly 14,400, nor did those on small accounts add up to 19,992. Neither did the new program calls total the exact number planned. Key accounts took more call time than small accounts. Distributor requirements varied. Geography of individual territories made a difference. But Acme's requirements of a weekly *average* of twenty-five calls per man was met. From the field salesmen's standpoint, the important change was that management gave them time to do their jobs and to execute their own plans with confidence.

Acme now revises its call budget each year as territories and customer requirements change. But the basic sales call budget is still working, and it has contributed to healthy growth not only in new products and markets but in volume from established customers, who are getting better attention than they did before.

The program has been helped considerably by Acme's use of *daily* call reports, mailed in each day by the salesmen. Each call report is a simple form, padded in quadruplicate. Immediately following a call the salesman records the customer's name, persons seen, action taken, and recommended action on the next call. He keeps one copy, one goes to his sales manager, and two go to headquarters. The latter copies are filed by salesman and by account for ready reference.

The daily call reports are also *read* by management—obviously not all 250 of them every day, but in sufficient number to keep track of salesmen's performance and the status of important accounts. Acme management concluded that its 1976 investment of $32 per call (today it's over $50) made the daily call reports valuable documents, worthy of attention. An occasional phoned or written response to a salesman from headquarters, commenting on an individual call report, demonstrates that the reports aren't neglected.

Considering annual costs, sales calls are worth budgeting. With the aid of your salesmen and sales manager, pinpoint the calls actually required to serve present accounts. Plan and schedule any new product and market development with careful consideration of the sales time available to support it. And set up a simple call report system.

You may discover you need a bigger sales force—or a smaller one. You will almost certainly gain in sales volume, satisfied customers, and better sales development. But more important, you will know a great deal more about the return on your investment in this year's sales calls. And you will be able to revise the call budget for next year—based on what you learn this year—with confidence that it will generate profitable new sales volume.

—BURTON SCHELLENBACH

TRACK SALES TO CONTROL COMPANY GROWTH

"If you can't control your sales, you can't control your company," says Abe Dranetz, chief executive officer of Dranetz Engineering Laboratories in Plainfield, New Jersey, a manufacturer of electronic instruments and instrumentation systems. Dranetz should know. By 1977, his company's sales were doubling annually and they were growing too fast for him to monitor the performance of the fifty independent reps and rep organizations that sold the company's product lines. As a result, the company didn't have the information necessary to put together reliable forecasts for upcoming years. "We liked the growth," says Dranetz, "but we didn't care for the confusion."

So they did something about it by installing a sales tracking and forecasting system. Since then, Abe Dranetz has had the data he needs to keep his company under control and get a better handle on sales patterns and his reps' performance. At the end of the first quarter in 1979, for example, the sales data showed clearly that one of Dranetz's rep organizations was way behind on its quota. Sales vice-president Tony Orlacchio and his regional manager met with the manager of the rep firm to discuss the poor performance. "Either they needed our help, or we weren't getting our fair share of their time," says Orlacchio.

In this case, the rep manager actually thought his staff was giving Dranetz a sufficient amount of time. Using the sales data, however, Orlacchio proved that the organization was giving Dranetz only 5 percent, when 11 percent was needed to make quota. "Before the end of the year," says Orlacchio, "we were getting twelve percent of their time. They became one of the company's top producing groups."

The basis for Dranetz's sales tracking and forecasting system is background information on finished goods inventory, customers, and reps. Each finished item has a part number, product code, and "house product line" number. Information about customers includes name and address, credit limit, classification, and purchase order number. Each of the company's reps has a number, both to make sure sales are credited to the proper rep and to facilitate compilation of performance measurements.

Incoming orders are transcribed onto a master sales order entry form—a list of the items ordered, information about the customer, a purchase order number, and the code number of the rep who handles the account. (Domestic orders are usually made directly to the plant; other orders are placed through the reps. By matching domestic orders with the reps who handle the account, Dranetz makes sure commissions are paid where due.)

Information compiled from the order forms each week tells the company total sales by product for the current month, year-to-date, and unit sales for each item on the price list, and total sales for each of the company's three product lines. This information can be broken down into market segments—domestic, U.S. government, and international. Every month, Dranetz also gets a report that shows bookings by each rep in each product line.

Abe Dranetz points out that these figures are useless unless the information itself is manageable. "You need the data first," he says, "but you also need it in a form that's understandable." To accomplish this, the company regularly plots the sales tracking data on graphs. (See sample on page 156.)

The company's sales tracking and prediction charts, for example, allow Dranetz and Tony Orlacchio to monitor sales and forecasts by product. A company without a sales tracking system might wait several months before noticing a sales decline, particularly on a specific product. Now the company gets the information quickly so that it can respond appropriately.

Each product is tracked on a cycle that shows total unit sales by month as well as projections for the next full year. These forecasts are revised every three months and extended for a new quarter. Since sales forecasts for each product are always up to date, developing an overall sales forecast for the company takes management much less time than it used to.

Total monthly sales are also plotted on graphs by product and by market. In the last few years, these graphs have shown curves with exaggerated peaks and valleys that represent wide fluctuations in sales volume. This data has kept Dranetz from overreacting to seasonal changes in sales. The company deals in markets with vastly different ordering cycles, and it needs to know where the potential business is in each market during the year. "We know not to expect any orders from Europe in August," says Abe Dranetz. "Things are dead there then. But we can expect a flood of European orders in November and December."

On the other hand, the company knows that electric utilities in the United States place a majority of their orders between February and April because that's when they've budgeted their outlays. "Every market and geographic area has its own characteristics," says Dranetz. "We have to be sensitive to that."

The information has also helped the company solve problems that

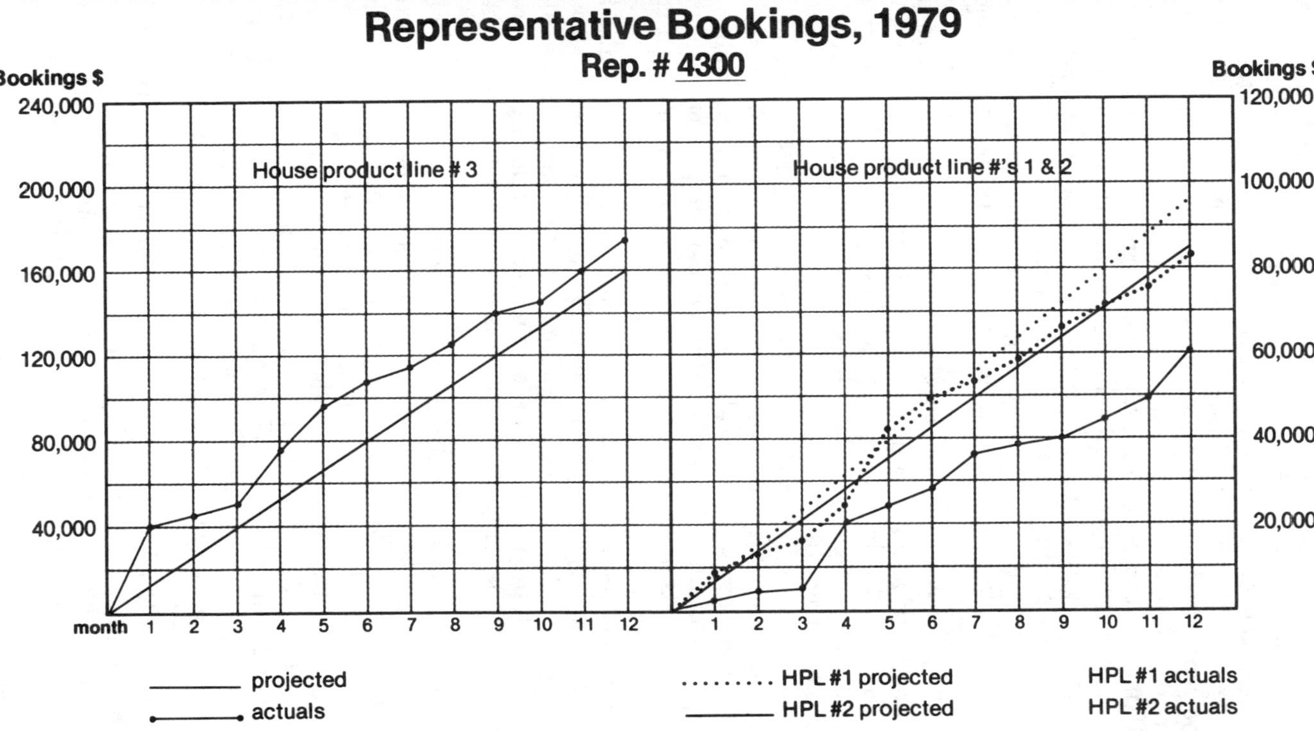
Representative Bookings, 1979
Rep. # 4300
Bookings $
240,000
200,000
160,000
120,000
80,000
40,000
House product line # 3
House product line #'s 1 & 2
Bookings $
120,000
100,000
80,000
60,000
40,000
20,000
month 1 2 3 4 5 6 7 8 9 10 11 12
1 2 3 4 5 6 7 8 9 10 11 12
projected
actuals
HPL #1 projected
HPL #2 projected
HPL #1 actuals
HPL #2 actuals

at first seemed inexplicable. For example, after peaking in March 1978, sales suddenly went dead in all areas, then rose sharply again after a two-month lull and remained relatively stable for the rest of the year. When a similar pattern developed in 1979, Dranetz was able to trace some of the downswings to price-increase announcements.

From the historical sales data, Dranetz has found that the best lag time between announcing a price increase and putting it into effect is six weeks. This six-week lag gives the reps time to contact customers who can take advantage of ordering before the price hike goes into effect. And it means that there's plenty of time for prospects to get used to the new prices.

Sales vice-president Orlacchio says that by orchestrating small price increases in the spring and fall, instead of one large annual increase, the company can actually create two periods of higher sales as customers order to save money. Moreover, the company's ability to anticipate the ebb and flow of orders greatly improves production planning and inventory control.

The historical sales data also gives Dranetz excellent support in dealing with its reps. It provides a working base from which to set sales quotas. If a rep balks at a proposed quota, Orlacchio or one of the sales managers can demonstrate how realistic the new quota is with accurate information about the rep's past performance.

Graphs are also used to track reps' performances. After a quota is set for each rep, the projected sales levels are plotted on a graph to provide a base line for tracking sales in the next year. At the end of each month, a member of the sales staff plots the month's actual sales for each rep for each of the three product lines. As the year progresses, Orlacchio can tell at a glance how closely a rep is progressing towards his quota in each product line.

The reps get photocopies of their charts each month, along with comments from Orlacchio about how he thinks each rep is doing. If one of them is significantly off his quota, Orlacchio or one of his regional managers contacts the rep to try to discover the reasons.

And though neither Dranetz nor Orlacchio expected it, the sales tracking and forecasting system provides another benefit. It serves as the base for the company's sales incentive program. "If we get the fifty reps we have to make one more call a week, that's the difference between night and day," Orlacchio says.

The heart of the Dranetz incentive program is a 2 percent commission bonus paid to each rep on his sales for the balance of the year, after he has made 80 percent of his quota in all three product lines in the first ten months. Bonuses are paid after quotas have been met instead of on total sales alone, because one of the company's lines is more complex and harder to sell than the other two and Dranetz wants total sales to come from all three product lines. With the sales tracking and forecasting system, the bonuses are relatively easy to administer because the information is provided in the reps' monthly comparison reports.

Dranetz uses a Xerox time-sharing system to make its information gathering and reporting easier. But Abe Dranetz says that the computer isn't a prerequisite for an effective sales control system. In fact, the company first went to a computer primarily for inventory control; they added sales tracking and forecasting later. "A smaller company, or one with fewer markets or product lines, could easily implement a sales control system without using a computer," says Dranetz.

The company spends about $15,000 a year for its entire sales tracking and forecasting system, including the computer printouts. Sales have doubled in the two years since Dranetz has been accurately tracking its sales, which are now at $12 million. But the costs of handling the sales information have increased only 20 percent.

The ability to control sales as Dranetz does demands reliable, up-to-date information. Abe Dranetz and Tony Orlacchio emphasize that you need to know total sales by product for the current month, unit sales for each of the items on the company's price list, and year-to-date totals for all the company's products. You also need to know whether your company's reps are devoting proper attention to prospects and customers, and whether sales are going through a normal seasonal lull or a major downturn. Timing price increases is part of controlling sales, too. And you should know what sales levels will be in the future.

"Whatever system you use," says Orlacchio, "you've got to have something that lets you know what's going on with your sales. If you don't know who's supposed to be selling what where, or what should be selling where when, you can't spot sales problems until they've gotten out of hand. But if you have the information and use it wisely, you control your sales, they don't control you."

—David De Long

PUTTING YOUR PITCH IN WRITING

Robin Brewster uses flip charts, David Bentley paces the floor, and Len Ross tries to achieve an atmosphere of informal intimacy. All three have the same purpose: to sell advertising space for *Marketing & Media Decisions (M&MD),* an advertising trade magazine published by Decisions Publications Inc. in New York City.

But Brewster isn't counting on her flip charts alone to make a sale. Neither is Bentley relying only on theatrics, nor Ross on personal charm to influence clients to buy thousands of dollars' worth of ads. The three salespeople all depend on another tool to back up their verbal presentations. On every major sales call, as they enter the room, they hand out neatly bound, carefully researched, written presentations.

The typed presentations, which usually run from ten to twenty pages, contain not only the material the salespeople will review during their meetings with prospects, but also the details about their product, including circulation figures and documented comparisons showing why their magazine is more effective than those of the competition.

Written sales presentations can be used successfully by a variety of businesses. Whether it is a Xerox copy of a flip-chart presentation that costs a few dollars to produce or an elaborate summary of the facts printed in full color, the written presentation reinforces a company's selling points. For example, Berk Swezey, national sales manager for Erisco Inc., a $15-million New York City company that leases and sells software packages for benefit and health claims programs, uses written presentations to reinforce his verbal pitches to his clients on how his company's products, industry position, and personnel can benefit a client in a cost-effective way.

"Any company making big dollar proposals will benefit from written presentations," says Swezey, whose company's software packages sell for $150,000 to $400,000. A written presentation, he adds, not only forces the writer to be specific about the client's needs, but also demonstrates to the prospect that the salesperson has done his or her homework. Furthermore, putting the pitch in writing allows the prospect to pass information along to other key decision-makers in the company.

Norman Glenn, founder of Decisions Publications, has long believed in written sales presentations. Such presentations, which he did himself for many years, helped him build his magazine to $3.9 million in ad sales in fiscal 1982, a 30 percent increase in a year. When Glenn hired David Bentley three years ago as publisher and executive vice-president, part of the job was the responsibility for training the eight people on the sales staff to write their own presentations.

Bentley's background in advertising and hotel convention sales helped prepare him. "In the hotel business, we'd determine a group's requirements—how many people would attend, for example, or whether they planned to hold seminars or larger, general sessions, serve coffee or dinners. Then we'd make a written presentation outlining how we could accommodate the group, noting our special features and price."

At Decisions Publications, Bentley found that the salespeople shied away from written presentations. Len Ross's reaction was typical. "My forte was to pick up the phone, make an appointment, and go over to talk to prospects," he says. "From those meetings, I'd gather data and go back [to a prospect] with specific proposals. But the crush of the number of accounts we were calling on made it seem unfeasible to do written presentations."

To increase confidence and experience, Bentley asked reticent salespeople to write follow-up letters to customers after each sales visit, reviewing what was covered during the meetings. Problems generally arose with structure, focus, or the use of repetitious words.

Once the salespeople began writing presentations, Bentley stressed the importance of prior research and standardization. Salespeople began asking account representatives, by telephone or in person, about their marketing objectives for the year. This research provides the information needed to tailor presentations to a particular client. Usually the personalized portion of the presentation, says Bentley, runs from several paragraphs to several pages.

The balance of the presentation includes standard information about the magazine's benefits, data to support those claims, and information on how the magazine outperforms its competitors. Standard company brochures and other promotional pieces are also incorporated. A dollars-and-cents proposal for the actual business desired from the client concludes each written presentation.

Giving salespeople time to write proposals is important, Bentley emphasizes. "It helps those who would otherwise feel they should be 'out selling,'" he says. "Our salespeople soon learn that they are selling when they're writing proposals, because their proposals get results." Bentley adds that most industries are cyclical; if you identify the planning and buying cycle for your industry, you can organize your proposal writing around that.

Last fall, for the first time, Len Ross made written presentations to eight regular accounts, including *Forbes* magazine, the *Boston Globe, Playboy,* and CBS Television. The advertisers increased their business with *M&MD* 10 percent to 50 percent. One longtime account doubled its advertising in the magazine to $104,000 for 1983.

"When you present the client with documented reasons why they should go with a specific dollar proposal and why they should do business with you rather than your competitor," says Ross, "they tend to go with your proposal." Jerry Maystrik, group promotion director of Hearst Magazines Division, which advertises in *M&MD,* confirms that a written presentation can be the decisive factor when two or three competitors are running neck and neck. "Sometimes the most effective presentations are sent several days later as a follow-up," says Maystrik.

Writing for Results

To help refine your written sales presentations, Deborah Dumaine, a Boston-based writing consultant and author of *Write to the Top,* published by Random House (New York), advises:

- Put the crux of what you are proposing at the beginning of the proposal, then give your reasons why it makes sense. Zero in on the client's needs rather than saying what "I" can do.
- Include a personal handwritten letter or note with a sales proposal, as well as a memo to guide the reader through the material. Use headlines, bullets, and lists to organize the memo and the proposal. Most people have a short attention span, and they will bog down in the middle of a word-covered page. White space gives the reader a chance to breathe and the strength to start again. Use visual representations, such as charts, tables, and graphs, for clearer explanations and for variety. For a sampling of useful charts, see David Ewings' *Writing for Results* (New York: John Wiley, 1974).
- Mirror your writing style to the client's. For example, if the client is very formal, make sure your writing is proper and formal. If the client is more casual, use contractions and short sentences that capture the rhythm of ordinary conversation. To test your style, read the material aloud and see how it sounds.
- Don't beat around the bush. Say things directly and write most sentences in order of subject, verb, and object. Avoid such words as *possibly, maybe,* or *perhaps.* Emphasize the positive: For example, instead of saying, "We hope you will not be disappointed," say, "We're sure that you will be pleased." Avoid inflated words like *utilize, commence,* and *converse,* when simpler ones—*use, begin,* and *talk,*—will do.
- Proofread everything. Don't give the impression of not caring about details. Put the material away for an hour or a day, then review it with a fresh eye.

  Often writers think they have said something but haven't actually put it down on paper. Have a second person edit your writing. Even professional writers need editors.

—CAROL ROSE CAREY

TURNING SALES INSIDE OUT

Rogers Hazlehurst, Jr., vice-president and sales manager of Beaver Industrial Supply, a distributor of pumps, compressors, abrasives, and other industrial supplies, believes in going the extra mile for a customer. Before making a sales call, Hazlehurst likes to ring up the customer from Beaver's Jacksonville, Florida, office to ask if he can pick up anything on the way out of town.

Such personal attention from field salespeople—particularly those dealing in commodity products—may become the exception rather than the rule as companies increasingly rely on the telephone to generate sales. "The sales guy with the balloons and suckers in his pocket isn't making it," says Larry Shay, president of Midwest Safety Products, a $3-million distributor of gloves and safety equipment in Grand Rapids, Michigan.

Telephone selling, which has generally played second fiddle to face-to-face selling, is catching on with many companies as a good alternative to field sales. According to a recent report prepared by Arthur Andersen & Company for the Distribution Research and Education Foundation (DREF), the research arm of the National Association of Wholesaler-Distributors, the ratio of field salespeople to inside telephone salespeople has shifted and will continue to do so. By 1990, notes the DREF report, "Future Trends in Wholesale Distribution," inside telephone salespeople will comprise 50 percent of the average wholesale distributor's sales force, compared with less than 30 percent in 1980.

"It's become a lot more difficult to maintain a profitable road force," says John McCaslin, president of J. Fegely & Son Inc., a fourth-generation, closely held industrial distributor based in Pottstown, Pennsylvania. (McGraw-Hill's marketing communications department pegged the average cost of an industrial field sales call at $178 in 1981, up from $137 in 1979.) McCaslin began a telephone selling program, with help from AT&T, long before the word *telemarketing* became a buzz word. The telephone, McCaslin reasoned as he watched field expenses soar, could become a useful tool for generating sales as well as for taking orders.

In 1968, McCaslin selected one of his top field salesmen, Earl Jamison, to head up a telephone selling program at Fegely. "I was nervous," recalls Jamison. "I'd been doing eyeball-to-eyeball selling for fifteen years." Despite his apprehension, Jamison found he could establish the same rapport with a customer over the phone as in person. By year end, he had rung up $115,000 selling predominantly to marginal accounts that didn't justify the expense of a field call, as well as to inactive accounts the company wanted to reactivate and to new prospects drawn largely from industry directories.

Today Jamison supervises four telephone salespeople in Fegely's Phone Power department, as well as the thirteen customer-service personnel who support the company's thirteen-person outside sales force. For the year ended April 1983, Phone Power brought in about $1.4 million from 1,850 active accounts in Pennsylvania, New Jersey, Delaware, and Maryland, and the department reported gross profits nearly five percentage points higher than the outside sales force. Fegely's best telephone producer, who averages forty to fifty calls in an eight-hour day, sold $447,696 worth of industrial supplies.

Developing an effective inside selling program, says McCaslin, requires commitment from top management that goes far beyond initial development work with the telephone company or seminars on telemarketing. "Telemarketing isn't just how to talk on the phone," emphasizes Peg Fisher, a telephone sales consultant in Racine, Wisconsin, who claims a telephone selling program can easily take three to six months before it starts to pay off. A company has to analyze, for example, which accounts can best be sold by telephone and which demand the hand-holding and personal contact of a field salesperson. Sales results must also be recorded and analyzed. Jamison, as well as Fegely's director of sales, Tom Carr, receive a daily review of each salesperson's call report, telling whom they reached and the results of each call.

According to Jamison, personality combined with training in company policy, product lines, and phone selling techniques contribute more to success than previous selling experience. Among Fegely's current Phone Power staff are an ex-customer-service representative, a former warehouse worker, and a truck driver. "We look for people who are enthusiastic, motivated by the opportunity of receiving a commission, and thick-skinned enough to handle dozens of rejections in a day," says Carr. Each is paid a salary, plus a commission based on the profitability of the business for which he or she is responsible. "Just as in field selling," notes Fisher, "the carrot has to be there."

The local Bell Telephone Company of Pennsylvania has helped provide the Phone Power department with a foundation in telephone selling techniques, and salespeople periodically attend refresher courses. They also receive product training from factory suppliers. Finally, Carr and Jamison meet weekly with the Phone Power staff to discuss new products and the best way to promote them by telephone. These promotions are followed up with a mailing to all active accounts.

The company also coordinates telephone selling and direct mail when developing new accounts. Before the company calls a prospect, it sends a letter with a photograph of the account's salesperson, followed by a phone call and, several days later, a company catalog and brochure.

Although Jamison notes that some customers have to be sold on the idea of telephone selling, most accept the idea. "There is a general impatience among people today," notes John Waltersdorf, president of Tristate Electrical Supply Company, a $38-million electrical-products distributor in Hagerstown, Maryland. "They don't want to wait for the salesman to show up next Wednesday." Adds Fisher: "Today's customers place increasing value upon having information. The person who has access to the most information is the person on the inside." A growing number of companies now have desktop CRT terminals that provide a salesperson with inventory and order status, as well as such information as the customer's sales activity or the contact's nickname.

Despite the increasing prominence of inside selling, few people believe that the field salesperson will become obsolete. In many cases, however, his or her role will change to that of a troubleshooter or consultant, providing technical and business assistance to customers. "Our salesmen used to be order takers, goodwill guys," says a hardware distributor in Buffalo. "Now they have to be advisers to dealers. They need to know about asset turnover, gross margins, return on investment, inventory control, and merchandising."

Says Tristate's Waltersdorf, "Field salespeople are starting to handle only the accounts that require hand-holding and tenacity to write orders." They have to be experts, handling technical problems, systems applications, and new product demonstrations. At the company's Baltimore branch, a high-technology training and demonstration room with videocassette recorder, television monitors, and other audio-video equipment is being built not only to provide an extra service to customers, but also to keep field and telephone salespeople informed about new products and technology.

Using Technology to Serve Customers

Inside salespeople, who traditionally have been responsible for taking orders, can now focus more and more on generating sales, because of a variety of new systems that allow buyers to place orders electronically.

At Cameron & Barkley Company, an employee-owned distributor of electrical and industrial supplies headquartered in Charleston, South Carolina, an IBM 4341 computer is hooked up with the company's twenty branches, which are, in turn, connected with more than 200 terminals in over thirty states at customer locations. With a terminal, each customer can access C&B's computer through phone lines, to check stock, get prices, place orders, and check the status of those orders. The cost of leasing and maintaining the terminals—assumed by C&B for its best customers—keeps falling, from $150 a month in

1980 to $65 a month in 1983. In some cases, C&B's computer is linked up with a customer's computer, which is programmed to check inventory, enter orders at the right time, and process billing automatically, thus ending the need for a person to get involved in the process.

In 1981, Larry Shay, president of Midwest Safety Products, a $3-million distributor of gloves and safety equipment in Grand Rapids, Michigan, was able to offer an electronic order-entry system to his customers even though he didn't own a computer. Shay subscribed to a computer time-sharing company, Industrial Network Systems (INS), that did it for him. Now Midwest Safety will negotiate a contract every two years with its eight key customers that also subscribe to INS. Each contract specifies the products and the prices at which they will be bought from Midwest over the next two years. That data is stored in INS's main computer in Toledo. The customer simply enters its order in its terminal, rented from INS, which is transmitted through phone lines to Shay's printer.

"When we receive an order on our printer," says Shay, "we can count on it being accurate, because the computer won't accept anything that isn't specified in the contract." For Shay, order processing has been vastly simplified: Each printed order serves as an invoice, as well as the shipping, sales, and accounting copy. For his customers, INS's service eliminates the lengthy requisition process, since prices and items have been prenegotiated, and allows them to communicate, through a single terminal, with all of their distributors that are INS subscribers. Delivery time is less than twenty-four hours.

In addition to an initial fee of $500 that Shay's company paid to join INS in 1981, the company also pays a fixed monthly fee of $100 (the cost for new subscribers is $250) to cover the rental of a phone modem and printer, plus a variable monthly cost—usually around $225—depending on the number of transactions. Costs vary among distributors, depending on the number of sales regions covered and the number of industrial accounts on-line.

In Roanoke, Virginia, Sands Woody, president of Woody Distributors, believes that a talking computer—an order-processing system that responds to callers in a natural-sounding human voice—will be a cost-effective way for his $10-million floor-covering distributorship to process orders. Last spring, Woody purchased a voice-response system, the VCT Series 2000, from Voice Computer Technologies Corporation in Arlington, Virgina. The microcomputer, says VCT, can handle two to eight orders simultaneously over an ordinary touch-tone telephone, twenty-four hours a day. "We're not open Saturdays, but our customers are," notes Woody. He hopes not only to eliminate the need for a new-customer service representative as a result of the new system, but also to free up current order-takers so they can make more outgoing sales calls.

VCT's voice-response system costs $25,000 to $47,000, depending on the number of incoming calls it can handle. The computer prompts the caller to enter orders by pressing appropriate buttons on a touch-tone phone. Various contingencies are accounted for. For example, if an item is not in stock, the computer can be programmed to suggest an alternative. If that substitute is unacceptable, the recording will ask the caller if he or she would like to speak with a salesperson. According to VCT, its new "box," introduced last June, can also check and automatically update inventories if the VCT is connected with the company's computer.

—SARA DELANO

TECHNIQUES FOR RINGING UP ORDERS

Stephan Perchick's suitcases bulged with wigs, invoices, and Rolodex cards. His calendar was filled with appointments with department store buyers. In 1966, fresh out of the Army and with a master's degree in marketing, Perchick had spent a month observing assembly line and stockroom operations at his cousin's hair goods company in Philadelphia. Now he was ready to take the boy cuts, fluffs, shags, pages, and perms out on the road.

But when Perchick's plane landed in Richmond, Virginia, one buyer after another canceled or postponed the appointments. Perchick looked at the wigs and began to wonder if he would be an early candidate for one himself. He decided to cancel his last appointment and talk to the buyer by phone instead. The call resulted in the only sale of the trip—a $3,000 order for hair goods.

When Perchick returned to Hair Fashions Inc., he called the other buyers who had refused to see him. He received orders from five out of six of them, all by phone. Within a year, Perchick was doing $150,000 worth of business with this first group of stores. Moreover, the division he had organized to sell hair goods exclusively by phone was grossing $700,000.

During the next six years, Perchick perfected his techniques of telephone selling. Hair Fashions Inc. filled orders day and night for the semiwavy Pussycat and the straight, blunt Dutch boy, two of the country's most popular wig styles, and sales topped $2 million. By 1972, however, the "go-go years" of the wig industry were coming to an end. New technologies made traditional wigs obsolete overnight, and a flood of poor-quality imitations created public suspicion of the product. Half of the country's hair goods stores and companies closed their doors.

Hair Fashions Inc. took a close look at its overhead. Perchick's division, which sold products only by phone, had a limited overhead of salaries, cost of goods, and telephone expenses. Other divisions, which were engaged in face-to-face selling, had to bear the expenses of airline fares, hotels, meals, and entertainment.

When Perchick suggested that he set up a joint venture with his company in which he would buy half the stock of the division, his impressive record of keeping expenses down through phone sales won over the owners. Nine months later, he used his share of the profits from this joint venture to establish his own company, L. Stephan Perchick Sales Agency Inc. In 1980, Perchick merged with his subdistributor to form Amekor Industries Inc.—a wholesale distributor and manufacturer of wigs and hair goods—and appointed himself chairman.

This year, Perchick expects to gross $1.5 million. Profit margins run about 30 percent, and Amekor had more than 800 long-term accounts. The company's six salespeople rarely venture outside its West Conshohocken, Pennsylvania, headquarters. In June, the staff rang up $110,000 worth of sales on a $3,300 phone bill. Perchick puts the cost of an average phone sales call at $2.

"There was no way we could have survived the vicissitudes of our industry if we didn't depend on the phone for sales," says Perchick, who estimates that overhead is half what it would be if he sent salespeople into the field. With the cost of an in-person industrial sales visit today averaging $160 to $180, more and more companies are looking to the telephone as a less costly sales tool. Perchick has developed key techniques for effective telephone sales that can be adapted by manufacturers, distributors, wholesalers, service organizations, and retail companies alike.

• ***Use some type of notation*** to organize your presentation. Perchick gives new salespeople an outline that describes points to be covered in the first call, such as introduction of the company, referral information, product description, price range and profit margins, marketing or promotional aids, and delivery time.

• ***Keep your presentation simple.*** Inexperienced telephone salespeople sometimes make the mistake of trying to emphasize too many details and technicalities. "I've heard people discuss the circumference of the wig cap, describe an intricate curl pattern, or give the weight of the wigs in exact grams," says Perchick. "All that is really needed is a description of the product's color, style, price, and market." Don't go off on a tangent, he adds. Too much emphasis on one topic, such as price, can make the call a failure.

• ***Put a time limit on sales calls.*** Perchick's goal is to complete a telephone sale in three minutes. It usually takes inexperienced phone salespeople three to four months before they can make their presentations both concise and substantive. "For a larger sale, you may want to stay on the phone longer. But you should be able to tell within three minutes if a lead is going to turn into a sale," says Perchick.

• ***Make contact with decision makers.*** Ask to speak with merchandise managers, store managers, owners, or company presidents, instead of buyers, for instance. "It's easier for the top person to exert influence on those beneath him or her. It can be very time-consuming to go through a series of clerks," says Perchick. He adds that people in more prestigious positions are usually more willing to cooperate and more accessible than lower-level employees.

• ***Avoid asking direct questions*** when determining a customer's needs. Salespeople should check their files to see what a customer ordered before. Then they can suggest related products—new colors or more expensive versions of a style the customer is already carrying. To determine the needs of new customers, ask questions regarding consumers' ages, geographic location, and price points at which they sell merchandise. If you ask outright what the customer needs, the answer will probably be "nothing," says Perchick. "Instead, try to make the call interesting with relevant suggestions."

• ***Start with a small order.*** Amekor's salespeople select several products to talk about instead of trying to sell the whole product line on the first call. They offer to send samples of these along with brochures and other detailed material. "Once you understand your customer's market, you can try selling them a larger cross-section of products," says Perchick.

• ***Establish a regular calling pattern.*** After making a sale, tell the customer you will be calling on a specific day of the week. Frequency of calls depends on the volume of sales you expect from the customer. But once the customer knows he or she can expect to hear from you every Wednesday, for example, you should start receiving orders regularly.

• ***Use sources for leads.*** "We'll wait at least a month before asking a new customer if they have any friends in the business to whom they can refer us," says Perchick. "We also approach companies that are going out of business and ask if we can be of service to their accounts. People who sell products similar to ours but who aren't competitors, as well as suppliers, are also good sources for leads." Half his leads come from referrals, the other half from the *Yellow Pages*.

• ***Gain market information.*** "In the process of making our normal sales calls, we found we're actually doing market surveys, learning what is and isn't selling," says Perchick. "This tells us how to order and how to price our goods. Such information enabled us to survive when we formed the company in 1972, and it continues to give us a competitive edge."

• ***Extend credit sparingly.*** Phone sales can yield a high volume of bad debts if you are not careful. Perchick extends credit to only 5 percent of his customers and does most of his business by cash or certified check. He won't accept a company check unless the customer can provide four credit references. He asks for three credit references and a bank reference. His bad debts run about 0.5 percent.

• ***Hire good salespeople.*** While Perchick has hired people without prior sales experience, all have attended or graduated from college. "I look for a patient person who can take both direction and criticism, produce a productive presentation, handle a customer well on the phone, and isn't afraid of hard work. An overly gregarious person would be a bad choice because he or she would have a hard time putting a time limit on calls. Someone who shows a lot of skepticism about the phone as a sales tool would also be a bad choice," says Perchick. New salespeople get intensive training for a week, which includes observing veterans, learning about the products, and mastering the techniques outlined above. Less intensive training lasts another month.

Perchick claims to have a 90 percent reorder rate with new accounts that have purchased initial samples. For Amekor, telephone selling has offered the opportunity for maximizing the salesperson's productivity and efficiency—a winning combination in these inflationary times.

—CAROL ROSE CAREY

GETTING READY FOR SHOW TIME

Perhaps the single most important selling medium available to small companies is the trade show—which makes you wonder why so many of them use it as everything *but* an opportunity to sell. Ask ten different companies why they attend trade shows, and you'll likely get ten different answers: image, contact with customers, getting a sense of the market, and so on. Almost as an afterthought, they will add "generating leads."

That makes for a lot of futile activity: A company that does not come to sell rarely winds up doing very much selling. "Too many companies attend a show and wait for something to happen," notes Allen Konopacki, a leading trade show sales trainer. "No objectives have been set. They're not really sure why they're standing in this mass of people, other than the fact that their competitors are in the next booth. Without selling objectives, they get very symbolic. They give away visors and bags. They hire a woman in a bathing suit to pass out brochures. That has nothing to do with the purpose of trade shows, which is to find qualified prospects for your products and services."

This is not to deny that trade shows offer other opportunities as well—to create an industry presence, to build an image—but those are ancillary benefits. "Unless you try to generate leads from a trade show, the medium is inefficient," says Konopacki. "You spend thousands of dollars for a one-time exposure to an audience. That's like buying one television ad and expecting your message to be heard by every person in your target group."

On the other hand, trade shows can be extraordinarily efficient for identifying prospective customers and making sales, provided you keep those purposes in mind and prepare accordingly. That question means asking yourself certain key questions long before you set foot on the trade show floor:

- ***Do you know why you're going?***

Before you can sell effectively, you have to know whom you want to sell to, and why. You need a strategy that identifies market segments, targets potential customers, and allows you to integrate the trade show with your other marketing efforts—direct mail, telemarketing, advertising, and public relations. All this may seem obvious, but a surprising number of companies try to wing it at a trade show, and wind up getting lost in the clutter.

• ***Are you sure you've got the right trade show?***

Picking the right show is harder than it used to be, if only because there are many more to choose from. Last year, more than 9,000 exhibitions were held in the United States, up from 4,500 in 1978. To be sure, some industries are still dominated by a single national trade show: If you're selling to restaurants, for example, you'd be well advised to go to the popular National Restaurant Association's trade show. But what about the increasingly popular regional trade shows? Are they worth the time and expense?

The answer depends on your overall marketing strategy. Three years ago, for example, Unadulterated Food Products Inc., in Ridgewood, New York, decided to get its Snapple beverages into chain supermarkets. For distribution, it targeted beer wholesalers, which were suffering from the general decline in alcohol sales, and were looking for new products. So UFP began attending regional and national beer wholesalers' meetings, eventually signing up more than 170 distributors.

Strategy aside, it helps to have solid advance information about a show: the number of attendees, their positions in their respective companies, their purchasing influence. Unfortunately, few shows are formally audited by independent agencies, and the data provided by trade show management firms leave much to the imagination. Of course, you can always hire a marketing research firm to do an audit, as some *Fortune* 500 companies do, but that's beyond the means of most small companies.

The alternative is to do the legwork yourself. Armor Elevator Company, based in Louisville, exhibits at three major national trade shows and fifteen other smaller shows each year. Before adding a show to its roster, the company sends a representative, a year in advance, to do an on-the-scene evaluation—getting attendance breakdowns, talking to exhibitors and attendees. "It's too risky to go into a show with only a little information about who'll be there," says Marjorie Floyd, Armor's marketing services manager. "If the people who go to a show can't buy your product, it doesn't make sense for you to go."

• ***Do your customers and prospects know you're going to be there?***

If they don't, they may not find you. "When you rent exhibit space, you're essentially leasing a space in a shopping mall," notes Konopacki. "If you opened a store in a mall, you'd expect to do advertising and promotion to get people in the door. The same is true at a trade show."

It's particularly true if you are attending a major show for the first time, because you're liable to wind up off in a corner somewhere. At his first National Restaurant Association show, in 1980, Guy Kitchens, of Royer Corporation, in Madison, Indiana, found himself next to the garbage cans. He has since cajoled the show management into giving him a better location, but he learned his lesson. Nowadays, Royer's salespeople prepare for the show by sending personal letters to prospective buyers of its custom-designed plastic name badges and swizzle sticks, and then follow up with phone calls. The company also notifies current customers of its booth location with stickers on every mailing that leaves the company two months prior to the show.

Joe Gantz, president of Empire Brushes Inc., in Greenville, North Carolina, goes a step further, setting up appointments with key buyers weeks before the National Housewares Manufacturers Association's show. "It's hard for them to plan their time," he says, "but if you don't try to do it before the show, you may miss them there."

• ***Do you have specific, realistic objectives?***

If your goal is to generate 1,000 leads at a single show, don't be surprised if you fail. In a ten-foot-by-ten-foot booth, you might make eight contacts an hour. That adds up to about 180 people over the course of a two-and-a-half-day show.

The trick, of course, is to come up with challenging but reachable objectives. Armor Elevator, for example, set out to sign up two additional distributors at the 1985 exhibition of the National Association of Elevator Contractors. "That may not sound like much, but—in our business—it was a hefty goal, and we met it," says Floyd. "It helped all of us working in the booth to have the objective in mind." Guerdon Industries Inc., a Denver mobile-home manufacturer, asks its salespeople to set individual sales goals for trade shows. "It gives them more motivation to hit a target," says David Fuller, Guerdon's product-design manager.

If you go into a trade show with reasonable expectations, moreover, you come out in a much better position to assess the results. At LK Manufacturing Corporation, a Westbury, New York, housewares manufacturer, president Robert Lutzker sets sales projections for new products based on their initial acceptance at the housewares show. "Knowing a show is coming gives me focus for the business," he says. "It's a regular event in the life of our company, one of the few things I can count on."

• ***Are your people adequately prepared?***

In order to reach your objectives, you need a strategy that your booth personnel understand. Guy Kitchens, for one, spends the day before the National Restaurant Association's show in caucus with Royer's sales staff about their show goals. "If everybody's delivering the same message in the booth, we have a more successful show," he says.

Trade show marketing planner Robert Francisco suggests assembling a preshow bulletin including your selling objectives; a selling scenario, complete with dialogue; the layout of the booth; and all preshow customer mailings. "Distribute it to everyone who will be in the booth a month before the show, to get them thinking about it," he advises. "And break down the costs of attending the show. If you let your people know how expensive the show is, and how important it may be to the company, they will take it more seriously."

Michael's of Oregon Company, a manufacturer of shooting accessories, provides its booth personnel with advance information on competing products. "We want everyone to know what they're up against, particularly at a trade show, where they're surrounded by the competition," says Jack Durrett, the company's vice-president for marketing.

Above all, you should be sure that your people understand what they're selling. According to the Trade Show Bureau, a recent study found that the major complaint of attendees is that booth personnel don't know enough about their companies' products and can't demonstrate them on the spot. Michael's of Oregon addresses that problem at a meeting the day before a show, during which Durrett and others demonstrate new products, talk about industry conditions, and go over the company's objectives. Then, at the end of the first selling day, the group meets again to discuss and refine the sales pitch.

• ***Are you ready to follow up?***

A successful trade show is an exhausting experience. After spending nine hours on the floor, the show team can usually look forward to an evening of entertaining important customers and prospects. To combat fatigue, large corporations rotate their staff during the day. Unfortunately, that is a luxury few small companies enjoy.

The good news is that trade shows seldom last more than two or three days. The bad news is that the work doesn't end there. To make the most of your trade show investment, you have to follow up right away. Some companies even bring direct-mail pieces to the show and send them out so that a prospect will have the information waiting on his desk when he returns. So there is no rest for the weary. "Don't plan a vacation right after a show," says Konopacki. "You'll probably need one, but it's the wrong time to leave."

—RICHARD KREISMAN

PART III

PRODUCT MARKETING

Selling toothpicks at a corn-on-the-cob convention might seem as easy as falling off a log. After all, people invariably get corn stuck between their teeth, and toothpicks are hardly a new invention for prying it loose. Still, you're up against some tough competition. Your toothpick is round. You're convinced that feels better, and you know round toothpicks are sturdier than the flat kind. Your research of ten test groups from major U.S. cities shows that people you tested agree. But don't forget the dental floss contingent. Waxed or not waxed, thin or thick, mint or regular—a spool of thread, it seems, could knock your wooden wonders out of the game. Ultimately, though, you believe in your product, and you know that when it comes to toothpicks, if your marketing techniques succeed your business will succeed.

In this series of *Inc.* articles, we look at some subtle and not so subtle factors that can influence the success of a new product and can even transform a standard product into a status symbol.

Many new products begin as an idea, a use of a new technology, a quest for a better mousetrap. But a Stanford University study of why products fail or succeed shows that a more logical starting point for the development of a new product is determining its need. Does the customer *want* a better mousetrap? Communication—between consumers and manufacturers, product engineers and marketing forces—can mean the difference between attempting to reach an amorphous target and hitting it dead center. Our first piece, "Why Products Fail," takes a look at some of the questions manufacturers should ask before sinking precious capital into any product, and drives home the most important marketing lesson: Listen to the customer.

We'll also see how a simple food product, yogurt, was approached by two men—one who tasted and one who tested—and why neither method brought lasting success. But if their efforts to make a killing in the grocery store were for naught, there is still a success story, over on aisle four, beneath the Shake 'n Bake. There, an innocuous farm boy with a penchant for poultry has turned his father's chicken farm into a multi-million-dollar industry. In his more than fifty years in the business, Frank Perdue has made a few mistakes, but they are nothing to squawk at compared to his success. *Inc.* investigates this marketing guru and his straight-talk advertising that springs from his respect for the customer.

Yogurt and chicken present a similar marketing challenge—neither commodity is new, so selling it successfully is a matter of getting the public to think of it in a new way. But what about selling a new product to an established market that, reasoning seems to indicate, would clearly benefit from it? "Who Wants Your New Product" looks at a software product that made a false start but whose developer had the good sense to pull back, sharpen his aim, and find the right market. Incidentally, the right market turns out to be another department in the same companies that rejected the software in the first place.

If selling a new product to an old market works, then what about selling an old product to a new market? Folks in Tennessee have a favorite candy bar—the Goo Goo—but above the Mason-Dixon line, not many candy eaters have had the privilege of tasting the popular Southern confection. "Sugar Baby" delves into the Goo Goo and the young company president who has had some success with Yankee markets and is planning more with an advertising budget that most companies would laugh at.

Perhaps the most fascinating group of consumers to ever come of age are the young professionals who now live and spend in every region of the United States. Highly educated and highly paid, these consumers are the target of a savvy product developer named Frank Berger, whose forte is turning the ordinary into the extraordinary by changing images. His story is the sixth in this series.

We also look at naming new products, not by what sounds cute or after an old family member, but by an analytic method used by a company called NameLab.

The article "But Will It Fly?" provides practical advice on how to develop a sound marketing plan for your new product, as well as some invaluable tips on how to test a product prior to rolling it out. "Buying High, Selling Low" and "Cultivating Growth" look at two very different companies and their success or failure at marketing their product.

The competition often dictates marketing strategy. Price wars, product changes, flamboyant packaging, expensive promotions—all are familiar tactics employed to capture or maintain a product's market share. What are the factors that go into successfully marketing a product? There are a few hard and fast rules, and no guarantees. But a combination of basic questions and listen-to-the-customer common sense with just the right touch of finesse is where to start, according to these hard-earned *Inc.* lessons.

WHY PRODUCTS FAIL

It is a report with implications that should reverberate throughout the American economy. It looks at a new industry and asks an old question: What are the most important factors in a product's success or failure? The study—sponsored by Stanford University and due out later this year—happens to focus on high-technology products, but its conclusions hold true across the board. Whether your product is a breakfast cereal or a silicon chip, the surest guarantee of new product success is to learn to listen to the customer.

"If you're a technologist, it's easy to delude yourself into thinking that it's the gadgetry that makes the success," argues Modesto A. Maidique, one of the principal authors of a study entitled *Towards an Evolutionary Model of the Product Development Process*. "But looking back at the research, I now realize that the key was that the product added value to the customer. It's not the technology that matters, but how you shape it for the customer."

Maidique bases his conclusions on research into 224 product innovations at more than 100 electronics companies with median sales of $20 million, as well as on interviews with company presidents, vice-presidents, and functional managers, conducted by himself, his coauthor Billie Jo Zirger, and a team of forty-eight Stanford University Business School students. Why, the executives were asked, did your successful product introductions succeed? Why did the failures fail?

It is interesting to note that their answers had little to do with technology, and a great deal to do with the skills necessary to succeed in any business. Technological lead and technical capability were named by less than 2 percent of the study sample. Instead, some 16 percent of the executives cited marketing as the single most important factor distinguishing success from failure. Another 13 percent cited the benefit/cost ratio for the customer. Seven percent cited the ease or difficulty of market development.

For Maidique—a forty-four-year-old doctor of solid-state electronics from Massachusetts Institute of Technology and a graduate of the Program for Management Development at the Harvard Business School—the answers came as something of a surprise. Not that he is an ivory tower academician; his résumé includes stints as vice-president and division general manager of Analog Devices Semiconductor (a then-independent subsidiary of Analog Devices Inc.), responsible for supervising the development of twenty-five new products; and as interim chief executive officer of Collaborative Research, a Boston-area biotech company. "But we are all prisoners of our experience," he admits. "And although it wasn't clear to me at the time, most of the new product ideas and the sensing of the market was done by very experienced hands at Analog Devices. [At the division level] we worried about the technology of products, the designs, the motions, the marketing, the advertising, the organizational aspect, the accounting. But most of the product ideas were suggested by Analog's president, Ray Stata. That led me to the illusion that the important thing is to hit the target, not to identify the target. But after talking to literally hundreds of people, I came to the conclusion that it is probably more important to do the right thing than to get things right."

Maidique believes the study identifies three practical steps to help managers "do the right thing" when trying to develop a new product:

1. Get a very clear understanding of the customer's business. Learn what he is doing and what he wants to do.
2. Stress internal coordination. In particular, make certain that there is easy communication between marketing, engineering, and manufacturing.
3. Be sure top management is fully committed to the new project. To develop new products, a company's decision-makers have to be willing to take money away from the current line of business.

These three steps, Maidique insists, are relevant guidelines for product development in every type of business. "I think the principles we found are basic and one hundred percent applicable outside high technology," he says. "The difference is only in degree, to the extent that the rate of change in electronics is so much faster. But with the movement of computers into so many industries, it's becoming harder to find many old, stable, buggy-whip companies anyway. Technology is affecting every industry today."

Characteristically, the peripatetic Cuban-born professor is not content to present his findings solely for the edification of his academic colleagues. He plans to leave Stanford in the fall for a post as professor of management and director of the newly formed Institute for Innovation and Entrepreneurship at the University of Miami. He also plans to apply his principles as he continues his ten-year interest in seed venture capital, searching for investments for his firm, American Technology Fund, and for Hambrecht & Quist, the San Francisco–based venture capital firm that recently appointed him a senior partner with special responsibility for southern Florida.

Inc. contributing editor Joel Kotkin interviewed Maidique this spring at his home in Los Altos, California.

INC.: How did you come to study the success and failure of individual products, rather than focusing on the success or failure of the companies themselves?

MAIDIQUE: I realized that the reasons why companies were successful were varied and numerous, making the analysis of any particular company's success a rather complex affair. There could be economic conditions, pressures from one product to another, politics within the company, an enormously complicated set of factors. So, at that point, I decided to change what researchers call the unit of analysis to an easier unit to study. I decided to study products rather than companies. Even though the United States produces about two-thirds of the significant innovations in the world, there had never been a study of this type done in the United States.

INC.: Did you set out in search of ground-breaking products?

MAIDIQUE: No, and—as it turned out—all the 224 products we studied were either minor or significant innovations. None of them were radical innovations like the CAT scanner or the transistor. They were improvements, changes, modifications, and extensions. None of them radicalized an industry the way the first calculator did, for example. Products like that are produced by intense research and development work, which sometimes results in useless products and sometimes results in innovation. But for 99.99 percent of the world, it is the minor and significant innovations that really make the difference. Very few innovations really result from a state-of-the-art breakthrough. Breakthroughs are too difficult to predict. No matter how much good sense you have about the market, the breakthrough is going to create conditions no one can anticipate. So the risks are much higher.

INC.: Then again, isn't it also true that the payoff on a successful breakthrough product is likely to be considerably higher?

MAIDIQUE: I'm not trying to discourage people from trying daring things. What I'm trying to say is that the more daring you are, the more important it is to know what impact the thing might have, rather than just doing it for the sake of being there.

INC.: In any case, one of the strongest points in your study seems to be that it is not the state-of-the-art breakthrough that really matters. Your results instead stress the supreme importance of communication.

MAIDIQUE: Internal *and* external communication. We need to perceive a company the way Chester Barnard [former vice-president of American Telephone & Telegraph Company and author of *Functions of an Executive*] perceived it half a century ago. He was one of the great management thinkers of America, and he believed that the customer should be viewed as part of the organization. We need to close the boundaries within the company, and between the company and the customer, so that we better perceive what is of value to the customer. The strongest factor in predicting new product success was product planning, developing a product that satisfied the needs of the customer rather than the needs of some engineer. Maybe the customer didn't give a damn about speed, didn't give a damn about accuracy, but just wanted something he could plug in and forget. If that's what the customer values, by golly, that better be the thing you deliver to him.

INC.: That's *external* communication. What about internal communication?

MAIDIQUE: If you have a multiproduct company, it is probably surviving on established products, which require resources, time, machines, equipment, and manpower. Well, a new product will require those as well. So someone has to make the trade-offs. If manufacturing has a goal to ship a certain amount of old product at a certain cost, and if the new product needs part of that manufacturing system to be tested and developed on a pilot run, there is incompatability of goals. So competition for resources will develop in any multiproduct organization. And that has to be resolved by management if the new product is going to see the light of day.

INC.: Those precepts of internal and external communication seem to be as applicable to low-tech businesses as they are to the electronics manufacturers you studied.

MAIDIQUE: I think most of the lessons we learned are worthwhile outside electronics. We chose electronics because it was economical, it was convenient, and it's an area where we had a lot of background. But I think if you look at Thomas J. Peters and Robert H. Waterman, Jr.'s, study of a much broader segment of American industry [*In Search of Excellence*], you'll find very similar conclusions. The person that establishes the value of what you do is not you internally; it's not some panel of blue-ribbon scientific advisers or scientific judges; it's the customer. And if that's the person that's setting the value of your activities, you just have to be very close to him as a philosophy and as an intricate part of the way you manage your business. I think that cuts across all segments of American business.

INC.: Did you find any significant differences between new companies and more established companies, in terms of new product success?

MAIDIQUE: A new product development, whether in a new or old company, will be successful for the same reasons. To succeed, a company must consider the new product as if it were a totally new venture.

INC.: What about differences between large and small companies?

MAIDIQUE: We broke the sample into two groups, large and small companies, with small companies being companies that were less than $20 million, and we found that those small companies rely more on technological advances to synthesize useful performances for customers than did the large companies. They seem to take larger risks in trying new technologies. That paid off for them because it is one of the few ways they have to compete. If you can't compete against IBM in marketing and service, you have to compete with technological superiority.

INC.: But did you find any difference between large and small companies in the way they market a new product?

MAIDIQUE: Small companies do so well because they are essentially new products with a corporation wrapped around them. And small companies tend to be very close to the customer because the marketing guy, the guy who visits customers, the guy who does the design, the guy who makes the decision is often the same person. But in a large bureaucracy, you're likely to have the decisions made by someone who hasn't seen a customer in years.

Let me give you a small vignette. I went to see the CEO of a $30-million to $40-million company, and I asked him how often he saw customers. He said, "I really don't have too much time to do that. I have to represent my company to the stockholders; I have financial issues; I have organizational meetings; I have my staff that I have to compensate and a lot of administrative tasks. So I leave it to my vice-president of marketing."

So then I went and I talked to the v.p. of marketing, and he said, "Well, I have a rather considerable staff. I have a sales force; I have advertising; I have promotions. So I really don't have the time. But we have a very highly trained sales force, and they are talking to customers all the time, bringing back ideas."

Then I went and talked to the salespeople and asked them if *they* could sense customer inputs and perceptions. They said, "We get them all the time. But nobody in management listens."

INC.: So how can a company avoid that pattern?

MAIDIQUE: Let me give you a counterexample from another company. In this particular company, the concept of the product was developed by the CEO. The CEO also worked on the design with the v.p. of engineering. When the first order came in, the sales v.p. referred it to the CEO for ultimate negotiations. So the CEO got on the phone and modified some of the specifications for the first major customer, a customer who wanted to order a couple of million dollars' worth of the product. Then he got off the phone and talked to the engineer to determine whether the changes were possible. Then he called the customer back and closed the deal. I don't think it has to be the CEO doing this, but whoever has a responsibility to move around the resources that are going to be combined to make new products and processes has to be involved closely with the company's lead customers. Otherwise he is delegating away the potential for success.

INC.: Have you seen larger companies that have been able to keep the necessary closeness?

MAIDIQUE: At Hewlett-Packard, close interface with the customers seems to be a religion all the way from the general manager down to the youngest engineer in the line. It occurs in other companies, too, but the fact that it occurs at one point in time doesn't ensure that it will occur tomorrow. We found that success creates fantasies about why the success was attained, and those fantasies cause companies to decouple themselves from the environment. Take Marine Technology [a pseudonym for one of the companies studied]. They were increasingly successful selling ever smaller versions of their product, until they felt they had the secret of success—to make their product smaller and smaller. So they guarded their secret perfectly, withdrew from the environment, and produced a whopping failure. They didn't realize that they had already made the product smaller than their customers really needed.

INC.: You mean they had become enamored of their ability to manipulate the technology but had forgotten the real-world needs?

MAIDIQUE: Exactly. The Concorde supersonic jetliner is another good example of performance for performance's sake. It turned out that people weren't willing to pay two or three times the cost in order to fly somewhere two or three hours faster. Another classic case is the Lockheed L-1011, perhaps one of the best jetliners ever produced. The L-1011 had more backup than any other plane. For example, it had four or five hydraulic control systems while the DC-10 had only three. It was an overdesigned product, an extraordinarily good airliner, but, at the same time, it was priced out of the range and had to be dropped by Lockheed as a commercial airliner. Meanwhile, Boeing was continuing with their everyday 747 and just ate up the world market with it. Boeing did a lot of incremental changes to make the 747 better and better over time, but they didn't win a lot of awards for designing it.

INC.: I guess a classic example of a company decoupling from the real world is Apple Computer, and the way it botched first the Apple III and then the Lisa.

MAIDIQUE: Well, the Apple III didn't fail because they misread the market; that's a somewhat different situation. With Apple III, they realized the need for an eighty-character display, a self-contained disk drive, any number of things customers are clamoring for. But the Apple II had been a very easy machine to make—open it up, and there was very little inside. So they became arrogant. They said, "Hey, we can do anything. We're Apple Computer. We were successful making Apple II, and we'll be successful making Apple III. It's no big deal." So they were rather cavalier about the way they handled manufacturing, and that came back to haunt them with a vengeance. At one point, some 20 percent of the Apple IIIs didn't work. And, as a consequence, Apple lost critical time and allowed IBM to really come into the market. They're still paying for that. What is interesting about Apple III, though, is that that failure caused a thorough revamping of Apple manufacturing, so when Lisa came out it was a product that worked and had high quality.

INC.: But wasn't the Lisa also a case of decoupling? In their rush to produce the best personal computer, they produced one that the market did not want.

MAIDIQUE: That was part of the problem. But, with Lisa, Apple was still paying the price for having done so poorly with the Apple III. The Lisa was already unappealing to customers because of the negative experiences with the Apple III. Then they corrected the problems, but they created new problems by creating a flashy technology that was high-priced. I think what they needed in the Lisa was a streamlined and economical product with a lot of service and software support, something that would communicate to the customer that this is a completely different deal than Apple III.

INC.: So how can companies avoid this kind of trap?

MAIDIQUE: You can rotate people around, rotate engineers to marketing and marketers to engineering. You have to reduce the normal cultural boundaries that exist between the different pieces in a company. When a new product is about to be conceptualized, get the manufacturing people involved early on. Get a group of people that have different views of the product-development process involved so that you don't wind up later with a product that has extraordinary performance but can't be manufactured, or a product that has just the extraordinary performance but that no one needs. As the president of one company told me, the thing you have to watch out for is that the most difficult performance parameter to achieve may not really be the one the customers value the most. Often engineers will go after some objective that is very important to them technically but that is far less important than perhaps ease of use or size or some other secondary characteristic. At Marine Technology, they had an internal communication problem. The marketing guys weren't even involved with the product. It was done secretly by engineering with the support of the president, so there'd be no leaks.

INC.: But isn't there a tremendous risk when you are developing a new product that by involving so many people you might end up by tipping your hand to a competitor?

MAIDIQUE: It's a far greater risk not to know the secret of success in the customers' minds than for your competitors to know the secrets of your technology. I would argue in favor of an open company that may let information out but that certainly brings critical information in. The real competition is not against each other, but it's a competition to see who can best understand what the customer would value.

INC.: What did your survey discover about the importance of a company's level of R&D spending in relation to the odds of their producing a successful new product?

MAIDIQUE: I don't think there is anything we learned about R&D spending. What we did learn is that it took about as much money to make a failure as it did to make a success. On the average, the successes seemed to cost about 20 percent more than the failures, but some of the failures were abandoned midstream, so the difference between the funding of a success and a failure wasn't significant. So money is not the answer.

INC.: Doesn't that contradict the common argument that increasing R&D levels is the key to America's future industrial competitiveness?

MAIDIQUE: A lot of the arguments with respect to a lack of industrial competitiveness rest on the implicit assumption that we should dominate every field. But realistically, other developed economies are bound to tie us or even lead in certain areas. By saying that our success depends simply on investing more in technology masks the real issue. Our competitors internationally now spend a lot more money, so what we have to do is not simply spend more, too; we have to learn from what they are doing, just as they learned from what we were doing when they were spending a lot less. What the Japanese have shown is that if you're really good at communicating and at extracting knowledge from other societies, you don't need the big breakthroughs in order to be successful. You can take the knowledge from other companies and other organizations and turn it into products. I think that challenges a long-standing U.S. belief that he who has the ability to make the significant breakthrough will always capitalize more than those who follow.

INC.: To what extent did the managers in your survey point to Japanese competition as causing new product failure?

MAIDIQUE: We had 500 responses, and not one mentioned Japanese competition as the reason for the failure of the new product. What that says to me is that the real issue is designing a product with value to the customers and having that product in quality and quantity out there, not whether the Japanese are in the market or outside the market.

INC.: That certainly contradicts the conventional wisdom. It seems that, in the last decade, virtually every industry—steel, autos, computers, apparel—has, at one time or another, blamed their problems on the Japanese.

MAIDIQUE: The Japanese serve as a good whipping boy. But that is just one of a whole bunch of old saws that people try to use to explain product failure. Some will argue that the product failed because we didn't have patent-protected technology, but we didn't find that to be significant. Another one is problems with government regulations, but that turned out to not be significant. Another one is that the economy just wasn't moving at the time. We found that that was insignificant. Still another says that the product failed because it didn't technically perform in an extraordinary way. But we found that extraordinary technical excellence, per se, is not one of the main levers of success. Those are all favorite whipping boys, but the answer lies elsewhere. They key is to find something that will make a difference in your customer's business. Successful products provide instant economic success to the users.

INC.: Yes, but only if your marketing program is effective at bringing the product to the user in the first place.

MAIDIQUE: Remember that marketing has to encompass the definition of what a product is. Marketing is not just promotion, sales, and advertising; marketing also includes product planning. When I start my course on marketing at Stanford, the first thing I say is: "Any engineer who does not see himself as a marketer is not doing his job."

INC.: Why?

MAIDIQUE: Because part of an engineer's role is to make design trade-offs, and every time an engineer makes a design trade-off, he is doing a marketing job, if not a general management job. So marketing starts with the definition of product characteristics, and often engineers unwillingly take that into their own hands without realizing the enormous impact that will have on the overall business. The tendency of technical people is to achieve technical performance for performance's sake; that leads to journal articles, but it doesn't necessarily lead to successful products. You can't go in saying, "Well, we've got a superfast technology, and obviously speed's going to do a lot for this guy, and if he realizes this, then he'll pay us these wonderful prices for our product." You've got to go in and say, "What's your business all about? What are you doing? What do you need? What is it in the market that you'd like to see that isn't there?"

INC.: What about market surveys? Were your successful products often launched on the basis of more formal research?

MAIDIQUE: The people who learn the most about your customers through an externally conducted market survey are the people who conduct the survey. I think that market surveys are useful in two circumstances. First, if you want to get an aggregate idea of where a market is going and how big it might be. Second, if you already have an established market, say, selling cereals, and you want to know whether increasing the sugar content of your product by 2 percent will turn the market on or off, and whether that cost is justified within a particular market segment. So tests can be worthwhile with huge, already existing, and gradually growing markets, not with markets that are very new. The best survey for that kind of rapidly changing market is for a group of people from the company—including the management people who are going to make the decisions—to go out and sit down with three or four customers for a period of two or three days. You can't beat that, particularly if those customers are lead customers, customers that are doing today what the industry is going to do a few years later.

INC.: One of the most provocative points in your study is your stress on the value of failure. What is it about failure that contributes to success?

MAIDIQUE: I think that one of the best ways to learn is to fail. People who are successful often don't know why they're successful, and all of a sudden they run into a situation that's different from what they have been in, and they're surprised to find out that they've failed. People who have failed a couple of times know where the weak links are and know exactly what are the things that must be avoided. After you fail, you tend to dwell on the failures and do everything you can to compensate for them, but if you're very successful, you tend to say, "Hey, I'm just absolutely great, and I'm going to succeed no matter what." So I think failures have a way of indelibly creating in your mind traces that prevent you from failing again in the same manner. Whereas successes often encourage you to fail by decoupling you from reality, creating illusions of what reality really is.

INC.: Still, no one shoots for failure. Is there any single lesson that companies can learn that might help them launch a new product successfully?

MAIDIQUE: There is no single thing that can guarantee product success. But the things that cause product failure are several, and, thank God, they're almost all malleable; they respond to managerial practices. A new product begins either as an unfelt need or as a requirement of your customers. It starts as an idea. Then it has to be taken by your marketing or engineering staff and turned into a blueprint for action, then into a prototype, then into a product that can be manufactured and that the company can sell. For all that to happen, there's an enormous amount of communication that needs to take place among many constituencies—customers, engineering people, manufacturing people, and marketing people—each with different goals, backgrounds, and cultures. Integration of those different constituencies is essential because cultures typically tend to block the new, and by definition a new product requires new procedures, new organizations, and new pecking orders. It will inevitably destroy some of the status quo. So, in order to do that, you need managerial power to make those changes as easy as possible, to integrate those various cultures and make sure they communicate.

There is no single way to accomplish all that; there is no way to take out the risk. Niccolo Machiavelli acknowledged that centuries ago in *The Prince:* "There is nothing more difficult to plan, more doubtful of success, nor more dangerous to manage than the creation of a new system." But you need to take those risks in order to succeed. You not only have to do the right thing; you have to do the right thing right.

CREATING A NEW PRODUCT: Two Paths to the Same Marketplace

Take two brands of the same product—yogurt. Both are introduced about the same time in different parts of the country, by two entrepreneurs who have had their share of marketing experience. One bet on his intuition, on *his* judgment of what his customers wanted. The other bet on research and testing, on what his *customers* said they wanted. Each knew the odds were against him; at least two out of every three new consumer food products fail.

Bill Bennet bet on intuition; his brand of yogurt was Yoplait. It's now the second-best-selling brand of yogurt in the country. Though he succeeded with his product, Bennet made some mistakes and lost his company to a big corporation.

David Goldsmith bet on research; his brand was New Country. Although it sold big when introduced in 1975, New Country started to falter two years ago. Goldsmith still has his company, but now he's introduced another new product to augment New Country's sales.

Both Bennet and Goldsmith say they would still use the methods they used the first time if they had it to do over again. Their stories, along with the commentaries that follow, make it clear that there's no one right way in the risky business of developing new products.

Bill Bennet Says, "Follow Your Instincts"

Bill Bennet is tenacious when he's convinced he's on to something good—like French-made yogurt. "Once I get fired up with an idea," he says, "I just put the blinders on and keep moving in one direction."

Bennet's single-mindedness paid off. His Yoplait (pronounced yō-play) yogurt is outsold only by Dannon and will bring in estimated revenues of $50 million this year. Unfortunately, Bennet won't share in the bonanza. He was forced to sell out to General Mills two years after Yoplait's successful introduction left his company in serious financial straits.

When he first tasted French yogurt ten years ago, Bennet was already in the dairy manufacturing business. He had bought Michigan

Cottage Cheese Company in Otsego, Michigan, in 1967 after leaving Jewel Companies Inc., a Chicago-based supermarket chain, where he had been a buyer and marketing specialist. Although his high-priced, premium products were bringing in $8 million a year, Bennet knew the cottage cheese market would never grow dramatically.

A large French dairy manufacturer offered Bennet his first taste of French yogurt—and the chance to introduce its products to Americans. Other U.S. dairy manufacturers (including large ones like Borden) had turned the company down, because they didn't feel American consumers would buy the product. Bennet was convinced they would. He spent two years in Paris working on the U.S. introduction, only to watch the deal fall through when the French dairy maker was bought out by a conglomerate.

But Bennet didn't give up. His instincts told him the product had tremendous potential. The flavor was full and fruity, the texture creamy yet thin enough to make the yogurt drinkable. Health-conscious Americans were just discovering yogurt, and Bennet simply knew that the French version would a hit.

He began developing his own French-style yogurt, which he called Mais Oui. On a trip to France to get ideas for packaging Mais Oui, Bennet discovered that Yoplait, a major competitor of his first French partner, now wanted to get into franchising. He jumped at the chance to move French yogurt into American hands sooner than he had planned, and dropped plans for manufacturing Mais Oui. Michigan Cottage Cheese became Yoplait's first licensed manufacturer and distributor in the United States.

Nine months later Bennet had altered the product to meet his own vision of what would capture the American consumer. Yoplait's French parent had commissioned product research, both in France and then in its new U.S. market. The report on the American market came to a basic conclusion: Yoplait's taste would be appealing to consumers, who actually preferred it to Dannon, but the peculiar shape of the tapered package would not.

Bennett didn't entirely agree. He'd worked with product research during his stint at Jewel, but he was never completely sold on its validity. "I'm cautious about research," he says. "You can't be blind to it, but you can't be its prisoner either."

So he ignored some of the research conclusions. He was pleased that the research confirmed his own judgment about Yoplait's taste appeal, but he liked the odd-shaped container. He wanted his product to stand out on the supermarket shelf. So he made only one minor change, expanding the size of the cup from four to six ounces. He could still advertise a lower shelf price than Dannon, whose standard cup is eight ounces, even though Yoplait sold at a higher price per ounce.

Bennet was convinced that the product had to be "all natural" to capitalize on the American consumer's preoccupation with healthful foods. So he eliminated the taste enhancers and stabilizers used in the French product.

Finally, to keep the French connection right in front of consumers' eyes, he had the cup printed with English on one side and French on the other.

Bennet had neither the money nor the temperament to conduct methodical tests on any of his changes. He focused his resources on those aspects of the product that he viewed as most critical, relying, as he says, "on what was in my head and my heart, based on observing the marketplace for years."

Once he had a product and product presentation, Bennet hit the road to find investors. The money he had used from Michigan Cottage Cheese to finance the Yoplait franchise was running low. He'd had to invest $1.5 million in a plant and equipment, and only part of it was financed through French and U.S. government loans. Finding investors took much longer than he'd expected, almost two years.

At the same time, he and his sales manager visited retailers in Michigan to sell them Yoplait. Their basic technique was simple, says Bennet. "We just made everyone we talked to—venture capitalists, dairy buyers, bankers—taste it. I didn't care if they were allergic to milk or hated yogurt. I was so convinced that I had the right product that I was sure it would sell itself once someone tasted it."

As Yoplait moved into a few supermarkets, sales proved Bennet right. Consumers and retailers were happy, but Bennet needed cash for production, advertising, and promotion more than ever. His equipment loans and the profits from Michigan Cottage Cheese couldn't take Yoplait the rest of the way. Finally, in February 1976, Bennet sold 51 percent of his company to a group of investors in return for the $1.5 million he needed to keep going.

Then came a setback. Some of the waxed-paper cups began to leak. The problem surfaced only intermittently, making the task of finding the cause and a solution difficult. "It would come and go, and we couldn't even track it down to a specific phase of production or design," says Bennet. "We even had the French packaging equipment manufacturer flying back and forth, and their people couldn't come up with a solution either."

Meanwhile, sales continued to grow stronger. But as they increased, so did the instances of Yoplait oozing onto supermarket shelves and inside consumers' refrigerators. It began to get an awful reputation as a "leaker."

Bennet now knows that the leaking was caused by a combination of problems: a seal that wasn't strong enough, warehouse distribution, and the material of the cup. When Bennet took the stabilizers out of the Yoplait, he hadn't thought to check how the new formulation would behave while held in a warehouse in waxed-paper packages. In 1977, he was faced with the consequences of his oversight. Putting the stabilizers back in the formula would have been an easy solution, but he was determined to keep the product "natural." So Bennet turned to his last hope: changing the package from waxed paper to plastic and designing a better seal. His solution came too late. Unlike Bennet, his nervous investors lost confidence in the product. Out of funds and out of time, they accepted an offer from General Mills in October 1977.

General Mills proceeded with changing the Yoplait cup from waxed paper to plastic. It took six months to come up with the right cup that would hold the yogurt in its place. Within another twelve months, H. Brewster Atwater, Jr., president of General Mills, announced that during its introduction in southern California, Yoplait had outsold Cheerios, General Mills' longtime best-seller in terms of units. And today Dean Belbas, vice-president for corporate communications, puts Yoplait's market share at 10 percent of the retail food-store market, which he pegs at $450 million.

So Bill Bennet's instincts were right. He beat the two-to-one odds against finding a successful new product. But in the process of bringing that new product to market, he lost his company. Could he have done it any differently? Probably not, says Bennet. "The cup problem was a bad break," he says. "I still feel that when you see an opportunity and believe that it's right, you should go for it. I ask a lot more questions now, but basically I like to shoot from the hip."

Bennet is still shooting from the hip. In 1980, he and a partner bought the Michigan franchise for King Cola, the latest entrant in the cola soft-drink market. No other buyers had been interested because of the distribution problems caused by Michigan's strict bottle bill. His solution? Michigan Container Redemption Service, a new Bennet company that picks up returnable soft drink bottles and cans.

David Goldsmith Says, "Ask Your Customers"

David Goldsmith doesn't like assumptions. So he tested his new yogurts every which way and back again. "We felt it made more sense to let consumers tell us what they liked," he says. "That way we could be sure that we weren't going to make any disastrous mistakes. I believe in the old carpenter's adage: Measure twice, cut once."

Goldsmith and his partner, Robert Finnie, unveiled their New Country yogurt in March 1975 only after they had spent eighteen months and over $200,000 testing the product in focus groups, testing the package, the concept, and the taste with consumers, and testing whether it would sell. When they put New Country on the market, it did sell; it captured a 7 percent share of the New York metro market after a year on supermarket shelves. But New Country ran into problems on the way to a solid share of the yogurt market. Now its New York metro market share is down to 2.1 percent and it's listed under "all other" on most A. C. Nielsen's market reports because its share is so small.

Goldsmith didn't make any disastrous mistakes such as those that cost Bill Bennet his company, but some people might say he lost perspective. Goldsmith and Finnie were used to doing market research. Before they formed Venture Foods Inc. to develop New Country yogurt, they worked together as business consultants for large consumer-product companies. Goldsmith had been an account manager for an advertising agency and Finnie a product-development manager at Procter & Gamble.

In May 1973, they formed Venture Foods with the help of one of their consulting firm's former clients, the Sentry Insurance Company, which invested $1 million in the company. "We looked for a joint investor," says Goldsmith, "because we knew we were going to get involved in some very expensive product development and testing. We decided that if we could come up with innovative packaging, create some exotic flavors, and give yogurt a whole new fun feeling, we had a reason for being."

Once they had a market, a company, and financing, all they needed was the product. They felt market research would serve them well in developing one. All the testing they did over the next eighteen months hinged on their belief that the customer knows best; to create the perfect product, you need to ask your customer what he wants and then produce it.

Despite their mixed success, Goldsmith thinks they got their money's worth. "Market research saves time, saves money, saves people, and above all, it saves emotional anguish," he says. "It's basically risk reduction. You spend a little money early on to toss out the bad ideas—the ones that consumers tell you won't make it—before those ideas see the light of day."

Before they could start eliminating any ideas, they had to come up with some. They went straight to the consumer to get them. The first step they took was to gather focus groups of twelve yogurt eaters in three cities—seventy-two yogurt eaters in all—to talk with a moderator about what they wanted in a yogurt. While Goldsmith and Finnie listened behind mirrored glass, the moderator started with a broad topic and then "focused" down to yogurt.

The focus groups produced more than sixty ideas for new kinds of yogurt, as well as a general idea of consumer perceptions about the product. "The consumers said to us, 'This is what we want,'" says Goldsmith, "and we had to take their ideas and translate them into products. That was our mission."

They spent the next few weeks going over the list of ideas with a team of seven consultants whose specialties ranged from packaging to food technology. When they had narrowed the field down to those ideas that sounded interesting and could be produced economically, the partners asked the food technologist to create small batches of each of eight different product concepts. Then they taste-tested these product concepts on groups of 200 consumers in New York City, upstate New York, Boston, and the Hartford/ New Haven area.

Three of the concepts were panned; one was a yogurt made with soybeans that tasted as bad as it sounds, and another was a yogurt flavored with carob that reminded at least one taster of sour chocolate milk. The three that got the most enthusiastic response—a fruit-and-nut yogurt; a rich, custardy yogurt with fruit rippled through it; and a fruit salad yogurt—were sent back to the dairy to be mass-produced in different flavors.

Meanwhile, the packaging consultant tested different shapes and graphics on 500 consumers. He ended up with a standard shape for the cup to keep production costs down. It was made of heavy-gauge plastic with brightly colored graphics. He recommended that the product be a "natural" one, because of trends he saw in consumer tastes. But he was voted down by Goldsmith and Finnie. They wanted to use stabilizers in the yogurt to enable them to keep it in warehouses and to get an edge with retailers who didn't want to worry about quick spoilage.

As soon as the food technologist was ready with the flavor variations of the three winning concepts, the market research consultant set up taste-testing booths in five shopping malls in the Northeast, where more than 500 consumers tasted flavors like Date Walnut, Hawaiian Salad, and Blueberry Ripple.

"At each stage of testing," says Goldsmith, "we were making what I call 'go/no go' decisions. The most important one came at the very beginning when we had to decide whether there was room for a new product in the yogurt market. There were minor 'go/no go' decisions on each of the eight product concepts, the flavors, and the packaging. If we began to get negative feedback anywhere along the way, especially if New Country hadn't sold well in test market, we were prepared to pull out."

The last measure Goldsmith took of New Country was to place it in thirty supermarkets in Binghamton, New York, in order to track sales during a six-month period. It was like opening a show on Broadway. "The critics had to review it," he says, "and our critics were consumers paying dollars to buy the product."

The results were encouraging. New Country actually attracted new users and expanded the yogurt market in Binghamton by 30 percent. There were also some negative results. One of the ideas that had come out of the focus groups was to segment New Country yogurt into three product lines: Rich 'N Ripply yogurts made with the creamy base were supposed to be eaten as a dessert; Fruity-Nutty yogurts were meant to be eaten as snacks; and Sunshine Salad was supposed to be a lunch yogurt. Attitude and usage tests showed that the Binghamton shoppers completely disregarded this marketing ploy and ate the yogurts whenever they felt like it. Goldsmith dropped the segmenting and at the same time changed the Rich 'N Ripply formula to the more typical low-calorie yogurt since it was no longer going to be marketed as a dessert. "The original Rich 'N Ripply formula ate so well," he says, "that I had to restrain myself from producing it."

After these final touches to conform with consumers' reactions, Goldsmith unveiled New Country yogurt in the Northeast in March

1975. Although sales started out strong, New Country's performance in the last two years has been disappointing. Goldsmith points to three reasons: a growing demand for plain, not fruited, yogurt; a proliferation of brands; and serious problems with the food broker Venture Foods first used to distribute its product. To make New Country stand out on grocery store shelves and to increase sales, he decided to lower the price of his yogurt from the standard 49¢ a cup to 39¢ a cup in January 1979.

Goldsmith still hasn't given up his belief in market research: "It's easy to say that we may have gone overboard with our market research, but there are a lot of guys who have tried to make it in this business who aren't around anymore. We're still here, and it's because we did market research."

Would he do anything differently if he had another chance? Goldsmith had that chance in early 1979 when Venture Foods acquired the license to the brand name Sweet 'N Low and began developing a new, low-calorie yogurt. "We took a shortcut on some of the testing, because we already had the basic data," he says, "but essentially we followed the same market research and testing procedures that we had used for New Country."

IS THERE A RIGHT ROAD TO THE MARKETPLACE?

I'm no expert in product development, but twelve years of running my own businesses tells me that neither Bennet's approach nor Goldsmith's is the best way to develop a new product.

I think a certain amount of elementary research is necessary to prevent a monstrous mistake. But, beyond a certain point, market research can be like hearing the weatherman report that it's 62.478 degrees downtown today. Those three extra digits aren't worth anything to anybody.

Here's the pattern I'd recommend for elementary market research. First, accumulate information on existing products and how successful they are; in other words, take a close look at the field. Second, send a straightforward survey to possible customers using only two or three questions: Do you eat yogurt? What do you like about it? What would make you like it better? Third, do some test marketing, because there's no way to know if people will buy something without trying to sell it to them. If you can't make the product a winner based on this information, you probably can't do any better with more information.

Lee Hecht teaches a course in new enterprise development at the University of Chicago's Graduate School of Business. The business he currently owns sells audiovisual products for corporate communications.

Even though I help other people do their own market research, in this case I favor Bennet's entrepreneurial approach. Goldsmith's research seems exaggerated, left over from his and his partner's corporate days. Such extensive research is appropriate for a large company where results are often used politically to push an idea through the bureaucracy.

But an entrepreneur needs to rely on his instincts. After all, nothing is stronger than an idea that is a real vision. Think of Edwin Land and his sixty-second Polaroid camera.

Market research is not an effective substitute for inspiration. It has its uses, though. Neither of these men used market research at the beginning, when many people find it most helpful in answering a key question: Where can I most profitably invest my funds? The answer isn't always as clear as it was in this case.

Robert Reitter, a former market research specialist at General Foods, heads his own New York research firm, Reitter, Wilkins and Associates Inc., which works with smaller companies.

Goldsmith's experience reminds me of an old one-liner: If the horse had been designed by committee, it would have ended up looking like a camel. I think that's a pretty accurate description of the process Goldsmith got caught up in. He got sixty different ideas from his focus groups and then tried to fit them all into his product, without stepping back to look at the whole picture. Did *he* ever sit down and taste the stuff while he was developing it? Common sense tells me no one would want a yogurt with soybeans thrown into it. I think Goldsmith could have used market research more efficiently by starting with a defined product or marketing concept, *then* testing to see if the idea was a good one.

Bennet had the instinct to recognize a good product and the guts to believe in it, no matter what. If only he had thought to have a food technologist check the new formula in its package, he might have prevented the leaking. But that's the risk inherent in his approach. You can put everything together to make a great product, but it's easy to miss one little thing—and that's the thing that can kill you.

Doug Benson, a graduate of MIT's Sloan School of Management, heads the Boston office of A. T. Kearney Inc., a general management consulting firm.

FRANK PERDUE: Face to Face

At a time when marketing has suddenly become the hot topic from Wall Street to Silicon Valley, one of the most effective marketers around is a slender, laconic, whiny-voiced, balding, droopy-lidded, long-nosed, sixty-four-year-old company president named Franklin Parsons Perdue. Although scarcely known in most of the country, he is something of a cult figure in the Northeast, where he does most of his selling. More to the point, his name is a household word—a status he has achieved by personally hawking his product on television almost every day for the past twelve years.

That product, oddly enough, is chicken. Not packaged chicken dishes or fried-chicken eateries, but the raw, naked flesh of the plucked bird itself. Indeed, he has taken this quintessential commodity and peddled it so plausibly that he has raised brand recognition of chicken to heretofore undreamed of heights. Not coincidentally, chicken has emerged as the country's fastest-growing meat category during this period, and—for the 22 percent of Americans who see his commercials—Frank Perdue has become to chickens what Calvin Klein is to jeans.

Thanks to such notoriety, Perdue Farms Inc. of Salisbury, Maryland, sold some 260 million birds last year—up 525 percent from 1968, when the company first began marketing fresh chicken. Revenues for fiscal 1984 (ending on March 31) are expected to be well over $500 million, ranking Perdue Farms within the top fifty private companies in the United States.

Frank Perdue owns most of that company and is its chairman. Although his father founded it, he is the one who has made it grow, under the banner of one of the great advertising slogans of our time: "It takes a tough man to make a tender chicken." Clever phrasing aside, the slogan's appeal owes much to Perdue himself, who doesn't come across as tough, so much as smitten—with chickens, that is. One ad, for example, shows three hens sitting at a dining table impeccably set with piles of feed, complete with a bottle of 1972 Chateau Du-Well wine. Perdue declares, "My chickens eat better than you do. If you want to start eating as good as my chickens, take a tip from me. Eat my chickens."

Such advertising has been undeniably effective. Perdue insists, however, that advertising has not been the key to his company's success. Rather, he says, "the quality of the product is number one; our advertising is number two. . . . In advertising, you have to tell people why [they should buy the product]." That means "you have to have a product that's better than most—if possible, the best in your field. . . . Too many people take a mediocre product and fail. Eighty percent of all newly advertised products fail. The manufacturer decides the consumer is a fool. That's why it fails. They think advertising is a cure-all. But when you advertise something, you stick it in the consumer's mind that [your product] is better. They expect something a little more."

It is precisely this heartfelt concern for quality that comes through in his ads—which is, of course, the genius of the whole campaign. Frank Perdue really *is* smitten with chickens. He is the sort of man who can wax romantic about something like a chicken hot dog, his latest product line. "I love and adore the chicken hot dog," he declares to a visitor. "Why, it's thirty percent cheaper [than beef or pork hot dogs]. It's got thirty percent less fat. It's got seventeen percent more protein. It's got it all!"

And he stands by his words. At the age of sixty-three, he still dutifully attends supermarket openings—"because they ask me to." On one recent Sunday, he went to two such affairs located one hundred miles apart. "My father wouldn't do it," he notes, "but I'll do anything it takes for this business because I consider it more my baby than it was his. I was totally into it without any letup for twenty to thirty years. I've been the principal force in its growth."

You might say that Perdue was born to raise chickens. The year of his birth, 1920, was the same year that his father, Arthur W. Perdue, shelled out $5 for his first set of laying hens. By the time Frank was ten, he, too, was in the egg business, earning $20 a week after expenses—which certainly was not chicken feed back in the early days of the Depression.

In 1937, he headed off to Salisbury State College—an institution more renowned for its wildfowl museum than for Perdue's matriculation—but quit after two years and joined his father's business, which was then a two-man operation. Meanwhile, he continued to keep his own flock on the side and, by 1941, had expanded his personal hen holdings to 800. "I probably didn't have to work more than two hours a day," he says. "I remember writing my girlfriend that I was making forty dollars a week. That impressed me." It also impressed his girlfriend, who married him soon after. (They were divorced in 1974.)

Perdue may not have *had* to work more than two hours a day, but he generally put in a good seventy hours a week in earlier days. Like a kind of chicken-hawking Willy Loman, he would rush off to New York or Boston on a lonely selling binge. "In the beginning we just sold to butcher shops. I'd run my production meeting Monday morning, a sales meeting Monday afternoon, jump on a plane about five o'clock, eat dinner in the Baltimore airport, and go to work the next morning, calling on meat buyers. All of them."

Perdue Farms was not built on hard work alone, however. From the beginning, it has been a tightly run organization, thanks largely to Arthur Perdue. "My dad was a tremendous influence in my life," says Perdue. "He was a man of great integrity and very religious. . . . He taught me to be thrifty, not to waste money." Almost to a fault, one might add. Arthur Perdue made his son wear high-top shoes so that—when the bottoms wore out—he could fix them with patches cut from the top leather. "A metal plate wouldn't have cost more than a penny, but he figured he was utilizing something he already owned," explains Perdue. " . . . When you grow up around that kind of thing, you can't help but be influenced."

That same spirit carried over into the business. In four decades, Arthur Perdue never borrowed a dime. "He was a check book-balance man," says Perdue. "If he had money in the bank and didn't owe any, it didn't bother him how much we lost. But if he owed money, it didn't make any difference if we were making a million a week—we had to get that paid off before we expanded. Which, of course, is not a proper use of money; I came to understand that slowly."

To a certain extent, the realization was slow because business was good. After the Depression, the company pretty much grew by itself. But the egg business had limited profit potential. So the Perdues decided to phase out of egg production and into an integrated breeding operation, which required hatcheries and feed mills. "I wanted to build a soybean plant," Perdue recalls. "When we finally borrowed money, I was forty-one years old, he was seventy-six. Knowing the nature of the individual, I have to be appalled in retrospect that he put his name on a five-hundred-thousand-dollar note. I guess he decided that he'd seen enough of me to believe that maybe I wasn't crazy. Now we have long-term debt, and we have rarely failed to grow because of lack of money."

Indeed, the company has rarely failed to grow for any other reason, either, and the motivating force has been Perdue. "I wanted to enable the company to grow to the maximum extent possible. I wouldn't be satisfied with number two. I have driven very hard to increase production, because the business was there. But I will spend money on our quality quicker than I will to decrease production cost."

As a case in point, Perdue recently put several hundred thousand dollars into a machine that would increase shelf life by a single day. "One day's shelf life!" he exclaims. "Well, that's important to me, because I don't know what happens to my chicken when it gets off my trailer. The woman picks it out of a case which may not be cold enough, because they're trying to save money in the store to keep from going broke. Boy, it's trouble. It was stinking when she got it, let alone when she took it out of the refrigerator three days later. So she writes a letter: 'Perdue chicken stinks! I want my money back!' And we give it back. We write her a letter thanking her for her attention to detail. So

I've *got* to get that extra day. I don't waste my time thinking about something like that. It might be the difference between stinking or not stinking."

Not all capital expenditures work out so propitiously. Perdue once bought a fleet of live-haul trailers. Each had thirty motors designed to circulate air. It seemed a kind thing to do for a doomed flock. "But," complains Perdue, "you'd have chickens in there packed tight, and suddenly they'd all be dead. The transformer blew out, and the motors quit. It would have taken an MIT graduate to keep the thing running. My God, if you're going to have a hundred [trailers], you'd need a *hundred* MIT graduates! It was a cool million dollars wasted. I mean, everybody makes mistakes, but some things are just ludicrous."

Although Perdue claims to possess no particular business genius, it is his undeniable instinct for marketing that is costing more and more roasters and fryers their brief lives (fourteen weeks and nine weeks, respectively). "I saw what advertising could do in the third year," says Perdue, referring back to 1968, when the decision to go retail was made. In that third year, the company spent $80,000 on television and another $80,000 on radio, and the premium tripled. "That's when I decided we needed the best advertising company in the business. I knew we already had a superior product in the chicken, but we weren't getting paid." Perdue screened more than forty firms, and finally hired Scali, McCabe, Sloves, a small, New York City–based agency that showed the good sense to put the shy, rather shrill, but unflaggingly sincere Perdue on the air.

The rest is history: Perdue has since appeared in over seventy spots, and sales have doubled every two years. Meanwhile, his success has encouraged a number of prominent chief executive officers to flood the airwaves in similar pursuit. Perdue's favorite is Eastern Air Lines Inc.'s Frank Borman, who comes across as "the most real," he says. Chrysler Corporation's Lee Iacocca, though, is "very tough. I don't think I would say, 'If you can find a better chicken, buy it.' It's not my style. I'll tell you why it's good and how it's better, but I'm not going to challenge you. . . . Well . . ." He pauses. "I might say it with a little smile and take the onus out of the hardness. You've got to have humility in your delivery."

With less than two years to go until the traditional age of retirement, Perdue already forswears quitting. His father came to work every day until his death at age ninety-one, and at least one Perdue associate predicts that Frank will, too. Perhaps it is his diet: "I like chicken," he chirps—quite credibly.

—Robert A. Mamis

WHO WANTS YOUR NEW PRODUCT?

When Cullinane Database Systems Inc. introduced its first computer software product in 1969, the $10,000 package—named CULPRIT—was aimed at data processing departments of large companies. The only problem, recalls John Cullinane, chairman, president, and founder of the Westwood, Massachusetts, firm, was that data processing managers didn't like the software primarily because it required programmers to use a shorthand computer language they weren't used to. Product sales floundered.

"The five hundred thousand dollars that we had raised on Wall Street was running out by 1969," Cullinane recounts. "We had no time or financial resources. We had to figure out what to do."

Instead of abandoning the product, Cullinane realized that the capabilities of his system were virtually identical to those of auditing software used by internal auditors in large companies. And the auditors had a greater need for CULPRIT's simplified programming language than did the more sophisticated data processing departments.

So CULPRIT was renamed EDP-AUDITOR and marketed to the audit departments of the same companies whose data processing units had rejected it. Cullinane held special training programs tailored to auditors, established a library of statistical sampling routines for their use, and formed a users' group that allowed auditors working with the computer programs to swap ideas and knowledge.

"The net result," Cullinane says, "was that auditors were so successful in using our product that they were producing reports and analyses in a matter of days, while their data processing departments would take months." Soon after, the auditors' success convinced the once-reluctant data processors to buy the CULPRIT software and start producing reports themselves.

Today, the company sells nearly twenty software products. For the fiscal year ended April 30, it posted net income of $4.6 million on sales of more than $29 million.

While not all technology-based firms can turn a marketing failure into success so neatly, Cullinane's experience illustrates the importance to a new venture of identifying its most productive market segment, then focusing scarce marketing dollars on these prime prospects.

"The key thing is to identify the market," says Samuel Wiegand, an experienced marketer in high-technology start-up ventures, who is senior vice-president for marketing of Grid Systems Corporation of Santa Clara, California. Grid plans to introduce its first product, a portable personal computer system, in January. Previously, Wiegand has been involved in start-ups at Diablo Systems—a Hayward, California, manufacturer of printing devices that was acquired by Xerox Corporation in 1972—and Tandem Computers Inc., a Cupertino, California, computer manufacturer.

"The main mistake made in start-up situations is heading off in all directions," Wiegand continues. "It's much more important to take whatever resources you have and apply them intelligently to the small subset of the market you hope to tackle."

When William Stevens began Triad Systems Corporation, a Sunnyvale, California, computer systems manufacturer, in 1972, he initially segmented the market both vertically and geographically, aiming at auto parts wholesalers in the San Francisco Bay area.

"Auto parts wholesalers were independent business people, there was a large population in the area, and there was a good chance that most of them would have a cost justification for a computer," recalls Stevens.

To reach his prime prospects, Stevens worked through trade associations, attended trade shows and conventions, advertised in trade journals, and sold face-to-face, aided by two other salesmen. Later Triad applied the same approach to retail hardware stores and tile outlets and branched out geographically.

Today the company still maintains separate divisions for each of the three markets. "Each group of customers thinks Triad is only in that business," Stevens explains. The company reported net income of more than $5 million on sales of roughly $56.5 million in 1980 (ranking number forty on *Inc.*'s 1981 list of the country's fastest-growing companies).

A key problem faced by start-up marketers with little time or capital to waste is distinguishing between inquiries that can lead to hard sales and those that are merely curious.

A good way to begin, says Suzanne Grey, a consultant with International Resource Development Inc., a marketing research firm in Norwalk, Connecticut, is to identify "applications environments" for your product or service, such as business office, assembly line, mailroom, and so on. The next step, she adds, is to peg these applications to a particular business, industry, or occupation.

For example, Cullinane Database Systems recognized that its report-generating software, rejected by data processing departments because they were not used to its simplified computer language, might appeal to internal auditors who weren't generally knowledgeable about electronic data processing.

With the EDP-AUDITOR package they could generate reports

themselves, rather than having to go through the data processing department, and thus could maintain the cherished "integrity of the audit." There would be no possibility, however small, that the data processing department could manipulate information or try to cover up wrongdoing. "Here was a tool that gave auditors the independence that they needed," says Robert Goldman, Cullinane senior vice-president.

Cullinane further zeroed in on its prime customers by recognizing that, at the time, financial institutions, such as banks and brokerage firms, were farther ahead in the area of internal auditing. "A lot of manufacturing companies didn't even have internal auditing functions in the early seventies," Goldman recalls.

To overcome the unfamiliarity of many auditors with computer use, Cullinane hired people with backgrounds in accounting to sell the EDP-AUDITOR software. They were backed up by advertising in trade publications.

Users were invited to seminars where they heard presentations by the company and auditors on product improvements and new uses for it. "Getting a user to tell about successful uses of the product can be a powerful sales tool," Goldman points out.

The first such meeting in 1972 drew just eighty people. Similar gatherings today, aimed at users of all Cullinane products, draw as many as a thousand.

—Dave Kemp

SUGAR BABY:
A Regional Product Goes National

James W. Spradley, Jr., twenty-eight-year-old president of Standard Candy Company, walks in his factory amid brimming hoppers of peanuts and huge vats of caramel, watching a 7,000-gallon tank pour warm chocolate onto clumps of peanuts riding a conveyor belt. The floor is sticky and the atmosphere frenetic as each day the production line churns out more than 150,000 pieces of the company's main product—a round, caloric amalgam of chocolate, peanuts, caramel, and marshmallow with the whimsical name of Goo Goo Cluster.

"When I first got here, this plant was making fewer than fifty thousand Goo Goos a day," shouts Spradley, straining to be heard over the din of gurgling chocolate and clanking machinery. "We're still operating at less than forty percent capacity, meaning we can meet demand once business *really* starts to take off."

Take off is precisely what Standard Candy, located in Nashville, plans to do. Despite scant cash for advertising and only limited test marketing, Spradley wants to take his southern-based Goo Goo Cluster and sell it all over the country. One day, he dreams, the Goo Goo will be battling with national top-selling brands like Snickers, a rival synthesis of peanuts and chocolate that is America's number one candy bar.

For Standard Candy, with only $7 million in annual sales—and for Spradley, who has been in the candy business only two years—it is a heady aspiration. Nationally, candy sales are growing at less than 8 percent a year, a pace that isn't expected to pick up anytime soon. And although there are hundreds of candy companies in the United States, only two of them account for nearly 70 percent of the entire candy bar market—M&M/Mars, the candy division of Mars Inc., and Hershey Chocolate Company, the candy subsidiary of Hershey Foods Corporation. The twin behemoths—each of which did more than $1 billion worth of business in 1983—manufacture all of the nation's ten best-selling candy bars and most of the top twenty. Yearly sales of Mars's Snickers alone, estimated at more than $300 million, approach the revenues of some *Fortune* 500 companies.

What seems like a quixotic quest, however, must be measured against Standard Candy's two indisputable assets. One is the Goo Goo itself, which enjoys a clientele that is almost cultlike in its devotion. The other is Jimmy Spradley, who is considerably drier behind the ears than either his age or his ambitions might suggest. Put together, they make a combination that may yet elbow one or another of the giants' bars off the retailer's shelf.

Back in 1912, Standard Candy founder Howell H. Campbell invented a candy bar—naming it, so the story runs, after the sounds uttered by his baby son. Since then, the Goo Goo Cluster has been as intertwined with the region of its birth as twanging guitars and misty-blue mountains: Ask a Tennessee good ol' boy to recall his childhood, and Goo Goos are apt to be right up there with hunting and hoedowns in the fond-memory department. Standard has always cultivated this down-home image, mostly by advertising heavily on Nashville's famous *Grand Ole Opry Show,* a country music spectacle that is heard in about thirty-five states. "The South's Favorite Candy," the boxes of Goo Goos are labeled.

Until recently, you couldn't buy a Goo Goo more than 200 miles or so from downtown Nashville. But that didn't stop word of the bar or samples of it from trickling into the outside world. Candy aficionado and author Ray Broekel, who consumed two years and over 1,000 candy bars to write *The Great American Candy Bar Book,* announced that the Goo Goo was his all-time favorite. Tourists visiting the Opry—and there are busloads of them every week—tasted the Tennesseans' delight and brought word of it to the folks back home. All told, some $100,000 in annual mail-order business around the world reflects the Goo Goo's mystique. Singers Dinah Shore and Pat Boone, both former Tennessee residents, regularly receive shipments of the bars, as does Hollywood tough guy James Garner. The company gets as many as a hundred letters a week either pleading for Goo Goos or singing their praises.

The Goo Goo has turned up in some other unlikely places as well. In 1982, Bloomingdale's ordered some for its Americana exhibit, as an example of a product indigenous to the South. The exhibit is long gone, but the Goo Goos remain: So far, the store has sold more than $15,000 worth. Recently, too, the bars have become a minor fad in Washington, D.C., endearing themselves to prominent lawmakers like Senate Majority Leader Howard Baker (R–Tenn.), and even, reportedly, to Ronald Reagan himself. Whether the candy has supplanted jelly beans as the favorite snack of the powerful can't be determined for sure. But if its growing trendiness is any indication, Goo Goos could be the hottest Tennessee product to invade the North since Jack Daniel's whiskey.

This possibility is not lost on Jimmy Spradley. Since his candy has already shown such appeal to the jaded palates of New York shoppers, Washington pols, and Los Angeles glitterati, Spradley reasons it ought to find acceptance throughout the land. "In the next two or three years, it's possible for us to be selling about five million dollars' worth of Goo Goos in the New York market," he says, "and from there, spread to Boston."

Spradley's informal timetable for this coast-to-coast market expansion is five to eight years tops. But although such ambitions are easy to write off as the impossible dreams of youth, Spradley is not your typical twenty-eight-year-old CEO. When he began working at Standard Candy in May 1982, the company was coming off a long history of mediocre sales and marketing and, in fact, was facing bankruptcy. He has since not only turned the company around, but has also strengthened its distribution channels and tapped additional markets. "Once the company was on the upswing, things got easier," he says with a chuckle. "Turning it around was the tough part."

Spradley wasn't the first to attempt a turnaround. In the early seventies, Howell Campbell III, the founder's son, was getting bored with the candy business, and his own son had no desire to pick up the reins. So Campbell unloaded Standard Candy for $1 million to two Nashville entrepreneurs, James Miller and James Fischer. The company's sales, at roughly $2.5 million, were steady but moribund, and Campbell's lack of enthusiasm was obvious to the new owners. While other candy companies of similar size had shifted at least a decade earlier from direct salespeople to food brokers, for example, Standard Candy still employed a force of about twenty-one salaried salesmen. Like a tired army of Willy Lomans, they sold the company's products out of the trunks of their cars. Although many had been with the company for more than forty years, in 1975 then-CEO Miller took the traumatic step of letting them all go. With a new broker-based distribution system in place, sales grew by about 5 percent a year from 1974 to 1979.

In 1979, the company moved from its antiquated, deteriorating, and grossly inefficient plant in Nashville to a 65,000-square-foot facility on the outskirts of the city. Right about then, however, things began to go wrong. Adapting the new building and moving the operations cost far more than the company had expected, plunging Standard Candy into debt just when interest rates were shooting as high as 21 percent. In the summer of 1980, a drought blazed across the Sunbelt, devastating the peanut crop and sending the price of peanuts, Goo Goo's second most plentiful ingredient, from 30¢ a pound to $1.50. Then the company foolishly moved to its new facility during the back-to-school season in late summer and early fall, thereby closing down production during the busiest candy-buying months of the year. Standard Candy lost $400,000 in 1980, the biggest loss in its history. It kept losing money in 1981 and 1982.

Enter Jimmy Spradley. In 1982, as the company's nosedive gathered speed, Miller and Fischer came under a great deal of pressure from their bankers to make drastic changes in the company or turn it over to new management. Spradley, with the ink on his 1980 University of Chicago MBA degree scarcely dry, was a manager for a real estate syndicator in Nashville at the time; he learned through the grapevine that Standard Candy might be up for sale. Bored with the work he was doing and nurturing a long-standing ambition to run a company, he sought help from his father, James Spradley, the former president of Stuckeys Inc., an Atlanta-based roadside-store franchise and large manufacturer of candy.

"I kept hearing how Standard Candy was getting into more and more trouble," remembers Jimmy Spradley. "It seemed like a perfect script had been written for me. I went to my father and said, 'Dad, there's a little company in Nashville that's having problems, and I'd like to get involved. Please come down and talk to the owners. Do it for me.'"

Spradley, Sr., obligingly played the role of sugar daddy. After several months of negotiations, he bought a 50 percent interest in the company and ran the business for a few months, with Fischer remaining as a silent partner and Spradley, Jr., learning the ropes. About six months later, Spradley, Sr., gave his son a 10 percent interest, crowned him president, and went into semiretirement.

Jimmy Spradley immediately focused his energies on marketing. He racked up sales with almost never-ending promotional campaigns. He motivated brokers with incentives such as bonus trips, and he enticed retailers with discounts. He took particular pains to fill distribution gaps in the company's original central Tennessee market, notably by contacting and bringing aboard important regional retailers that had been overlooked. In his first full week of work for the company, for example, Spradley called Wal-Mart Stores Inc., a major chain of discount department stores in the Sunbelt and the Midwest, and convinced its candy buyer that the Goo Goo Cluster was an indispensable item for any store that sold candy and professed to be Southern. Wal-Mart stocked the candy on a trial basis in 31 Nashville-area stores; when it sold well, Spradley discounted the Goo Goos for about three months, prompting Wal-Mart to put it in 123 stores. Wal-Mart now stocks Goo Goo Clusters in all of its 680 stores, encompassing an area from Oklahoma to Georgia.

By the summer of 1983, sales were strong, the price of peanuts had stabilized at about 50¢ a pound, and debt left by Miller and Fischer was being paid off. Then, with recovery apparently assured, Spradley made his first—and so far his only—major blunder. In an impatient desire to boost sales further, he doubled his usual discounts for some customers over a five-week period. Sales soared, but profits plummeted, and the company lost money for about a month before it put an end to the practice. "I had become hung up on sales growth," confesses Spradley, who has since discovered the virtues of moderation in price-cutting. "I've learned there's more to my company's health than fast growth."

Now, with an impressive turnaround under his belt, the young confectioner is preparing to play ball in the national arena. It is, as they say, the big leagues.

Candy bars, which account for about one-half of the U.S. candy industry, reaped over $5 billion in retail sales in 1983. That is enough to provide every man, woman, and child in America with one bar every week. Yet the business may be one of the hardest markets in the world to break into. "Most consumers of candy are guided by tastes they had when they were children," says Kenneth Rosen, president of American Candy and Tobacco Wholesalers Inc. in Landover, Maryland. "That creates fierce competition for limited shelf space. It's hard to get someone, especially an adult, to pick up a bar unless he recognizes the brand. A company has to throw massive amounts of advertising and promotional resources behind a product before it even gets noticed, and there's still no guarantee. Remember Nabisco's Reggie bar, and what a flop it was?"

Reggie wasn't the only one. Mars's Forever Yours bar, reintroduced with great fanfare in 1978, was a resounding failure. Hershey's Rally and Toffo bars struck out, too. All told, at least thirty-eight bars have disappeared from the market since 1977. One of the few to have made a hit is the Twix bar, a cookie-and-chocolate treat made by Mars; introduced in 1977, Twix has already muscled its way into the top-ten listing. Another is Hershey's Whatchamacallit, brought out in 1979 and now a $50-million brand, in seventeenth place.

What makes the difference between success and failure? If the giants have any theories, they aren't talking. "We conduct test marketing, hope we've landed on a good formula, and use lots of advertising," explains Bill Deeter, spokesperson for Mars. Hershey's Susan Graham echoes the theme: "Consumer tastes are fickle. If a product looks promising after a market test, we back it up with lots of money and take an educated leap."

Lots of money in this context means lots of money. Hershey's advertising budget is $68 million this year, or almost ten times Standard Candy's annual *sales*. Spradley's ad budget is $125,000. "To make advertising effective, we'd have to buy a lot of it, and we can only afford a little," says Spradley. "Some day, if our plans work, we'll be forced into using media like television. But that's down the road a bit. For our present purposes, the visibility we have is quite good."

A lot of the Goo Goo's current visibility can be traced to Spradley's shrewd and unconventional promotional tactics. In May 1983, for example, he made a deal with Delta Air Lines to supply Goo Goos as a snack with in-flight meals, bringing the candy bar to the attention of 200,000 travelers every month. Following up on the Bloomingdale's experience, he secured a berth for Goo Goos three months ago in Chicago's Marshall Field & Company. "Stores like Marshall Field and Bloomingdale's were the first to offer once-unknown things like cordless phones and hand-held calculators," says Spradley. "Being on their shelves gets attention, and people start talking about us."

Spradley is careful, however, to complement attention-getting techniques with solid marketing and distribution efforts. The Marshall Field's introduction, for example, was timed to coincide with the Goo Goo's entry into the Chicago market. And he has capitalized on the candy bar's strength below the Mason-Dixon line by carving out toeholds in chains that are prominent both in Tennessee and in other regions. The most recent addition to the fold is the Kroger Company, the nation's second-largest supermarket chain, with stores in southern, central, and southwestern states. The chain agreed to place Goo Goos in about 500 stores in the Tennessee area, where the candy's risk of failure was low. It proved popular, and last March Kroger placed it in all 1,470 stores. In the next twelve months, when Spradley tries to conquer such cities as Denver and Philadelphia, a key stratagem will be to plant Goo Goos in the local stores of large chains that reach to those cities.

Standard Candy has already appointed brokers in several new cities in addition to Chicago, including Kansas City, Oklahoma City, Houston, Baltimore, Pittsburgh, Cleveland, Detroit, and Washington, D.C. The brokers sell to the wholesalers, who in turn peddle the company's products to retail outlets like supermarkets, merchandise stores, and mom-and-pop candy stores.

Candy is known as an "impulse" item: The closer a bar is to a consumer's attention, the more likely that fingers will get itchy and grab it. Big companies like Mars therefore put a great deal of effort into point-of-sale merchandising techniques, providing retailers with such amenities as freestanding bag display fixtures and vertical candy racks, where candy is next to gum and not beneath it. Spradley's distributors, who can't afford to use such techniques very often, instead emphasize discounting and often use just plain cajolery to get Goo Goos near the cash register.

So far, all of these strategies have worked pretty well. Sales have tripled in the past eighteen months, suggesting a high repeat factor among Goo Goo initiates. According to a report put out by Distributor Concepts, a tracking service that measures confectionery sales, Goo Goos jumped during Spradley's brief tenure from number 136 on its ranking of the country's favorite candy bars to number 79 at the end of 1983. "There's nothing else like it on the market," summarizes Spradley. "Once we get people to try it, they're hooked."

To build up his marketing firepower for future guerilla attacks, Spradley has begun raiding the competition's camp. A year ago, for example, he hired David Jarrett, a sales manager at Hershey for the previous twelve years. Jarrett is now Standard Candy's senior sales manager, spending most of his time on the road and in the trenches, rallying the company's twenty-eight brokers.

"Introducing a new bar nationally can be very complex, like raising up a child from birth," Jarrett says matter-of-factly. He adds with a hint of disdain that the Goo Goo Cluster's only limitation all these years has been management's lack of vision. "The Goo Goo is not a new bar. It has a history, and it always had the potential to go national. Our brokers have already seen a dramatic difference, from almost no support when Jimmy first got here, to a great deal of it."

Spradley is also reorganizing his sales structure to prepare for the demands of territorial growth. Last January, a second sales manager, Bob Alexander, was hired away from Mars, and a slot for a third manager is in the works. Currently, sales work is shared by Jarrett, Alexander, and, to a lesser extent, Spradley himself. Soon, he hopes, the Goo Goo's territory will be divided into three regions of roughly equal size, each headed by a manager. By delegating most day-to-day tasks, Spradley is preparing to ease out of selling completely.

"When we hit thirty million dollars or so in sales, which is about all our present factory can handle, we'll start thinking about things like bringing aboard more sales managers and building factories in our regions," says Jarrett. "In the long run, the sky is the limit."

Spradley has not confined his innovations to marketing alone. One of his first moves was the introduction of a new product, the Goo Goo Cluster Supreme, a cluster loaded with pecans instead of peanuts. He says the Supreme has been "ecstatically received," and already accounts for 20 percent of the company's chocolate sales. To circulate the Goo Goo name even more, he prompted an ice cream company, Fantasy Flavors Inc. in Wheaton, Illinois, to devise a mixture called Goo Goo Cluster Ice Cream. Fantasy Flavors has been selling the ice cream's ingredients since March 1983, in return for a nominal licensing fee to Standard Candy.

"It's the fastest-growing new flavor our company has ever introduced," says Bob Anderson, Fantasy Flavors' marketing director, enthusiastically. The ice cream, already picked up by forty-seven ice cream manufacturers and dairies throughout the United States, has been such a hit that Standard Candy and Fantasy Flavors came out last February with the Goo Goo Cluster Ice Cream Bar, a gooey combination that some observers think will benefit dentists as much as it will Spradley. "Getting the name out in any manner is what counts," says Spradley. "I mean, let's face it: Goo Goo is a dumb-sounding name, but it sells the candy. No one ever forgets it."

Standing in his office, not far from the ceaseless bustle of his factory, Spradley dramatically sweeps his hand across a wall map of the United States. "Once we consolidate the areas we're already in," he says, "we'll continue to slowly spread sales coverage in overlapping circles." He pauses, then, with cheerful certitude, declares, "We can be a major candy company someday."

Perhaps. But for now, the real issue is whether Spradley's scheme can spark a nationwide mastication of Goo Goos, or whether the clusters rolling off his production line are destined to stay as provincial as grits. "Mars and Hershey spend millions of dollars on promotional work and advertising when introducing a new bar," says Lisbeth Echeandia, executive vice-president of American Consulting Corporation in Orlando. "But making it work Standard Candy's way is possible. I do know that the Goo Goo has a lot of Southern appeal. What I don't know is whether that Grand Ole Opry stuff will wash with New Yorkers."

—JOHN F. PERSINOS

A MATTER OF IMAGE

Frank Berger, founder and chairman of Viceroy Imports Inc. in Ramsey, New Jersey, says he would love to design a car that gets 150 miles to the gallon, has a roomy interior, and rides on tires that never wear out. So far, he admits, he hasn't discovered a product with such "tremendous USP," marketing jargon for *unique selling proposition*. In the meantime, however, he has developed an extraordinary talent for taking goods with no particular distinction and converting them into top-selling brands.

Such products include wine and spirits, soda, and cosmetics—the kind of items that "sell on image," says Berger, who speaks from direct experience. Three years ago, he left his job as president of Joseph E. Seagram & Sons Inc.'s North American sales and marketing organization to start his own investment and consulting business. The new company's first move was to buy Hazel Bishop Industries Inc., an ailing cosmetics company, which Berger restored to health within a year. Recently, he reentered the wine and spirits industry by forming his own importing company, which was well capitalized with bank loans, institutional investments, and his own resources. Berger, forty-five, had no specific product in mind when he started Viceroy Imports in August 1981. What he did have, besides seventeen years' experience at Seagram building such top-selling brands as Glenlivet and Chivas Regal, was a dogged determination to carve out a market niche in the liquor industry.

Within the burgeoning table-wine business, Berger quickly homed in on a relatively small but rapidly emerging market segment: imported sparkling wines. Case sales of these bubblies had increased approximately 260 percent from 1970 to 1980. Berger also noted that, despite inroads by a few sparkling wines—particularly Freixenet, from Spain, and Martini & Rossi's Asti Spumante, from Italy—no company had as yet gained the market share Berger believed possible.

"The category was small enough—about eleven million cases sold annually—that big companies were reluctant to gamble in a field" where potential sales volume was still unproven, says Berger. "Smaller companies didn't have the advertising dollars or the marketing know-how and distributor connections to gain a significant share." By last fall, Berger determined not only to gamble on the category by introducing his own brand of sparkling white wine but also to risk substantial losses by investing heavily in television advertising—more than $500,000 just for the product's initial rollout in New York, New Jersey, Connecticut, and Florida.

Berger; Richard Keller, Viceroy's newly appointed president; and Alan Portney, vice-president, searched for their first offering, a competitively priced product that would win over current consumers of sparkling wine accustomed to paying $4 to $10 for medium-price brands. Viceroy would also have to capture a large number of white wine drinkers by marketing its product as an elegant libation suitable for any occasion. The typical consumer of white table wine cut a demographic profile with some attractive characteristics: He or she was twenty-five to forty-nine years old, a middle-income, well-educated adult who represented the fastest-growing segment of the population in terms of both absolute numbers and income.

Developing a wine with a taste to suit the target group's palate and a concept that appealed to its collective psyche was based on painstaking research. "What consumers said they liked and what they actually preferred in blind tastings weren't always the same," says Berger. Although most white wine consumers said they preferred "very, very dry wine," they chose the sweeter varieties in taste sessions. Because research showed that French imports had the greatest cachet with the average consumer, Viceroy's officers decided to import the wine from France but travel overseas themselves to develop a formula rather than rely on a foreign producer. That way, they could blend a product that conformed to their taste-test findings, and assure that the grapes selected were plentiful enough to meet anticipated demand.

By April, Viceroy had its introductory product, a sparkling wine with a suggested retail price of $5.99, called Champs D'ore, packaged in an elegant champagne bottle with a cork that popped, a gold foil wrapper, and a wire basket around the neck. Berger paid attention to every packaging detail, down to the number of times—seven—France is mentioned on the label.

He also dealt with the discrepancy between what consumers said they liked and what they really preferred by allowing the maximum amount of sugar (1½ percent) for his product to qualify as a *brut,* the driest classification of champagne and sparkling wine. However, the television advertising message, which began airing in Viceroy's four introductory markets in mid-May, emphasized the very, very dry quality of the wine, following the marketing axiom: Sell the sizzle, not the steak.

So far, Viceroy has concentrated its promotion exclusively on television. "Although magazines and newspapers allow you to pinpoint your target audience better and make for a more in-depth explanation of a product, television gets the message out faster and to more people," says Eliot Glazer, account supervisor at Cadwell Davis, Savage/Advertising, Viceroy's advertising agency in New York City.

In addition, Glazer notes, television reinforces the message that Champs D'ore is a drink anyone can feel comfortable serving any time of the year, because the commercial spots reach a wide range of people and avoid any tie-in to a holiday season. Moreover, "television gives a product acceptability," says Glazer. "People tend to think if it's on TV, it's got to be right."

Besides a strong ad campaign, Berger can rely on the personal relationships he built up in the wine and spirits industry during his years with Seagrams. By the end of September, Berger projects, Champs D'ore will be selling in thirty-five states, distributed through a network of about seventy wholesalers, many of whom are friends of Berger's.

Such strong distributor support depends not just on Berger's ties in the industry but also on Viceroy's ability to help wholesalers and retailers sell Champs D'ore effectively. For example, the company will advise a distributor where to place the product on the floor or give a restaurateur a menu clip-on promoting the merchandise. At the wholesale level, Viceroy provides sales brochures, shelf labels, stickers, and case cards with the same selling message it uses at retail and consumer levels. Consistency of selling points, such as "very, very dry," frequently repeated on materials that are inexpensive and easy to display, makes it easier for distributors and retailers to sell the product. It also reinforces the message the consumer has heard on television.

Berger argues that strong distributor support, together with Viceroy's ongoing advertising campaign and competitive product price, will make the company a "fierce competitor." He cites E. & J. Gallo Winery as a "private, well-run company with high spending levels and low price points that drives everybody in the public companies that compete with them just crazy." Because Viceroy Imports is small and privately held, Berger has another trump card: "I can operate with smaller margins because I don't have to worry about a board of directors or shareholders asking me about quarterly profits."

For the next five to ten years, in fact, Berger plans to plow 100 percent of any gross margin on Champs D'ore back into advertising. He concedes that there will probably be no profits for some time: "If I have a major brand doing five to ten million cases in ten years and haven't made any money on it yet," he notes, "I'd be happy."

—SARA DELANO

NAME-CALLING: Finding the Right Name

It was Shakespeare, of course, who recognized that the value of a good name exceeds the crass considerations of cash. In the abstract, that is still true. But in the Bard's day, a good name didn't cost upwards of $35,000, as it can today. At least that is generally the price San Francisco–based NameLab, a prominent commercial-names factory, assigns to one of its creations. A bit steep, perhaps, for half a dozen or so letters, but a successful brand or corporate name can put a new company on the marketing map, set a product head and shoulders above competitors, and even make its way indelibly into the language. On the other hand, left to chance or collective company wit, a misnamed entity either gets accepted into the Edsel hall of fame or risks becoming just another whatsis.

Not that good names save bad products, admits NameLab founder Ira N. Bachrach, but in these days of product me-tooism, a dull or inappropriate christening is undoubtedly a handicap even to the best of the lot. Individual pride of ownership often influences a whole line of ineffectively described goods, like, say, Osborne. And corporate presumption can insist on such dubious items as the Apricot, a microcomputer brand name patterned after the Japanese manner of speech in pronouncing the first two words of the product's manufacturer, Applied Computer Techniques. NameLab is devoted exclusively to ensuring that such a fate doesn't befall its clients—including such market makers as PepsiCo, Procter & Gamble, Honda Motor, Hiram Walker, Miles Laboratories, Gillette, Chrysler, RCA, Federal Express, and other big-timers to whom an effective brand name clearly is a prized asset.

In the four years of its existence, NameLab already has left major marks. To position a Nissan Motor Corporation of America entry, it came up with Sentra. For NYNEX, one of the companies to emerge from the American Telephone & Telegraph Company breakup, NameLab came up with the name Datago for the company's chain of retail computer stores about to open in the Northeast. And although NameLab deals mainly with packaged goods and business entities, lately it has been dabbling in movie titles, which, like any other packaged good, also must hazard the economic consequences of drabness. For better or worse, NameLab recently changed ABC Motion Pictures' derivative *The Making of Emma* to *Foxtails.*

But despite some 130 jobs to its credit in areas ranging from cars to pastry, NameLab's most notable entry so far came in 1982 on behalf of a tiny start-up that intended to sell portable computers. The founders, two engineers from Texas Instruments Inc., were content to name the company and its product after a local address; hence, Gateway Technology. The little machine presumably could be sold as Gateway, inasmuch as a computer is a "gateway" to some vague, but assuredly noble, end. To scientists, the connection seemed clever enough. But not to the company's prime investors, a partnership headed by Ben Rosen and L. J. Sevin. Justifiably concerned lest Gateway mean little to consumers and even less to Wall Street, Rosen urged that NameLab be consulted. Enter Ira Bachrach, with his intensively linguistic and peculiarly totemic approach to naming things. Within a few weeks, Gateway was presented with several snappier choices, among them Cortex, Cognipak, and Suntek. Oh, yes—and Compaq.

No one can say for sure that the company might not have done equally well under the banners of Cognipac, Gateway, or even Tip-Top. Nonetheless, as Compaq, the corporation went on to sell $111 million worth of computers in twelve months, a U.S. record for first-year revenues. But this almost didn't come to pass, due to concern that the name might be challenged. In many of its particulars, trademark and service mark law is so vague, confusing, and regionalized that general counsel often prefers the discretion of another choice to the valor of stepping on toes, however unrelated. Gateway's attorneys felt that the proposed new trademark came too close to Compac, a registered service mark of a transatlantic cable switching network owned by ITT Corporation, and asked that it be reconsidered. But with a public offering at stake, the board of directors sought a hot name, and Compaq it stayed. "If you ask lawyers, 'Should I go outside?'" Bachrach complains good-humoredly, "they'll say, 'God, you could get run over!'"

An expert in marketing packaged goods from an earlier career in advertising, the forty-six-year-old Bachrach has discovered that the rules there apply to nonpackaged-goods fields as well. To this discipline he also brings an approach to language developed in his graduate thesis that involves relationships among semantic fragments, by which he tried to win the George Bernard Shaw prize for developing an English phonetic alphabet. (Thuh pryez rhemaynz unwon evun toodae.) As a result, many NameLab creations enjoy multiple effects, sometimes via neologisms with implications that are hidden within ancient but evocative roots. To be sure, Compaq computers could easily have been called Compacts, but with humdrum impact, weaker suggestiveness, and stage-sharing with cars and cosmetics.

The client had ordered up a word that would be memorable and at the same time "take command of the idea of portableness"—something that would distinguish itself from the other IBM Personal Computer compatibles. NameLab developed a table of basic word parts called "morphemes," of which some 6,200 exist in English. An unabashed morpheme addict, Bachrach fashioned Compaq from two "messages," one of which indicated computer and communications and the other a small, integral object. The *com* part came easily. The *pac* followed with more difficulty, since its phonetic notation included endings in *k, c, ch,* and, possibly, *q*. NameLab considered all four of them. When the *q* hit, Bachrach gasped eureka. As a bonus to the assigned burden, *paq* also was affectively scientific, he reasoned, strongly hinting of "somebody trying to do something precisely and interestingly."

As a significant benefit, the *paq* suffix fits neatly into what could become a product family name: Printpaq, Datapaq, Wordpaq, and the like. Combining a corporate name with a product name results, by mere repetition, in consumer acceptance of substance and reliability. "By naming subsequent products *-paq,*" Bachrach reasons, "they get added free exposure. It doesn't cost them a dollar in advertising."

When Compaq's board of directors asked what would happen if the company wanted to produce larger systems under the restrictive *paq* concept, Bachrach explained that all good solutions are limited. The more general a solution is, he philosophized, the less effective. "Look, if it works," Bachrach told the board, "your name will become the dominant symbol for portable computers, like Xerox is the symbolic identity for copiers. If that happens and several years from now you want to introduce a megasupercomputer, you can always change your company name or use a model that doesn't have a *paq*. In the meantime, you'll be crying all the way to the bank. A name that's any good," he lectures consumers, "is scary. If it isn't, it's not going to accomplish very much."

Names like Compaq and Sentra (and, adds Bachrach, generously commending the pioneering work of others, Kleenex and Jello) are what he calls "attributive nouns"—symbolically appropriate images or evocative sounds that are NameLab's stock in trade. Shoppers accept them as a quality of the product, Bachrach explains, like its color or size, but understand that there is more to it. (In Sentra's case, the idea was to denote safety and security.) Opposed to this effective concept is the limiting "argument"—a shampoo named, say, Gee, Your Hair Smells Terrific. The consumer assumes that is the *only* benefit of the product. Since a shampoo has a complex set of attributes, creating the assumption that the only thing it does is to make hair smell good is, according to Bachrach's way of thinking, "an unhandy identity to have." Bachrach tends to eschew cute phrases like "Shake-'n'-Drink," on the grounds that among other things, they lack "visibility," and thus "they go by and the brain doesn't cue in on them."

To get an angle on the product or corporate attributes NameLab needs to work with, Bachrach insists that each client take part in a three-hour meeting to agree to a ranked list of messages to be expressed in the chosen name. NameLab's entire staff is present: Bachrach, his two professional linguists, and a secretary. The other side usually consists of one or two executives.

NameLab then sharpens its pencils and taps a computer for an apropos combination of language and speech fragments, symbols, and metaphors that Bachrach has arranged by the thousands. Because a name can be made up of two or three of these, mathematically, there are literally millions of possibilities. Most, obviously, are nonsensical and can be dismissed. Eventually, sifting the words through screens of characteristics, Bachrach ends up with perhaps 300 more-or-less sensible combinations (the average is 150). These are culled for the twenty or so strongest candidates. Fashioned haphazardly out of fragments as they are, most NameLab names turn out to be newly minted expressions that ingeniously *seem* like real words.

About three weeks later, there is a second meeting, at which the expectant client is presented with the recommendations, each of which is analyzed symbolically—where it was derived from, how it positions itself among similar items, what it is apt to mean in public perception. The client picks one, pays an ownership fee after a search determines that it is legally eligible, and proceeds to use it.

One of the most recent companies to submit to that ritual entered NameLab's Marina Boulevard doors as undistinguished Digital Transactions Inc. (DTI), and departed a few weeks later as the assertively all-capital AMBI Corporation. But, as in most instances pertaining to novice name-seekers, the reidentification didn't come without second thoughts.

Started in 1982, the Stamford, Connecticut, company had one product, a modest-price computer-cum-telephone that, in the absence of a marketing muse, DTI's two engineer-owners had dubbed the Teleterminal. The name left Roy Dudley, the company's director of corporate communications, cold. So did the corporate identity itself, since the product wasn't really digital, and the *transactions* in this context was nothing more than an arcane electronics term appreciated only by fellow engineers. Somehow, DTI had to establish itself; the days of selling technology on its own merit were over.

Bachrach came to the rescue. Without a better name, he argued, the company would forfeit the all-important tactic of pervasiveness. "If you're selling against IBM or AT&T, the larger you're perceived to be, the better. If you're a small company, it makes sense to have the company name the same as the product name. There are thousands of companies all converging on electronic devices. If you make a corporate name that's embedded in the product name, you'll be seen as large and mentioned more often in magazines and newspapers. Every time the product is written about, the company is evoked." That, said Bachrach, was the issue.

Furthermore, he added, the strange hybrid had the rare potential, like Kerosene and Milk of Magnesia before it, of entering a generic term forever into the shoppers' lexicon.

The board decided to go ahead. At the meeting between NameLab and the company's executives, it was determined that what was needed was a name that was generic, that was virtually impossible to mispronounce, that immediately created a subliminal sense of recognition, that would be memorable when the company went public, and that symbolically conveyed the marriage of a phone and a computer. Further, if products with that name were to be marketed overseas, it couldn't translate into something embarrassing, as had a desktop telecommunications unit called the Chat Box in the United States that became the "cat box" in France.

Given the nature of the product, NameLab sought a packaged-goods structure that conveyed duality—a "fusion noun," in Bachrach parlance. "If we didn't give users an easily said, unique, and interesting word, they'd call it a telephone or they'd call it a computer. It's both, but you can't get people to talk about the thing on their desk as a 'telephone/computer.'"

In point of fact, it was almost called a BiSet, the runner-up proposal, but the maestro much preferred AmbiSet. "When you first encounter the word, your brain defines it by a process called 'association,'" explains Bachrach. "The primary association with *ambi* is *ambidextrous*. As complicated as it is, every child learns the word in elementary school." Even so, the folks back at DTI remained nervous. "These people were undergoing a personality crisis," Dudley assesses. "They had early attacks of insecurity about who they were going to be. Their corporate identities got mixed with their personal identities. It was very tense." Adds an inured Bachrach, "All clients feel a distaste for packaged-goods methods."

"Whether or not we like the name is immaterial to the fact that we're in business to achieve certain goals," Dudley reasoned. "We want high recognition. We want people to start using the name. Memorability is the key. It's not going to happen with Digital Transactions." Perhaps Dudley was supported by the serendipitous, subliminal effect of the characters hidden within the name—IBM and American Bell—but ultimately all agreed. They would go with Ambi.

Still, nerves remained jangled. One night, an executive was watching television when an ad for an Ambi soap came on. "They've stolen our name already!" he complained. "We thought it was exclusive." No matter, Bachrach explained patiently. You can't own a name. For instance, there are 200 applications of "Ivory," and one of those happens to be a soap, too. Other Ambis exist, but none pertained to an electronic product. "Ambi" was indeed, Bachrach reassured, theirs to exploit.

With that, Dudley went about literally reordering the corporate identity at a cost of several hundred thousand dollars. Hardly had he paid the lasting printing bill when the next crisis struck: the discovery of a *telephone* called an Ambiphone. There it was, neatly packed in a box in the window of a Stamford toy store. This Ambi didn't ring or interconnect; it simply squeaked, to the presumed delight of three-year-olds. Its manufacturer, a plastics company from the Netherlands, had also developed a fusion noun, based on the first two letters of Amsterdam. Dudley had to break the news to the boss, but this time it was taken in good humor: The *real* Ambi was already in strong demand.

Names are Ira Bachrach's second calling, as it were. After cashing out from his own advertising firm and subsequently dabbling in venture capital, his next-to-last undertaking was to enjoy the fruits of compound profit through early retirement. But the talkative Bachrach is capable of delivering off-the-cuff monologues for long stretches at a time, and his containment within the household didn't take. Please, Ira, his wife pleaded, find something to *do!*

That is when he dusted off his college thesis work on patterns that form words in English. He decided the same principles of linguistics could be applied to product descriptions—indeed, possibly quite profitably. And if nothing else, at least it would get him away from the house. By a good forty miles, as it turned out: For the first two years, NameLab operated in obscure secrecy out of a small office in Sonoma County, north of San Francisco. By sequestering the operation, Bachrach could exercise a hobby; he never intended to have to put in a full *week*. But alas, like many a covert operation, it was found out by a diligent reporter, Carrie Dolan, after NameLab's own name mysteriously kept cropping up in research. When Dolan's article appeared in the *Wall Street Journal,* NameLab's phone didn't stop ringing, much to the owner's consternation. "I kept trying to insist that the company didn't exist," says Bachrach, "but nobody believed me."

Forced out of the closet, NameLab moved to the San Francisco waterfront, where it presently occupies a hectic floor-through in what otherwise is the Bachrach's peaceful marital domicile. So for the beleaguered Mrs., it is back to square one. Except that now she helps out, too.

And with good cause: Bachrach's name-calling talents were so much in demand that more than once NameLab has had to turn down hefty contracts. One was for Time Inc., when it was launching a weekly television magazine. Time intended to call the project *TV Cable Week*. But just before the debut, the publisher got nervous; tests were showing that people expected an uninteresting guide like the ones in newspapers, not the elegant publication Time had just spent millions on. So at the last instant, they rang up NameLab.

Bachrach couldn't have agreed more. The title was flat and denotative. "But it was the kind of job that terrifies us," he recalls. "If you do it and it fails, everybody is going to know it was *your* name." Without the buffer of nine weeks to mull it over, NameLab turned down the chance. "Naming a magazine is really hard," admits Bachrach (who happens to think that the internally devised *Inc.* is "absolutely brilliant"). "To people who read, the issues of what makes a magazine more desirable are much more complex than what makes toothpaste desirable."

Such distinctions ultimately become the concerns of NameLab's linguists, who take the messages of the clients and formulate tables of morphemes—the cores of the semantic units within a word. They usually have to struggle too much, however, because Bachrach believes, like Mies van der Rohe, that less is more. In product and company titles, though, two syllables is about as less as you can go. The focus on brevity doesn't so much have to do with the soul of wit as with a concept called "visibility." Expounds Bachrach: "These things are part of your everyday life. Since you have to say them often, you try to do it efficiently, and you assign them short, friendly, familiar words. Your brand of beer isn't Budweiser, it's Bud. If you make a name which is short, friendly, and familiar, people will use it, and that becomes the thing, rather than the *type* of thing. It's because of having a familiar name, and a familiar name has to be short."

Along with NYNEX's Datago, which to Bachrach "utterly magically" at once suggests retail, volume, fast service, and because of the "go," a combination of "computers and communications," one of his favorite NameLab creations is "Mindset." The new West Coast home-computer company, known pre-Bachrach as RHB Computers, makes a sophisticated graphics system that uses a television set for its display. The word comes from yet another NameLab pool, a collection labeled "adapted metaphors." These are a category of words that describe complex concepts in condensed form. A prime example is Sears' Die-Hard—the best adapted metaphor in the history of brand names, according to Bachrach.

"It's a class that makes for brilliant brand names. What you do is take the literal meaning of the word and use it to describe your product. *Your* value overwhelms the metaphor." Not only is the Die-Hard battery long-lived literally, but in part it also is, as the metaphor has it, stubborn. "So you get to steal a word out of the language," Bachrach confesses. "Mindset" is like that. Not only does it literally reflect the sensation that there is a brain in the TV apparently thinking like a person, but the metaphor value of "strongly held opinion" gives the product credence as well. "The advantage to that is if you took an identical product and gave it a less accidentally clever name, say, 'Videocomputer,' you'd have to spend at least ten times as much [in advertising] per retained impression as for 'Mindset.' "

Sometimes it happens that effective names aren't names at all. Hewlett-Packard Company, for example, has successfully marketed lines of computers and calculators purely by catalog number, and only recently word-named a product—its new ThinkJet computer printer. Mercedes-Benz calls its cars by numbers as well. To automotive or electronics cognoscenti, numbers contain information that is direct, appropriate, helpful, and effective; such a hierarchical sequence as Mercedes-Benz's conveys more information than an emblematic name like the Diplomat (a 1950s automobile). "If you want an efficient-sounding car instead of a social emblem," Bachrach concedes, "240 is symbolically a good name."

One other numbered product that earns at least partial Bachrach approval is Lotus Development Corporation's microcomputer software, 1-2-3—a name that handily expresses its ease of use and triple function. Besides, as Bachrach believes, "you can't separate names from products," and 1-2-3, he grants, is a good product. And the naming approach was commendably distinctive within the "noisy" set of business software.

But 1-2-3 could have been a problem, because at the retail level, the software which generates the most sales has "fusion" names—*viz.*, Visi-, Easy-, Peach-, and so on. These promise a series yet to come; a series, says Bachrach, connotes big-ticket, big-time, highly profitable products to a retailer. Thus the name 1-2-3 lacks the promise of a long-run product that some formidable fellows share. As for Lotus itself, the name fails muster entirely. "It's a memorable, easy name," Bachrach acknowledges, "but it means nothing—maybe an automobile or a flower. There's a dissonance between the mechanicalness of 1-2-3 and the estheticism of Lotus. When you have dissonance, it's hard to remember the name. It's pretty, but prettiness isn't a characteristic of software."

But neither is apple a characteristic of microcomputers—except in the morpheme-laden eyes of Bachrach. "When Apple was created, there wasn't any computer market. Computers were awful things that screwed up your utility bills. They had to name a company, and the marketing issues were simplicity, friendliness, safety, and trustworthiness." Although to an untrained observer that describes a Boy Scout better than a computer, Bachrach proposes that an apple is a wonderful symbol of such qualities: a computer that *didn't* screw up your phone bills.

The ill-fated Texas Instrument TI 99/4 was a stubbornly held number-title that, in Bachrach's view, "helped kill the product." The now-defunct machine came off as being "complex and difficult to deal with technologically, more oriented toward mathematics than toward human things. A slash is a grammatical element that people who are less skilled in reading don't encounter very often and don't understand the meaning of. There was considerable pressure from retailers to adapt a real name, but they just wouldn't do it. A slogan won't take the place of a name."

But real names can be just as disastrous. Digital Equipment Corporation's Rainbow fares nearly as poorly in Bachrach's estimation. "When Apple happened, computers were seen as packaged goods that consumers would buy based on affective messages. DEC, which had insisted on calling its products PPP-11 and VAX, decided that here was a work station that was meant to be friendly. So what do they do? They copy Apple. They pick a nonspecific positive-affect symbol." No doubt that sounds just fine to a linguist, except, as Bachrach points out, it came five years after the fact. By then people had accepted the idea that computers were friendly, and they didn't need to be convinced by brand names. Worse still, in Rainbow, "they created the first feminine name in the history of computers. It said '*non*computerlike.' Yet they were selling it as a professional work station. They patently stuck a label on the thing; there was no 'rainbowness' at all. With Apple, the message is obvious and appropriate. With Rainbow, it's just terrible."

As for the noncomputerlike but masculine Adam, Bachrach allows that "there are worse names. It was meant to say, 'simple, archetypical, human.' If I were them," Bachrach adds, throwing Coleco Industries Inc. free advice from his packaged-goods past, "I would want a pair of products—an Eve eventually."

He also blesses PC, because it is "consonant with 'IBM.' They didn't have to put any competitive message on the name of the product. PC without the word IBM *still* indicates 'this is IBM's computer.' And it's meant to be generic—the definitive such product. If the rest bring out PCs, it won't do IBM any harm. IBM can get away with this; they're less concerned with trademark value than the others.

But it falls to the nonsensical (in English) Atari, though, to win Bachrachian huzzahs hands down. Atari "is pure gold in packaged-goods terms." The name given to Nolan Bushnell's small electronics company back in 1974 "was accidentally brilliant. It was the sixth name Bushnell tried on the list, but it's brilliant nonetheless. He created a word that is pure, has no combination of vowels that are difficult to say, and that's also unique. Because it wasn't a natural English word, he could develop strong rights to it, too." Another advantage of Atari is that it sounds Japanese, Bachrach feels. "He didn't think of that either, but to young people, all good things that don't come from the United States come from Japan. The Japanese are smart enough to have figured this out."

NameLab's notoriety draws requests from all over the country and from all levels of income. Naturally, not every business seeking a clever name can afford to indulge itself at tens of thousands of dollars a throw. It could try to play on Bachrach's sympathies, though: He feels it is unfair that only large companies have the resources to hire specialists. "A small company has to sit on a shelf competing against them. There's no way they can get the heavy muscle. There are so many people out there who have good products who should be in business but who don't have the resources."

One such product is manufactured by Kleen-All Products, Inc., a small enterprise in Oklahoma City. Recently, the folks from Kleen-All phoned in with a plea for assistance. The company had a product that removes chewing gum from clothes. For no apparent reason, it was called Turbo. Turbo was selling like frozen hotcake batter in local supermarkets, demonstrating such uncanny demand that the founders felt that they could go national with it. But they had been advised that the label was ugly and the name even worse. Bachrach had to tell them that NameLab was apt to be expensive for small companies; they could expect a fee of $30,000. "But," stammered the voice, "that's our annual sales!" Instead, Kleen-All proposed sending him a free bottle. "If you have any ideas what the name ought to be, let us know." After Bachrach got a look at the homespun creation, he was moved to send them a book on design and a few pointers.

Over the four years of its existence, NameLab's storerooms have steadily filled with products in similarly budgeted search of names. Such blandishments are not apt to do the trick, however. Bachrach already is facing a two- to three-month backlog, and demand is continuing to mount. For a person to whom the business was never meant to be more than a pastime, that is a severe problem. "The obvious solution," says the would-be retiree ominously, "is to raise the price."

—ROBERT A. MAMIS

BUT WILL IT FLY?

I received a telephone call a few weeks ago from a young woman who, in partnership with her husband, had just set up a company to sell a new consumer product. She told me a story that I've heard many times, and one that's worth repeating. They had quit their jobs, started their company, spent their savings, and sold their house. Now they were ready to get their product into mass-merchandising outlets such as Walgreen, K Mart, and the like, but didn't know where to begin. I listened to her tale of woe and began asking questions.

"Do you have a marketing plan?"

"No," she answered, "but we have a great product, and we know that once people see it they will buy it."

"How do you know that?" I asked. "Did you do some consumer research?"

"No, but all our friends told us it was a fantastic idea that would sell like hotcakes."

"Is the product ready for market?" I asked.

"Oh, sure, that's what we've spent all our money on. We're ready to go, but we're not exactly sure how we should go about getting stores to buy it."

I spent the next half hour or so telling her some of the things that stood between her and the customer. When I finished, she said, "Why didn't someone tell us all this before we spent our money?" I reminded her there were volumes written about marketing new products. "I know," she said. "I even plowed through a couple of books, but they were obviously written for people who already knew everything about marketing." After thinking about it, I realized that she was right. I couldn't think of anything I'd seen that might be called *Marketing for the Amateur.*

So I thought it might be helpful if I outlined a plan for those of you with new products but without degrees in marketing or the resources of a big company. At the very least, I call tell you some things you should find out before you quit your job and sell the old homestead. My plan doesn't take a lot of money, but it takes a lot of ingenuity, shoe power, and guts.

The first thing to understand is the terrible risk in introducing *any* new product. I doubt that 1 in 500 makes it from concept to market; in consumer products, the figure may be as low as 1 in 1,000. It doesn't make a hoot in hell whether you have a great product, a fantastic idea, or something that your friends say will sell like hotcakes. The rare product that does make it all the way does so only if it's the answer to a real consumer need. And even that isn't enough. You need to dot all your *i*'s, cross all your *t*'s, and have all the angels in heaven on your side. It also helps if you have 20 million bucks, which is probably the going price today for a large company to launch a new product. Don't think anything is going to happen just because you will it to or because you are prepared to pour your life into it. But if you are good enough and lucky enough to make it, the rewards are incredible.

Let's start out with your idea. The first thing you need to find out is if it will pass the most important test associated with any new product. I call it the "Well, I'll be damned!" test. For any product to be successful, it must have what marketing people call a unique claim. In other words, potential buyers must say, "Well, I'll be damned!" when they see it for the first time. If they don't, your product is probably headed for the graveyard. Big companies spend millions to find out if consumers think their new product candidates are unique, but since you don't have millions, and maybe not even thousands, let me suggest a do-it-yourself test.

To conduct this test, you must have a sample of your widget. Don't worry yet about mass production or perfection. If it's too expensive to make the actual product, then a sketch or drawing, or even a written description, will do. The important thing is to be sure that a prospective consumer can easily understand what your product is and what it's supposed to do. Now, take your sample to at least twenty people, the more the better—not to your mother, or your brother, or your best friend, but to people who will be objective and won't say things just to make you happy. If most of them don't say, "Well, I'll be damned!" or "Why didn't I think of that?" stop right then. You still have your job, your savings, and your sanity. Go no further; your widget is a dog.

If most of the people you ask say the magic words, you're on the right track. Now ask them, "What would you be willing to pay for this widget if it were on the shelf of a local store?" Insist on a specific price. The next question is multiple choice: "If this widget were available at the price you suggest, would you (1) buy it for sure, (2) might or might not buy it instead of the widget you now use, or (3) not buy it." Then continue your questions: "How many times a year would you buy it? What are you using now? Are you happy with your present product?"

Ask these and any other questions you can think of, along with the age, occupation, income level, marital status, and so on, of each person. Keep a careful record of each answer. I can't tell you how important it is to be sure you are getting the right answers, not the ones you want to hear. If you want to be absolutely sure about the validity of the answers, ask everyone who gives you a positive response if they would like to invest their money in your widget. If they all say no or if they hem and haw, they probably lied, and you should know that your widget has fleas.

Now, take all of your questionnaires and "spread" the information. If you don't know how, find some fifteen-year-old kid with a computer. First, you want to know what you can charge for your widget. To get that answer, go to the "What would you be willing to pay?" question, throw out the top and bottom 10 percent of the answers, and average the rest. That, whether you like it or not, is a rough idea of what the consumer thinks your widget is worth. Let's call it the perceived value. Now you have to subtract the approximate amount the retail store will want for its markup: around 25 percent if your widget is something you eat, drink, or clean your house with; 35 percent if it's a household item or an appliance or something you put on your face or hair or body; 40 percent if it's something that is normally sold in a hardware or specialty store. Because these percentages vary, to get more accurate information you should ask three or four local stores what the standard markup is for your type of product.

Then you'll have to subtract roughly 15 percent for what it will cost you to sell it to the store, another 15 percent for advertising, 10 percent for warehousing and transportation, 5 percent for administration, and 5 percent for miscellaneous things like interest and your salary. Again, all these percentages will vary by product category, so find the most accurate numbers you can. One way is to ask people who are in the widget business to give you a breakdown of their costs. They may tell you to drop dead or hang up on you, but it's worth a try.

After you subtract all these numbers, you'll have the amount left for manufacturing and profit, if any. When you compare the number with what you think it will cost to manufacture your widget, you either have a "go" or a "no go."

If the signs are go, the next thing you need to know is what percentage of the people who buy any kind of widget will buy yours. So go back to your would-you-buy question, and take 100 percent of the "for sures" and 50 percent of the "maybes." Let's call this answer the intent to purchase. If that total is over 50 percent of all the answers, you have a small fighting chance; 65 percent is okay; 85 percent or over, great. If it's under 50 percent, forget the whole thing. You are no go. Up to now, your only cost has been shoe power and guts, so it costs very little to quit.

If your numbers look good and you are still determined to go ahead, take a deep breath, because it's now going to start costing money, and you are still a long, long way from any income. Regardless of your results, don't be misled into believing that the research you have done is going to ensure the success of your widget. It most definitely will not. What it should have told you is whether or not your widget belongs in a kennel. If your answers and numbers are really good, however, it is just possible you are on the right track, so you can be cautiously optimistic.

I call the next step the "Rube Goldberg test." It's a bit makeshift, but it does the job. To get it started, you must have a small quantity of your widgets. It's not time yet to worry about building a factory or buying thousands of units, but it is time to get someone to make some widgets for you. If you can make your own, so much the better. Because of the low quantity, be prepared for the cost per unit to be high, maybe outrageous, but that's not so important at this point. You must, of course, develop packaging for your widget, which means that you need an advertising agency's services, if you can afford them. If you can't, go to a company that sells packaging. Most of them have a design department they make available to their customers. Show them your widget and ask for their creative help in exchange for future business. To do the Rube Goldberg test, you must have enough finished and packaged products to put up a small (or large) display in five or more retail outlets.

Now it's time to put on your selling shoes. Go to independently owned stores in your neighborhood and tell the owners you have developed the world's greatest widget, and ask them if you can put up a display in their store. And don't charge them anything for the product, which should be an incentive for them to cooperate. The price will be the perceived value you came up with earlier. The purpose of all this is to find out how many customers, for every hundred who buy any product like your widget, will buy yours. In other words, you are looking for your percentage share of the total widget market.

This test won't be easy to arrange. First of all, most store owners will think you are nuts. Remember, though, they own their own businesses, which means they may be entrepreneurs, and entrepreneurs have great difficulty refusing one of their own kind. Of course, you are going to get a lot of nos, but keep trying—sooner or later you're bound to find five people who will cooperate.

When your Rube Goldberg test is over, you will have a general idea of your market share. Of course, you didn't have any TV or radio or newspaper ads, but your widget was on display, which is almost as good. Anyway, old Rube never claimed this was a Procter & Gamble market test. It also didn't cost $2 million. Now, just before you leave, ask your friendly store owner to compare your sales with the slowest-selling competitor. If your sales were lower, you are probably out of business. Common sense says that no merchant will buy anything that sells slower than their slowest-moving product. On the other hand, if your widget sells more than their fastest-selling widget, you've probably got a winner. In either case, the moment of truth has arrived. Ask the store owner if, based on your sales, he or she would consider leaving the item in the store. If three out of five say yes, call me and let's celebrate. If all five say no, don't call.

The test is over, and you now have enough information to play a what-if game. Before you go back and find the fifteen-year-old kid with the computer, you must know the total dollar sales for widgets nationally. You can get that information by calling the appropriate national association of widget producers, or, if you have an advertising agency, ask it to find out. If all else fails, call some local widget salespeople. They know everything.

Now you can play with the numbers. If, during your test period, there were a hundred widgets of all kinds sold in your five outlets, and you sold ten of them, then you have some reason to believe that if you were national you could sell 10 percent of the total widget market. Of course, if you sold only one, then you would have 1 percent, and so on. By taking the total national sales of all widgets and applying your test percentage, you can determine what your dollar sales could be if your widget were available nationally. The percentages will work for any size market, including your own hometown. To figure potential sales there, all you have to know is its share of the national market, and your local newspaper will gladly tell you that. You can have a lot of fun with the numbers, and you can also get some idea about whether or not your widget can make it in the market.

Some general rules apply to every product category. For example, if your widget is destined for the supermarkets and your estimated annual national sales are less than $20 million, you have a problem. You probably would not be able to maintain distribution, because your small sales would not warrant space on the supermarket shelves. Besides, 15 percent of $20 million is $3 million, and that's on the low side of what you would need for advertising and promotion. Likewise, 15 percent would be needed to support a national sales organization. Again, $3 million isn't that much when you consider you must pay the broker and/or representatives between $1 million and $2 million (depending on the product), and you'd need all the rest for your internal sales force.

If your widget is a specialty item that can be sold through a K Mart or a department store, the annual sales requirement may be much less, even as little as $3 million or $4 million. But the lower the volume, the higher the commission would have to be to interest a broker or representative, and the less you would have left for all the other requirements, including profits and your salary.

You are still a thousand miles from success, but you have evidence that your product does answer a consumer need, and you have a general idea as to the share of market you may expect. If everything looks good, you probably owe it to yourself to take the next step, but not without professional help. You now need someone to design a marketing plan for you that includes a national rollout. Find someone who has had some experience in marketing products similar to your widget. If you don't know anyone, go to the *Yellow Pages*. If you can't find someone in your hometown, go to the nearest big city. If that doesn't work, run an ad in one of the many marketing publications or call up a couple of advertising agencies and ask them to recommend someone. A retired marketing executive from a widget company would be ideal.

When you find the right person, negotiate a firm price—it will probably be far less than you expected. The expert will study your questionnaire and the results of your Rube Goldberg test. With that information, along with all the other information available to him or her, a professional can tell you how much money will be required for what and when, how slowly you can roll out your product or how fast. By analyzing the competition, he or she can also suggest whether you can go market by market, which is the best of all worlds because you can use the profits from the first market to help pay for the second, and so on. The rollout plan will also determine the level and types of media for advertising and promotion, and it will establish the necessary introductory allowances. It will also tell you how much product will be required and when. With the expert's help, you can prepare a total business plan, including forecasts and financial requirements. When your marketing and business plans are complete, it's time for another go or no-go decision.

If it's no go, you'll feel terrible, and your savings account won't feel so good, either, but you still have your job and a place where you can lay thee down and bleed awhile until the next idea gets you up again. If it's go, I pity you and envy you, because the moment of truth is at hand. Now it's time to raise money. From the beginning of time, entrepreneurs have been faced with money problems, and I predict that you will be no different. But you own 100 percent of a product that has proven that it will sell against competition, and you have some indication of the final results. You also have a marketing plan prepared by a professional and a business plan that clearly shows your charted course, and you can project the kind of profits that can be anticipated. In short, you have done your homework. Maybe not quite as the professional would do it, but you are not asking an investor to take a shot in the dark—into the clouds, maybe, but total darkness, no.

Start your fund-raising as close to home as possible, with yourself. You must be willing to commit everything you own. Ask every family member who is still speaking to you to invest. After all, you're about to found a new dynasty for your children's children's children. If you are not willing to make this kind of commitment, then know with absolute certainty that investors will be hard to find. Although investors are being asked to invest money that they probably don't need, they will expect you to invest everything you own. It won't be easy, and you'll learn some new definitions of frustration, but if you are willing to make a total commitment, chances are that you will find someone who will fly with you.

If you can't get enough money to go all the way, be content to start the first market. Things get easier and easier as you prove the marketing plan. When you have raised the start-up money, it's time at last to quit your job, and sell your house and anything else you own.

Let me leave you with a thought: As you walk down the aisles of a supermarket or department store and see all those products on the shelves, stop a moment and think. At some time, way back when, there was another person, just like you, who was faced with the same situation. The name might have been Heinz, or Procter, or Gamble, or Goodyear, but at some point in time that person was you.

Have fun—I wish you luck.

—WILSON HARRELL

BUYING HIGH, SELLING LOW

David Lloyd is not discouraged. Even now—four years and $3 million in expenses later—Lloyd is convinced he'll be running a $100-million company soon. But his problem is getting started. Lloyd, now forty, has encountered virtually every problem that can plague a new enterprise. His company, American Discount Stamps Inc., in Houston, is proof that a brilliant idea is no guarantee of instant success. And Lloyd's idea *is* brilliant, if a bit unorthodox. He wants to buy first-class stamps from the post office for 22¢ and sell them for 17¢.

Plenty of companies buy high and sell low, but it isn't on purpose. For Lloyd, however, that strategy was a key part of the business plan, and it isn't as strange as it sounds. Lloyd will buy stamps for 22¢ and surround them with small ads. Projected revenues from the ads should offset the discount, cover overhead, and produce a tiny profit on each stamp. When he multiplies that fraction times the 20 million stamps he thinks he can sell each month, Lloyd sees a garage full of Porsches. That's why the former Coca-Cola Company consultant has been working on the idea since 1982 and still talks confidently about foreign markets before he has sold a single stamp here. But those four years have been filled with problems.

Lloyd had never thought much about stamps; then he heard a rumor that Coke and McDonald's Corporation had offered to print postage stamps for free, in exchange for placing an ad on each one. The government said no—stamps are considered currency and only the government may mint money—but Lloyd was intrigued. He began wondering, "How could we give advertisers what they wanted, make the government happy, and build a demand?" The answer: Sell the stamps at a discount, and the world would beat a path to his door.

Selling a 22¢ stamp for 17¢ would create demand, but where would shoppers buy them? When Lloyd went to such mass-marketers as department and convenience stores, their first question was, "Who is going to advertise? Prove to us you are for real, then we'll talk about shelf space." So Lloyd trudged off to see advertisers. Their first question: "Where will you sell the stamps?"

Lloyd figured he could get around this Catch-22. Perhaps advertising agencies could convince their clients to give him money for a test. He came to Madison Avenue, expecting that excited account executives would dash off mock-ups. But Lloyd had never worked in advertising and didn't understand the business. To his surprise, the agencies wanted to know how the tiny ads would look. So it was back to Houston to do sample ads. The prototypes persuaded 7-11 Convenience Food Stores to sell the stamps on an experimental basis. Armed with that commitment, Lloyd went back to potential advertisers. But instead of handing over money, businesses like Campbell Soup Company began asking hard questions, and Lloyd didn't always have the answers.

For example, advertisers had told Lloyd they wanted proof the ads would boost sales. So Lloyd designed test markets, using a few retailers in each. But by limiting distribution, Campbell asked, aren't you risking an antitrust violation? Lloyd's attorneys are reviewing that. The bills keep piling up as Lloyd waits. And even legal okays won't end his waiting, because Lloyd hadn't anticipated yet another problem. "We had no idea how far ahead ad people budget," he says. A company that likes Lloyd's idea may not write a check for a year. But things could be worse. Lloyd would have gone through considerably more than $3 million if he hadn't worked at holding down his operating costs. The company still consists of just five full-time employees.

Will he succeed?

Abe Borenstein thinks so. Borenstein is the Merill Lynch vice-president who has gotten senior management to consider the idea. Borenstein believes a small Merrill Lynch ad on the outside of a pitch for the company's cash-management accounts could get more people to open the envelope. "Ninety percent of the people who get our stuff put it in the circular file," says Borenstein. "This is an eye-catcher. It won't make the sale, but it will open up an opportunity for people to consider what we have to say."

George Mahrlig isn't so sure. Mahrlig, Campbell's director of media services, has experimented with everything from advertising on shopping carts (a winner) to ads on parking meters (disappointing). "We get ideas from all over creation," he says. "It is amazing the number that don't take off."

Assuming the business takes off, Lloyd faces a rather sobering competitive situation: Nothing about his idea is proprietary. If that's true, what does the future hold? A price war in postage stamps?

There's another problem: The stamps themselves may not be *legal*. That's right, four years and $3 million, and Lloyd doesn't know if he can sell the stamps. The U.S. Postal Service, which had initially given its blessing, recently unearthed a law that could be interpreted as forbidding Lloyd's idea. Lawyers are looking into that one, too.

Lloyd, as always, remains optimistic.

—PAUL B. BROWN

CULTIVATING GROWTH

White Flower Farm has an almost storybook look to it. The white cottage and horse barns converted to offices nestle amidst manicured lawns, colorful flower beds, and hedgerows. Although White Flower is in the mail-order nursery business, about 15,000 visitors drop by its retail store from April to October. Many want to see for themselves the place so handsomely photographed in *The Garden Book,* White Flower's catalog. Some plan their visit for the one weekend each summer when cucumber sandwiches are served outdoors, with owner Eliot Wadsworth II and his wife, Sandra, helping with the iced-tea pitchers. This year, the sandwiches required forty-eight loaves of Pepperidge Farm exta-thin white bread.

"Right now, we've got four hundred and fifty thousand perennials in the fields," says the forty-three-year-old Wadsworth. "And every morning I get up and run these fields with my dog, looking for things like disease problems and water problems. What a marvelous thing to be doing for a living. The idea of being paid to be out making notes in the trial gardens is indescribable."

Yet this is no starry-eyed horticulturist with a tendency to lean on his hoe and gaze across the fields. With planting in some cases a year and a half ahead of fulfilling orders, and catalogs printed months in advance, the mail-order nursery business combines the advance planning and seasonality of the fashion industry with the perishability problems of the restaurant trade. And Eliot Wadsworth II is as comfortable poring over a spreadsheet full of numbers as perusing a field abloom with phlox, as familiar with leveraged buyouts as with species of iris. He is a tough-minded businessman who has found exactly the right business to be in.

White Flower Farm, selling only select flowers, sets the highest standards in the industry. Still, it is far from the biggest seller of flowers and bulbs through the mail. Companies like Breck's, W. Atlee Burpee Seed, and George W. Park Seed ring up several times White Flower's annual revenues of nearly $7 million. But where many others merely buy in, mark up, and redistribute most of what they sell, White Flower is a fully integrated company. It does everything—growing, picking, warehousing, fulfilling telephone orders, shipping, even advertising. The decision to do everything has limited the growth of the company. It also has ordered its priorities. Wadsworth has put his capital into computers, greenhouses, fields, irrigation ponds, refrigerated warehouses, and shipping capacity. "When you add to all the physical investment a huge marketing investment," he says, "the equation just doesn't work." Hence, the overall strategy of White Flower Farm: dedicated service to repeat customers. White Flower showers its upscale customers with education, grooms them with unflagging service, and harvests the benefits—loyal repeat buyers who, at over $60 a shot, undoubtedly place one of the highest average orders in the business.

"In a helter-skelter workaday world, White Flower shows it's possible to start with the clients' needs, work back, and still have a substantial financial success," says board member Bruce Schnitzer, a private merchant banker. "White Flower Farm is one of those places that restores the faith."

Located just south of Litchfield, Connecticut, White Flower Farm began as a hobby of a *Fortune* magazine writer named William Harris. Harris and his wife would leave their Park Avenue apartment in Manhattan on Friday afternoons and head for western Connecticut; they soon were bent over the gardens of their weekend home, a late eighteenth-century cottage. The name White Flower Farm, apparently, came from their fondness for white blossoms, which were easier to see as they worked the soil well past dusk. Although Harris turned his avocation into a mail-order business in 1950, he continued to run it more like a hobby right up until the mid-1970s, which is when Eliot Wadsworth II showed up.

Wadsworth, out of business school, had spent a few years here, a few years there, without really finding his niche in the business world. He started out in investment banking in New York, where he got his first glimpse of leveraged buyouts. His next stop was Maine, where he co-owned several Kentucky Fried Chicken restaurants. While his partner oversaw day-to-day management, Wadsworth negotiated for real estate, built stores, hired and trained staff, and held the marketing reins. He was working nights and weekends, and, ensconced in the Maine woods, says he was "fearful of protracted bachelorhood." So he sold out to his partner, and went on to become an acquisitions analyst with now-defunct American Garden Products Inc., a Boston-based wholesaler and retailer. Wadsworth discovered then that "the guys who had the job I wanted were running nurseries." White Flower Farm, especially, caught his eye.

The place was beautiful, and it grew and shipped a quality product. It was also, in Wadsworth's view, "significantly undermanaged." Harris was close to eighty and in failing health. "Whatever else was going on," Wadsworth recalls, "they had not compromised their standards of taste and quality." At the same time, Wadsworth saw his peers, perhaps nudged by the environmental movement and back-to-the-earth sentiments, turning to gardening. In short, he saw the wind at his back and a perfect opportunity: a business with good rootstock, good opportunity for growth, and, not so incidentally, the chance to fashion a wonderful lifestyle. He signed up as general manager.

After proving himself "honorable" to Harris, Wadsworth bought the business in January 1977 for a price he describes "in the neighborhood of annual sales," which were then approaching $750,000. His Wall Street experience came in handy, for this, he says, "was a leveraged buyout with the *leveraged* in capital letters." To his small earnings from his restaurant business, Wadsworth added loans from local farm cooperatives and working capital and mortgage money from the Bank of Boston. And he talked Harris into accepting some two-year promissory notes.

Since then, Harris's 50 acres, 4 farmed, have expanded to 300, more than 100 of which bear some 1,000 different flowers and shrubs. Although total sales in the mail-order nursery business have flattened out in the past few years, and more companies have entered the market, sales at White Flower have risen 10 percent to 15 percent a year. The staff has increased from twelve employees and twenty seasonal workers to eighty-three full-timers and sixty seasonal workers. And Wadsworth recently purchased an old manufacturing building in nearby Torrington, Connecticut, which will provide 100,000 square feet for new offices for the sales, customer service, and finance departments, currently bursting out of their quarters in converted farm buildings and stables.

Wadsworth claims to be pleased with the growth he's so carefully nurtured. Yet he is also concerned: "I worry we'll be seen as a go-go operation," he says, " a rocket ship willing to sacrifice quality to growth. And that's just not true. Our corporate strategy is simple: We will be *the quality supplier*. Period." That means being a nursery first and foremost, and a mail-order business second.

A few words about pink lavender back up this contention. Not too long ago, this new shade, offering a dramatic contrast to lavender's traditional smoky blue, was the talk among nursery owners. White Flower quickly planted some in its test gardens, and lovely pink blossoms resulted. Everybody was excited, and plans were made to pair the pink and the blue and photograph them for the upcoming catalog. About then, Landon Winchester, White Flower's staff horticulturist, happened by, cut a piece off a trial plant, and held it to his nose. "We can't sell this," he said. The smell was only slightly bitter, but the point was, it was not the expected aroma of lavender. You can buy pink lavender from other mail-order nurseries, but not from White Flower Farm.

"Eliot has a very clear idea of what White Flower Farm is, and his standards come through consistently," says Lesley Nelmes, White Flower vice-president and general manager. "He loves beautiful things and respects them. I don't think anyone here is confused about what we do." Pointing to a recently cleared meadow and on to newly planted azaleas and rhododendrons, all of this far from the view of most visitors to the retail store and street-side gardens, she adds, "He wants us to be what we say we are."

The message is clear to White Flower's new production manager, Greg Jones, who was hired away from Gurney Seed & Nursery Inc., a catalog nursery easily three times White Flower's size. He left Gurney "partly because after a while, the plants become like nuts and bolts. At most places," he says, "nurserymen deal only with small plants or cuttings and roots. They really don't see the finished product. At Gurney, there was a guy who could identify many varieties of trees by their roots, but show him a leaf and he was lost."

Wadsworth himself likes to quote what he considers a great advertisement for a small brewery: "We drink all we can. The rest we sell." "That's the way we feel about the plants," he says. "The gardens here are allegedly for the benefit of our customers, but the fact is, they are for us. We are in it for the love of plants, not just to sell them." But sell they must, and at what appears on the surface to be a disadvantage. Specialty growers, limiting themselves to a few or a single species of flower, can almost without exception grow their product more cheaply than White Flower. Thus, many varieties, wholesaled to other mail-order catalogs, are sold at prices *The Garden Book* cannot match. White Flower has never even tried to compete on price.

There are other problems as well. This year, there are shortages at White Flower Farm. Wadsworth avoids the temptation to buy replacements at wholesale, for to do so would be to lower the guard on quality control, an essential ingredient if customers are to return to White Flower year after year. Wadsworth is similarly unyielding with perishable surpluses. When White Flower fails to sell what it grows, he doesn't try to wholesale the extra plants elsewhere. Nor does he hold fire sales or try to fine-tune demand with last-minute advertising. He buries his mistakes—literally. "We've tried a lot of things and essentially discovered it's throwing good money after bad. We've found it's best simply not to be too aggressive, not overcommit ourselves, not try to sell out every year to maximize the last dollar, because all we're going to do is offend the last twenty-five percent of the people who order."

Despite the problems, Wadsworth still believes in the White Flower way. He estimates that as many as one-third of the 250,000 clients who are sent White Flower's biannual catalog place at least two orders a year. "I think in the end, what the others are going to lose by their strategies is a clear identification with their product and an identification with their customers," he says, in an apparent—though unspecified—reference to Wayside Gardens, owned by George W. Park Seed Company and one of Wadsworth's most formidable catalog rivals. "When you become a shipping warehouse in South Carolina, in the scorching heat, with big semitrailers arriving from Ohio, it's pretty hard to identify with a little old lady sitting on her porch in Vermont wondering whether her peonies are going to make enough roots, or whether the full moon is going to mean a hard frost for her garden. We don't have any trouble empathizing with her—because we are doing the same thing she is doing."

In essence, the people who work at White Flower Farm are expected to sell education and service as well as to grow the biggest and best flowers. *The Garden Book,* for example, is not just a catalog. It is a beautifully written book filled with helpful advice and information for both beginning and experienced gardeners. The three most trusted words in home gardening these days may well be *The Garden Book*'s sign-off: "Sincerely, Amos Pettingill."

So graceful is the prose, so gentle the approach, so laid-back the sales pitch, that you practically forget you are a customer. Listen: "Tulips are the lipstick of the garden, adding a touch of color when and where it is most needed. They can be soft or bold, elegant or informal, but it's plain that if we didn't have tulips, someone would have to invent them. In our garden we made abundant use of a recent strain of tulips that can truly be said to be perennial. No, they will not last as long as peonies, but neither will we."

Wadsworth has made a lot of changes in his nine years at the helm of White Flower Farm, but there's one thing he didn't change. He kept Amos Pettingill in charge of prose and his gentlemanly mien the mode of doing business.

People who come asking to see Amos Pettingill may or may not be disappointed. "You're talking to him," Wadsworth says, should a visitor ask him to point out Pettingill. Wadsworth's predecessor, William Harris, created the persona. Wadsworth says he has just "shamelessly aped his style" and cooked up a signature to pen on letters. How does he envision this Pettingill fellow? "I see him as a seventy-year-old uncle, somebody who has been gardening all his life, who has undertaken the job of helping you start your own garden. He looks like the face out in the hall," Wadsworth says, referring to a photograph of a smiling, white-haired Harris.

"Actually," he continues, one foot up on his desk, "Amos Pettingill is not me. He's a distillation of the wisdom of everybody here. . . . We're just a bunch of swamp Yankees trying to grow plants carefully and ship them carefully—and we'll be tickled to death to do business with you." If that sounds a little bit like Amos Pettingill talking, it is hardly surprising, for Wadsworth admits it has become increasingly hard to determine where White Flower Farm stops and Eliot Wadsworth begins.

"I do believe companies have to have an internal consistency about what they do," says Wadsworth. "And for better or worse, that reflects the work habits and integrity of the boss." Walking to his car, the sight of a lone dandelion will have him stooped and grabbing. Wadsworth has the lawns mowed not once, but twice a week. "The place looks like a new penny three hundred sixty-five days a year," he says with pride. An unkempt nursery, of course, is a candidate for disease. "But I am also fussy, partly because it's a way of expressing your affection and respect for the people who work for you." He pays his people well. Managers earn top dollar and experienced tractor drivers make as much as $7.80 an hour, considerably more than at other nurseries. Wages, says Wadsworth, account for $1 of every $3 taken in. To be tight with salaries, Wadsworth knows, would be ruinous: He needs a dedicated, stable workforce, because farming is so labor-intensive and, most of all, because his emphasis on tending plants and customers with equal diligence demands it.

"White Flower trains its people well," says an envious executive of a competing mail-order nursery. "When I've called to place orders, I've found the operators qualified to handle many horticultural questions. I love companies like that. They are really good for the whole industry." The telephone operators at White Flower Farm, who take about one-third of the orders, attend regularly scheduled briefing sessions led by staff horticulturist Winchester, so they can advise and inform customers. In slow times, operators are sometimes given assignments in shipping and in the fields. This is not only to ensure a full day's work for a full day's pay, but to expose them to what they are selling. "If you stand in a field of thirty-five thousand phlox, you'll remember it for the rest of your life," says Wadsworth. "You may not remember all twenty-two of the colors or varieties we sell, but you will remember what they look like and smell like, and about when they were in bloom."

White Flower is such a customer-driven company that when Wadsworth talks about the probable impact of a big new computer on order processing, he speaks what others might consider a businessman's blasphemy: "The trick is to avoid the temptation to sell, sell, sell." Instead of programming the computer to prod telephone operators with slick, suggestive marketing aids, Wadsworth would rather it help solve gardening problems. "What would our director of horticulture, David Smith, say if he were on the phone?" He believes that, perhaps before the end of this year, the computer will be able, while processing an order, to flag potential problems: plants not hardy enough for a particular ZIP code; one sun-loving flower in an order of shade dwellers; a combination of colors that, if destined for the same location, might not blend well together.

Indeed, in the person of Landon Winchester, White Flower Farm functions almost as a clearinghouse for horticultural tips, pointers, and desperately sought advice. With close-cropped white hair, silver-framed glasses, and an unhurried, gentlemanly air about him, Winchester might pass for Amos Pettingill's younger brother. He came to White Flower about four years ago after a long career with the Brooklyn Botanical Garden and a stint as superintendent of horticulture for the city of New Haven. On a particularly busy day, he may take close to fifty calls, without ever ending a conversation with the words, "Sorry, we don't have it." He'll find out who does and call back.

White Flower Farm guarantees everything it sells, and Winchester is typically the one who placates dissatisfied customers. He is, to put it mildly, a soft touch with replacements, which he views as goodwill advertising. "Many people call with their boxing gloves on," he says during a lull between calls. "And you can't blame them. This seems to be part of what goes with the name *mail order.* Many people write me later and say, 'I'm sorry, I thought you people were like the rest.'

"Take that caller from Illinois earlier this morning. He ordered two hollies from us two years ago. He put them under a dense oak tree where they received too much shade. Now, there was no moral responsibility on our part to offer him replacements. They are not on our shade-tolerant lists, so they shouldn't have been planted there. On the other hand, he seemed like a decent enough Joe. I see the replacement of those two hollies, at about twenty-five dollars plus shipping, not as a minus, but as a plus. We'll have a person who was so surprised we would do this that he'll talk to everybody at the office about it, and we'll have a spokesman in Illinois."

Winchester signed on with White Flower Farm because he was impressed with the emphasis on quality by director of horticulture Smith and with the clear signal sent by Wadsworth. "He told me he wanted a horticulturist who could give the right answers. There was no implication I would have to bend to commercial pressures," says Winchester. "If Eliot was selling motor cars, I think I would have been tempted to work here."

The fact is, Eliot Wadsworth charms and impresses almost everybody who meets him. Perhaps because he attended prep school, Harvard, and Harvard Business School, or because of that roman numeral after his name, or because he's as apt to be reading Shakespeare as the business section of the newspaper, people assume he hails from money. In fact, his upbringing was strictly middle class—and New England Yankee. He is smart, handsome, and, in old-fashioned parlance, a "well-rounded individual."

If there is a sticking criticism of White Flower's owner, it is that he tries to do—and does—too much. All the recent logistics for a White Flower tour of English gardens were mapped out by Wadsworth, who personally scouted lodgings and restaurants. "It was fun," he says. A longtime follower of *Horticulture* magazine, and with no more publishing experience than his own mail-order catalog, he talked *The New Yorker* into buying the ailing magazine with him in 1981 and soon turned it around. Three years ago, White Flower was named a finalist in a magazine advertising competition sponsored by the Magazine Publishers Association. Listed alongside big Madison Avenue ad agencies as producer of the White Flower ads was the Isaiah Smith Agency of Litchfield, Connecticut. Who's Isaiah Smith? "Well, that's me, too," says Wadsworth.

"He has so much energy and enthusiasm that he has a tendency to say, 'I'll take care of that.' Then he gets a call and there's just not enough time," says Lesley Nelmes. "If he were perhaps a little more realistic about his limitations. He'll say he'll take the photographs [of a particular flower for the catalog], but when that flower is in bloom, he's in Boston." She feels he needs to delegate more authority to the top-flight managers he has hired. Because he so often "steps into somebody else's niche," Nelmes says, "he deprives them of the satisfaction of doing a job themselves."

Wadsworth pleads guilty, admitting he should have been entrusting more to others far sooner. Whether it's sooner or later, given his present schedule, some delegation seems inevitable.

Visited one morning last spring in his Litchfield office, Wadsworth—wearing a green cable-knit sweater, khaki pants, tasseled loafers, and socks closer to pink than red—had a healthy glow. There was no sign, as noon approached, that he'd been up for nearly eight hours. He'd left home in Brookline, Massachusetts, before five, and, with a hired student behind the wheel, had sat in the backseat under a reading light poring through his briefcase during the two-and-a-half-hour drive to Litchfield. Since moving his family from the cottage at the farm to Brookline, each week he shuttles from one side of New England to the other. Restrained by his Yankee notion of how to grasp purse strings (tightly), which also limits him to $35 motel rooms, Wadsworth travels in an American sedan so undistinguished it might moonlight as an unmarked police car.

With his workday now approaching twelve hours, Wadsworth quits his office for a late-afternoon walk. His son, Eliot, he says, has worked at the farm the past two summers, putting in a couple of hours a day and punching a time clock. Eliot is eight and already knows the names of two to three dozen flowers and perhaps half that many weeds. Wadsworth's oldest daughter, Eve, age five, will start next summer. Natalie, but two, will have to wait. The notion seems a bit old-fashioned, but it would not displease Wadsworth if one of his children eased into his rubber gardening boots one day.

He passes his cottage and heads through a newly cleared meadow toward some recently planted elms. He stops by one of them, and rubs his hand along a crack where the bark has split. "The south side," he says. "The tree probably needs water." On he continues, to a hill overlooking what some employees refer to as "Lake Wadsworth." The one-acre pond was formerly a swamp. Snowshoeing there one day, Wadsworth saw that it hadn't frozen over and realized it must be spring-fed. He recently had the swamp cleared and an irrigation pond carved out, which also doubles as a place to swim and fish. Nearby, under a stand of mature oak trees, he planted laurel, rhododendrons, and azaleas in what he calls "a knock-off of a hillside at the Royal Botanic Gardens in Edinburgh."

Walking back, a half moon shows in the fading blue of a brilliantly clear afternoon. Though it is barely sweater weather, Wadsworth worries aloud about the possibility of a frost that night. Back inside the office he asks for $20 from petty cash for the drive back to Boston. He's offered $30, but turns down the extra $10. "I'd probably just blow it," he says. After retrieving his overnight gear from the cottage, he is soon in his car and headed down the lane, past the gardens. Pasted on the back window of the sedan is a bumper sticker: "Amos Pettingill for President."

WELL-TENDED CUSTOMERS

In the mail-order nursery business, the volume houses depend on extensive marketing departments to keep bringing in new customers. White Flower Farm's marketing staff is only three people, plus owner Eliot Wadsworth II. At White Flower, the emphasis is on growing quality plants over marketing them, and on pleasing present customers over looking for new ones. Some random telephone calls to customers indicate that both of the strategies are working well.

Heather Bradley, thirty-seven, lives in the San Francisco Bay area and has been ordering from White Flower Farm for about four years. With a new vacation house to landscape, she recently placed an $1,800 order. "I first saw an ad for them in *House and Garden*. And when I received their catalog, it made me feel good. Catalogs from other gardening companies don't really say much about the plants and sometimes use only the common names and not the botanical names—and that gets confusing when you are trying to compare plants. I also like the helpful hints White Flower gives, like how to tie up gypsophila to make it compact and grow in a nicer way."

Andrew Koenig, thirty-three, who lives in rural New Jersey, had his parents send him a copy of White Flower's catalog, *The Garden Book,* when he moved into a twenty-five-year-old house on property that he describes as looking like a jungle. "I like to read anything where the English language is used well. The photographs are absolutely gorgeous. I feel I have learned quite a lot from the catalog. I'm particularly pleased by the absence of hype. We visited White Flower Farm during the fall of 1984, just when they were closing for the winter. We resolved to go back during the growing season when the chrysanthemums will be coming out.

"We ordered a lot of bulbs. Many were spectacular, but a few proved to be duds. They grew enthusiastically, but when it was time for the buds to open, they just shriveled and turned brown. I called [White Flower staff horticulturist] Landon Winchester and described the situation. He said it sounded like classic symptoms of bulbs damaged in transit by cold. I then remembered that all the bulbs that had failed had been in one shipment that had arrived just after an unexpectedly severe cold snap. They have said they will send replacements. I'm sure we'll be ordering from them again. What's important to me is they go out of their way to set things straight."

Ann Findley, forty-two, is a former Connecticut resident now living in Wisconsin, a gardener, she says, all her life. "One of the oustanding things about White Flower Farm is the excellent way they package their products. They wrap them in sphagnum moss and then some form of polyethylene, so the roots stay nice and moist. We have never received anything that was overheated or too wilted to plant. Their customer service is fantastic. If you ever have a problem, their records are kept so orderly that when you call, they find your order in a couple of seconds and solve your problem. If they are out of something, they don't substitute something else unless you tell them to. Their shortcoming, if they have any, is that they can't carry everything. I think the only reason I would go somewhere else would be to get a plant I couldn't get from them.

"White Flower doesn't sell you a two-inch shoot like so many catalogs. And I don't think that in the long run you are paying more money. If you start with healthy plants, if you can more or less assume that one hundred percent will grow, and if you don't have to worry about filing a claim, then I don't think that makes the price out of line. What's more, they will tell you how to plant it, what kind of soil it likes, and if it needs a lot of coddling. Their whole attitude in the catalog is very interesting. It's written by someone named Amos Pettingill. . . . There is no Amos Pettingill? You're kidding. I find that very depressing, frankly. Oh, I don't like that. I would give them an F for false advertising for that little ploy."

—John Grossman

FOLLOW THE LEADER

If you are like most company presidents I know, you stay up nights wondering what kind of marketing you should be doing. The answer is: as little as possible.

That may sound like heresy at a time when marketing is being widely hailed as "the new priority," the key to business success in the 1980s. Savvy marketing, it is said, will cure all your company's ills. The secret, we hear, is to be creative and innovative—to come up with some clever technique, slogan, or medium that will blow your competition away. Don't believe it. The fact is that the best marketing a company can do is often no marketing at all.

Marketing is nothing more than activity undertaken to promote the likelihood of sales. Period. It's as simple as that. Marketing is not an art form; it is a way to increase business. The goal is not to be ingenious or elegant; it is to build the top line. Frankly, if you can do that by doing nothing, you might as well avoid the expense. But most companies cannot increase sales without doing some marketing, and that's where problems arise. Instead of focusing on the real goal, they try to be creative and innovative.

This is odd, when you think about it. After all, few companies want to be known for their creativity in other areas of business—accounting, say, or operations. Rather, they want systems that work, that handle a function efficiently and well. And how do you come up with such systems? More often than not, you look at what other companies do and imitate them.

In this regard, marketing is no different from any other business function. There is certainly nothing new about it. All the important techniques were invented long ago and are being practiced by successful companies in every industry, every day. So how do you figure out what kind of marketing you should be doing? My advice is simple: Be a copycat marketer. Find out what works for other companies, particularly the leaders in your field, and do the same.

The notion, I admit, flies in the face of what you generally hear and read on the subject. That's because most experts in the field think of marketing in terms of the mass-market, consumer-goods giants. Talk to marketing specialists, and they will tell you stories about Federal

Express or Coca-Cola. Read the business best-sellers, and you will learn about the exploits of Chrysler or IBM. It's all very entertaining, and sometimes even inspiring, but it has absolutely no relevance to the vast majority of American companies.

When a huge corporation embarks on a full-fledged marketing campaign, it is like a battleship in action. The spectacle can be awesome, and the fireworks thrilling. You would be foolish, however, to think you could do similar things in your dinghy.

To begin with, most companies can't afford to market on that scale. Six hundred thousand dollars might sound like a lot of money to spend on advertising, but it's a mere drop in the bucket of big-time marketing—it will get lost so fast your head will swim. What's more, big-time marketing doesn't scale down well. Tonnage counts. The whole idea is to drive the marketplace by molding consumer attitudes, which demands a marketing budget in seven or eight figures. If you don't have one, you can forget about competing in that particular arena.

Thanks to the sheer size of their budgets, moreover, the giants are able to play by their own set of rules, turning the usual relationship between selling and marketing on its head. In big companies, the sales department executes to the marketing plan—marketing creates the right environment for selling, and the salespeople follow up. Almost everywhere else, the opposite is true. Sales does not support marketing; marketing supports sales. Indeed, marketing, at least as it is practiced in most companies, might better be called sales support or sales promotion.

That's only as it should be. In most well-managed companies, marketing means such things as keeping sales literature up-to-date, setting up a telephone system that can handle customer calls quickly and efficiently, or making sure that leads are qualified and followed. It means preparing good proposals and having backup material available. It means educating salespeople about where profits come from, who the best customers are, which ones are likely to account for the company's future business, and why, and how.

Granted, all this lacks the glamor and splash of a multicolor catalog with six die cuts and four gatefolds. Or a twenty-eight-projector slide show in an auditorium the size of the Astrodome. Or a six-story trade show booth whose space rental charge is roughly equivalent to that of a Manhattan city block. But that sort of thing is self-indulgence, not marketing.

Real marketing, the kind that successful small companies do, is not a glamorous activity. It's done one-on-one with key customers at sporting events, in restaurants, and around hospitality suites. It involves working a cocktail party for an evening while nursing a single drink. It's hard work, requiring long hours and careful follow-up, and it won't get you into the next business best-seller. But it might get you three new accounts and pay for part of a new building.

This is not to suggest that there is a single, "correct" way to go about marketing. There isn't. The general rule is to figure out how to get more by spending (or doing) less, but the specifics vary from industry to industry, and region to region. You can find some clues in your own experience. What has worked for you in the past? What has brought in new business? What have you found to be the best routes to the market? Do your printing bills exceed new account sales? Do you target your efforts to high-potential customers? Do you follow up, and follow through consistently and effectively?

Beyond that, you have to look to your competitors, your counterparts in other regions, your industry leaders. What has been working for them lately? What trade shows do the market leaders attend? To what extent do they rely on direct sales? Who are their sales representatives? How are they dealing with the marketing challenges that you are facing? Remember, the goal is not to be innovative; it is to be effective.

By way of example, consider the case of some New England car dealers I know, who found themselves caught in a bind when their market changed. They had grown accustomed to a world in which cars were traded every eighteen to twenty-four months, and service was just an extra. Then the cost of a new car began approaching that of a modest house, and the trade-in window opened to fifty months. Service was no longer an extra—it was crucial to the dealers' long-term survival. So what could they do to market their service departments?

Looking around the country, they discovered that other dealers were having success with a "planned maintenance" program, developed by a former Chrysler dealer named John Fisher. The program was built around a computer-generated booklet of coupons for preventive maintenance, each good for a prearranged appointment with the dealer's service department.

The idea was to encourage new car buyers to bring their automobiles in for regular checkups, thereby allowing a dealer to build long-term customer relationships, and to turn the service department into a strong profit center at the same time. Best of all, the program required no significant up-front investment, just a monthly service fee to Fisher, who would process the coupons as they were used and send the owner reminders of upcoming appointments.

It was a simple idea, and not an original one, but it went a long way toward solving the problem of the New England dealers, who signed up right away. They have been counting their service-department profits ever since.

You can find these kinds of marketing solutions in almost any industry. The trick is to watch what the winners are doing. Copycat marketing may be tough on your creative ego, but it is easy on your pocketbook. What it produces in results and income, moreover, should more than compensate for the fact that you won't be written up in *Ad Age*.

What Not to Copy

Copycat marketing makes sense for most small companies, but watch out for fads that don't build sales, merely reduce profit. Some other pitfalls to avoid:

- Forget about rebates or promotions unless they produce incremental dollars.
- Telemarketing is hot these days, but don't try to generate business with boiler-room tactics. You're better off using the phone to set up appointments, say thank you, and respond with information.
- Beware of hotlines as well, especially if you depend on relationship marketing; you can destroy almost any relationship with 800-numbers and bureaucratic procedures that are unresponsive to customer needs.
- As for computers, they're fine so long as they help you serve your customers; if not, get rid of the computer, not the customers.
- Above all, avoid the trap of building an image or program that makes you feel good but doesn't produce results. There's nothing wrong with being a well-kept secret in the marketplace.

In general, the best course is to focus on the activities that generate income. Do those well and let the rest go. Life is too short to be good at everything.

—JACK FALVEY

ONCE IS NOT ENOUGH

To Bruce Nevins, it was just another day in the limelight. Nineteen seventy-nine had been a good year for him, and he had become a regular on the media circuit—profiled in newspapers, mentioned in gossip columns, interviewed on radio and television. With his polished good looks, he had both the appearance and the demeanor of a celebrity. Now he found himself in the studios of KABC Radio in Los Angeles, waiting to go on the air to talk once more about the things that had made him famous.

Comfortable as he was in this setting, he was by no means a typical talk-show guest. He was not plugging a movie; he had written no books. Rather, his fame came from water—a particular kind of water, one that bubbled up out of the ground in Vergèze, France. There it was put in attractive green bottles and shipped to the United States. It was called Perrier.

Thanks largely to the efforts of Nevins, Perrier had become the toast of the American leisure class. A new generation of health-conscious, upwardly mobile young professionals were drinking it by the truckload, convinced that it was as special as the marketing campaign suggested. Admittedly, other carbonated waters cost less, but they lacked Perrier's natural minerals and its unique taste, or so the faithful claimed.

There were skeptics, however, and one of them happened to be KABC Radio's Michael Jackson, the host of the popular talk show on which Nevins was about to appear. Jackson was so skeptical, in fact, that he had planned a little surprise for his guest. Soon after the show began, he challenged Nevins to a blind taste test. If Perrier were truly distinctive, Jackson suggested, Nevins of all people should be able to taste the difference. Taken aback, Nevins agreed to give it a whirl.

Jackson proceeded to place seven paper cups on the table—six filled with club soda, one with Perrier. Nevins tried them all and chose one. Wrong, said Jackson; that was club soda. Nevins picked another. Wrong again. A third choice. Wrong once more. In all, it took him five tries to pick out the water from France—a result that gave Jackson no end of satisfaction.

Nevins, for his part, took the episode in stride. After all, the water was only part of Perrier's appeal. "It's hard to tell the difference between seltzer, Perrier, and club soda," he admits, "but in a restaurant, they don't just bring you a glass of water; they bring you a *bottle*. As a customer, you respond to the shape of that bottle, the feel of it in your hand, the design of the label. There's something to that, a panache. It becomes something you can identify with."

The water, in other words, was a commodity. The genius was in the marketing.

Marketing is hot these days, and its popularity has spawned a new breed of consultant, the professional "marketeer." Scores of them can be found roaming the business landscape, offering their services to companies, especially small ones, that lack the in-house expertise to win the battle for shelf space in an increasingly competitive marketplace. Many of these specialists come with hefty credentials. Seasoned veterans of such consumer product giants as Beatrice, Dart & Kraft, and Pillsbury, they tell war stories of big-time marketing campaigns for products ranging from Prestone Anti-Freeze to Green Giant vegetables. Some have been spun loose in corporate restructurings and cutbacks. Others have simply decided to strike out on their own. Whatever their reasons for leaving the *Fortune* 500, their backgrounds suggest a level of real-world marketing experience that would impress even the most hard-bitten of small-company presidents.

And perhaps the most impressive of the lot is Bruce Nevins.

Nevins is an acknowledged master of product positioning, a reputation built largely on his success with Perrier in the late 1970s. Since then, he has done a nice job of positioning himself as well. A forty-nine-year-old bachelor, he drives around in a white Jaguar XJS and is often spotted at trendy watering holes in the company of beautiful women, including Shelley Hack, of "Charlie's Angels" fame, and Margaret Trudeau, the estranged wife of the former Canadian prime minister. When he is not traveling, he lives in an elegant rooftop apartment just off Fifth Avenue in Manhattan. On summer weekends, he can usually be found at his house in East Hampton.

Nevins came to his present position via a circuitous route. A West Point graduate, he spent four years in the service—one year as a Green Beret in Southeast Asia. He then enrolled in the Stanford Business School and took an immediate liking to advertising and marketing. After business school, he did a two-year stint with Benton & Bowles Inc., the Manhattan advertising agency, before moving on to Levi Strauss as merchandising manager for international operations. Seeing growth opportunities in the Asia-Pacific region, where the company was doing less than $1 million in sales, Nevins set up shop in Hong Kong. By the time he returned to California in 1973 to become Levi's head of corporate planning and new business development, international sales overall, which had been a mere $10 million, had soared to $400 million.

But Nevins was becoming frustrated with corporate life. He soon left Levi Strauss to pursue other opportunities. For a while, he worked with a French apparel company and with the small Canadian manufacturer of Pony athletic shoes. Then came his big break. On a trip to Paris in February 1976, he met with a Pony investor named Gustave Leven, who happened to be chairman of Source Perrier. Leven invited Nevins to become president and part owner of Perrier's U.S. distribution company. Nevins accepted.

The challenge was certainly a formidable one. At the time, American sales of the beverage amounted to less than $600,000, and all signs pointed to a narrow niche. True, Perrier was available at fancy restaurants, but few stores carried it, and you could not build sales of a product that people could not buy. Clearly, Nevins had to expand distribution. The problem was that most major distributors were reluctant to tie up their own resources on an unproven product.

To solve the problem, Nevins proposed to promote Perrier like crazy, on the theory that a massive advertising and public relations campaign would pull consumers into the market and create an incentive for distributors to sign on. He had statistics to bolster his theory. Market research showed that a growing number of Americans were looking for an alternative to alcoholic beverages, on the one hand, and sweet, artificially flavored soft drinks, on the other. Perrier was the ideal beverage for these consumers, Nevins contended. His French sponsor bought the argument, agreeing to commit the millions of dollars required to support the campaign.

With the money in hand, Nevins went into action in the spring of 1977, promoting Perrier under the slogan "Naturally sparkling from the center of the Earth." He advertised. He flew a planeload of journalists to the Perrier "source" in Vergèze. He hired clean-cut young people to stand in stores and serve chilled samples. Within two years, Perrier was available in supermarkets all over the country, but Nevins had just begun. He arranged for Perrier to sponsor running events. He helped municipalities build more than a hundred Perrier exercise courses. He persuaded distributors to splash the Perrier logo on the sides of their delivery trucks. And he put Perrier umbrellas on sidewalk tables across America.

The program was bold. It was innovative. It was lavish. And it worked. In 1979, the third year of marketing, Perrier sold about $60 million of imported water in the United States, a mere drop in the beverage bucket perhaps, but more than double Nevins' five-year projection. Most impressive, he had established a whole new product category, one that was already attracting a host of competitors.

The Perrier launch was the stuff of marketing legends, as successful as they come. But in October 1980, Nevins abruptly called it quits and sold his interest of less than 10 percent in the American import company. It was time to move on, he says. His five-year contract with Perrier was up, and the "water wars" were threatening the product's future growth. Besides, he was hankering to get involved in other entrepreneurial marketing efforts. Managing a large company, he says, "wasn't nearly as much fun as getting out there and doing it."

So, with Jim Stevens, his senior vice-president of marketing and sales from Perrier, Nevins formed a company, Premium Products Sales Corporation, located in Greenwich, Connecticut. Together they began looking for small companies with promising ideas. Their plan was to come in as a marketing team and do for their clients what they had done for Perrier. For a piece of the action, they were even willing to invest in the businesses they advised. With their know-how, their contacts, and their capital, they were bound to hit some winners, and everybody could get rich and famous in the process. It seemed like a sure thing.

Nevins' first project was a new line of Italian table wines, to be sold under the name Bollini and priced at less than $5. The idea came from an Italian investor, who thought it a natural for the wizard of Perrier. Nevins himself was enthusiastic enough to put up his own money, but he soon discovered that introducing a new wine was nothing like opening up a new product category. For one thing, he was competing against a lot of established brands. To build a name, he had to rely heavily on special promotions and coupons, techniques that would motivate distributors. It was an interesting market, he says, but one in which it was hard to make money.

Undaunted, Nevins and Stevens continued to look for opportunities, and they found one in February 1981. Through Nevins' friend Tucker Frederickson, the former New York football Giants running back turned investment banker, they met a pair of entrepreneurs named Richard LaMotta, a former CBS video engineer with a law degree, and Sam Metzger, a lawyer. Their product seemed like a winning field goal waiting to be kicked. Called the Chipwich, it was a slab of premium-quality ice cream between two large chocolate chip cookies rolled in imported chocolate chips. The previous fall, LaMotta and Metzger had introduced the Chipwich at a street fair in Manhattan's Little Italy, and sold 25,000 in a single week. Now they were gearing up for a major product launch in May, when they would flood the sidewalks of New York with sixty street carts attended by college kids wearing safari clothes and bow ties. Their aim was to sell 25,000 to 30,000 Chipwiches a day, all of which would be made by hand at a storefront in Queens.

For Nevins, the Chipwich was love at first sight. He could see that LaMotta and Metzger scarcely realized what they were onto. Oh, Nevins gave them credit all right—LaMotta for inventing the product and Metzger for finding the money to get it to market. And the cart program, he thought, was just a super idea. But ice cream was a $4-billion category and growing. Ice cream novelties constituted about a quarter of that, and most of the existing products were commodities. Chipwich had the potential to become a major brand.

But to accomplish that, Nevins said, they would have to get the Chipwich into supermarkets and support the product with an imaginative marketing program. He and Stevens offered to supply the expertise. For $6,000 a month, they would coordinate the rollout in the New York area. Once the program was off the ground, they would charge a sales management fee of 14 percent. They also agreed to invest about $100,000 of their own money in the company.

LaMotta, Metzger, and their board were delighted. "We were so focused on our cart program," recalls LaMotta, "that it wouldn't have occurred to us to go into the supermarkets."

It soon became clear, however, that the new marketing plan would necessitate other changes in the operation. With the carts rolling all summer, LaMotta and Metzger had their hands full keeping up with demand. At the storefront in Queens, about fifty Chipwich makers were busy slapping together up to 25,000 units a day, but all of those were usually gone by the end of the next Manhattan lunch hour. Obviously, more capacity would be needed to produce enough Chipwiches for the frozen-food cases of supermarkets in the area. After exploring the possibility of farming out production on a contract basis, the company elected to expand its own production facilities, opening up a Chipwich factory in a 20,000-square-foot warehouse in Lodi, New Jersey. There they would install semiautomated equipment and lick the capacity problem once and for all.

But who was going to get the plant up and running? Neither LaMotta nor Metzger had that kind of experience. Nevins was pushing hard toward a December supermarket rollout. The more they thought about it, the more Jim Stevens seemed the natural choice. Although his background was in sales and marketing, first for PepsiCo, then for Perrier, he seemed to be savvy about operations. So Stevens was put in charge of operations and appointed president, for which he was paid additional fees.

But their problems continued to multiply, and—as December drew near—LaMotta and Metzger became increasingly nervous. It seemed to them that there were too many projects under way, too many *expensive* projects. Nevins, for example, had hired a major advertising agency to do the television commercials. "He spent about one hundred twenty-five thousand dollars just to produce it," says LaMotta. Then there was the plant in New Jersey, which LaMotta says was budgeted for around $600,000. "It came in at more than one million dollars."

By March 1982, LaMotta and Metzger concluded that they had made a big mistake. The supermarket program was up and running and generating sales, but expenses were rising even faster. Moreover, the marketing consultants seemed oblivious to the company's precarious financial situation. "We had one hundred to two hundred thousand dollars in the bank," says LaMotta, "and Nevins was talking about spending three million to build a brand, the way you'd do it at Perrier." They couldn't afford the television ads. They couldn't afford the cost overrun on the plant. Come to think of it, they couldn't afford the services of Nevins and Stevens. So they terminated the relationship.

It took Chipwich four years to dig itself out of its hole. LaMotta and Metzger raised some new money privately and almost did an initial public offering for $5 million to $7 million in January 1983. (The preliminary forms had been filed with the Securities and Exchange Commission, which challenged certain accounting details, and it was never sold.) By the middle of 1984, Chipwich had arranged to license the production and distribution of its product to four large companies. But that summer, Nevins' company joined with the ad agency in a petition to force Chipwich into Chapter 7. Twelve days later, the company itself filed for protection under Chapter 11. It finally emerged from reorganization last January with 40 percent of the stock owned by a Swedish company.

Some people might look back on such an experience as a cause for introspection, but—to hear Nevins tell the story—it was simply a case of getting mixed up with the wrong people. "These guys weren't businesspeople, they were *lawyers,*" he says. "You hope you have management in place that understands you and what you can do for them, and [that] can run a good part of the business. . . . But the expertise I thought was there wasn't. We find that people [often] begin to rely on you for everything, because you've done it before. They see very quickly that they have limitations, and you have talent." Instead of focusing on marketing, "my partner, Jim, [had to spend his time] running the company. . . . It was Murphy's Law—every problem imaginable." Once he and Stevens were fired, "nobody knew what the hell was going on. They were better off in bankruptcy."

As the Chipwich saga was unfolding, Nevins and Stevens had other irons in the fire—a fire that was being stoked with hickory. Nevins had a friend named Greg Cummings, who was selling hickory wood chips and cooking logs by mail order from his farm in upstate New York. Advertising in *The New Yorker* and other upscale publications, he was getting orders from all over the United States. In the spring of 1981, he began talking to Nevins about the prospects for selling his Hickory Cookin' Logs through stores.

Nevins soon warmed to the idea. Hickory had a nice flavor; it was cleaner than charcoal; and it didn't require the use of lighter fluid. All in all, the timing seemed right for a hickory rollout. Of course, the product category wasn't nearly as large as ice cream: The total market for charcoal, Nevins figured, was only around $150 million a year. But unlike Chipwich, the Hickory Cookin' Logs were ready to roll. "Cummings had done a lot of the up-front stuff himself," says Nevins, "and his packaging was great." Nevins saw the potential for $20 million of sales in five years.

So he and Stevens agreed to become Cummings' selling agent.

They would buy product from him and sell it to supermarkets in New York, New Jersey, and Washington, D.C. They also invested more than $100,000. To get the program under way, Nevins bought ads in grocery publications and *The New York Times Magazine.*

But a funny thing happened on the way to the first $1 million. The logs shrank. State officials, making routine checks of grocery products, discovered the problem at a supermarket in the New York area, less than six months after the logs first appeared in stores. According to the package, the weight was seven pounds; the actual weight, officials found, was often less. Apparently, some of the logs had been packaged before they had fully dried. As the moisture evaporated, the packages got lighter. As soon as the problem surfaced, supermarkets began yanking the product off the shelves, effectively killing the program.

Cummings would just as soon forget the whole experience. "It was a costly mistake," he says, and he places some of the blame on Nevins and Stevens for taking the product into the mass market prematurely. Nevins' forecasts were much too optimistic, he says. What sales they had were disappointing. "He had a real New York attitude," Cummings says, "and sometimes New York isn't the best barometer for the rest of the country." Then again, he also believes that Nevins and Stevens botched the rollout. "They should have been in the market by December, and they waited until April." Cummings is now successfully selling Natural Wood Smokin' Chips through mail order and in stores.

Nevins and Stevens see things a little differently, of course. Stevens says that Cummings "wasn't what I'd consider a strong business type. . . . He was naive about what it took to make the manufacturing side happen." Nevins, for his part, suggests possible sabotage. He thinks a large charcoal manufacturer may have played a not-so-passive role in getting the state regulators to examine the new product. "There was concern in the [charcoal] industry," he says—a concern that was heightened, he adds, "when they saw who was behind [the product]."

So another opportunity had bit the dust. It was, without doubt, a disappointment. Lesser men might have given up after two such ignominious failures, but Nevins and Stevens were not to be denied. While they continued to look for a big score, they did some consulting work for a variety of large companies and for a business acquaintance of Nevins who was developing a line of salt-free condiments. Then, in the fall of 1982, they were approached by an investor with an idea that had the glimmer of another Perrier.

The investor's name was Steve Adams, and he owned some property in California's Napa Valley. He was interested in bottling the spring water from beneath his land. Nevins and Stevens, whose noncompete clauses with Perrier had just run out, flew to Aspen, Colorado, in November 1982 to discuss the project with Adams and some other investors. They discouraged the investors from getting into the bottled-water market. Instead, they proposed that the group put its money in the next growth segment of the beverage business: soft drinks containing fruit juice. Such a product, they argued, would appeal to the same people who now drank Perrier but wanted more flavor.

The investors agreed to put a few million dollars into a start-up called Adams Natural Beverage Company. Nevins and Stevens, who committed more than $100,000 to the company, were hired to run the business for the first eighteen months or so. The plan was to launch the product on the West Coast, then roll it out nationally, and eventually sell the business or take it public.

To develop the product, Nevins and Stevens hired a well-known formulation consultant. They also arranged to have the beverage produced at a large bottling plant in Sacramento. Meanwhile, they had retained an advertising agency and were plotting their distribution strategy. After a year of careful planning, Napa Naturals was finally ready for its debut.

The rollout began in northern California in March 1984, and it was picture perfect. Customers were wild about the product, which came in four flavors, each containing 67 percent fruit juice and no preservatives. It was billed as the "world's first natural soft drink." That summer, Nevins told reporters that Napa was breaking Perrier's sales record for the first six months.

Then the cans began to explode.

Nevins remembers getting a call in September reporting that cans of Napa Natural were bulging ominously and, in some instances, blowing their lids off. What he heard next was "the sound of my jaw hitting the table." It turned out that the beverage was fermenting because of the high juice content. Nevins says that the trouble should have been discovered before the product was released. He blames the formulation company for not doing its job. "They said they did things they never did."

Be that as it may, Nevins and Stevens were forced to recall thousands of cases of Napa Natural and then did not ship any product for a period of two months, during which time the product was reformulated and the juice content reduced from 67 percent to 51 percent. When shipments finally resumed, some supermarket chains, including Safeway, refused to take the product back. In 1985, it was introduced in Oregon, Washington, and Arizona, and last January was reformulated yet again with 30 percent juice. The new formulation was launched with an advertising campaign featuring O. J. Simpson as the company spokesman.

Meanwhile, the market had grown more competitive. PepsiCo has come in with its own juice-based beverages called Slice, containing 10 percent fruit juice. As a result, Nevins has had to concentrate on differentiating Napa Natural and making sure the company is not constantly going head-to-head with PepsiCo. In some areas of the country, that has meant switching from warehouse distribution to store-door delivery, in order to get better coverage. In others, it has meant turning to beer distributors. "It's a matter of trial and error," says Nevins. "You look at your costs and you do what works."

To date, Napa Natural has cost plenty. Most of the original $8 million is gone, including about a quarter of a million dollars invested by Stevens and Nevins. The business is close to breaking even on sales of just over $5 million, says Nevins, but it hasn't been easy. Both he and his partner have had to stay in the business far longer than they had planned. Stevens, in fact, has been running it out of Sacramento on a full-time basis for about two years.

Nevins makes no bones about wanting to get out. Last September, he says, they were "ninety percent down the road" on a deal to sell the business to Schweppes, but the latter backed out at the last minute. "We'd like to go national as soon as possible," says Nevins, "but until we do another round of financing or find a partner or acquirer, we need to limit our spending to make sure we can continue." In the meantime, Nevins and Stevens are stuck with the company.

On a sunny day in July, Nevins sits by the pool outside his house in East Hampton. He is dressed nattily in white pants, a faded blue shirt, and Italian loafers without socks. Lunch is over, and he is reflecting now on his experiences since he left Perrier. Things clearly have not worked out as he planned. The money ran out; the supermarkets balked; the logs shrank; the cans exploded. Not that he blames himself. "You want to believe everything's in place," he says. And maybe in big companies, it is. Then again, big companies may simply have the resources to cover their mistakes. That is seldom the case in small companies, as Nevins' experience bears witness.

There is, no doubt, a lesson in all this. Many entrepreneurs have fantasies of bringing in a hot-shot consultant to work miracles and make dreams come true. But success rarely happens that way. The most brilliant marketing program in the world can't make a product any better than it is, or let a company go on spending more money than it has. In the end, all you have to fall back on is your own resourcefulness.

As for Bruce Nevins, he's had it with trying to find the next Perrier. He's sick of prodding distributors and retailers into pushing products. He's tired of worrying about the quality of the things he sells. So, after five years, he is winding down his marketing business and moving on to something he thinks will be more manageable. Car washes.

He's going to work for a company in Philadelphia that has already set up twenty-one streamlined facilities, called White Glove Car Washes. It was started by one of his classmates from West Point. Nevins will be an operating partner, helping to expand the business across the country. He's excited about the possibilities. The time is ripe, he says, for a more sophisticated approach to car washes, and White Glove has a well-developed system that will allow it to take advantage of marketing opportunities not available to mom-and-pop operations.

"The people who wore Levis in the sixties are into images," he says. "They want to look good. They're smart. They're willing to spend money to keep a car looking good so they can keep it longer. They think about the economics of their cars."

It is not just the market that appeals to him, however. "The beauty of a car wash," he says, thinking perhaps of his other recent ventures, "is you don't have to go through two or three levels of distribution. You can take your product directly to the customer. I like that. . . . If you blow it, it's just you that's blown it."

—BRUCE G. POSNER

THE GREAT TEXAS WATER WAR

In any other state, it might never have come to this sort of shoot-out between the two men. But this was Texas, after all. Texas has always bred its men stubborn.

They squared off in the supermarket aisles of the boom towns of the old Southwest. One was a city kid up from the streets, brash and feisty, a shameless self-promoter who in his ads had promised "to kick Perrier in the derrière" when he introduced Artesia Sparkling Mineral Water in 1980. His challenger was a soft-spoken country boy from the hills, a fourth-generation Texan who hoped to save the family ranch by selling the water he used to dip from his daddy's spring. As a pair of Texas archetypes, they might have stepped out of the pages of some potboiling saga of sweat and dust and family feuds.

Their disagreement was nothing much more than a public spitting contest, waged through the columns of the local press. But by the fall of 1985, it had escalated into a full-blown legal brawl. The charges included copyright infringement, unfair competition, fraudulent advertising, and violations of federal racketeering statutes. At issue, really, was nothing more than bragging rights: which man could claim that his was the more genuine of the homegrown Texas waters.

Even today, there are people in San Antonio who think Rick Scoville and Ron Bownds a bit squirrelly, who wonder if this water feud of theirs has gone too far. On the other hand, water has always been a precious commodity in these parts. In the past century, it was sustenance for thirsty cattle and hard-driving cattlemen who made the yearly trek north to Abilene. Today, it is a pricey designer drink. Water, in fact, is now big business in Texas and in every other state, the fastest-growing beverage on supermarket shelves. And with profit margins ranging to 25 percent, neither Scoville nor Bownds was eager to relinquish his claim.

San Antonio boasts that it's the most entrepreneurial of American cities, and the story of Rick Scoville and Artesia Waters would be instantly recognizable to any student of the entrepreneurial revival. Scoville had been transplanted at age five from West Hartford, Connecticut, to Kansas City, Missouri, and then San Antonio, where he grew up a scrappy, redheaded Anglo attending working-class Mexican-American schools. By the third grade, Scoville had a newspaper route and an egg route, and he had cornered the market on painting fluorescent house numbers on the curbs of his neighborhood's streets. An erratic student, Scoville flunked out of the University of Houston and served a tour of duty in Vietnam before returning to complete his degree. Launched into the corporate world at H. B. Fuller Company, a manufacturer of industrial adhesives, he rose quickly to become one of the company's top ten salesmen. And just as quickly, he found himself very bored.

Inspiration came in 1979, while Scoville was cooling his heels waiting to make yet another sales pitch. Picking up a magazine, he read about Perrier's dramatic rise in the mineral-water business in the United States. He didn't know much about water, really, except that the water in San Antonio, purified by its 176-mile journey over the limestone of the mineral-rich Edwards Aquifer, tasted pretty good to him. He had seen the health-conscious crowds at his exercise club. He had heard the refrains of club-soda-with-a-twist at his favorite bars. If Perrier could make money shipping bottled water all the way from France, Scoville figured he could make *beaucoup d'argent* right at home.

The initial tests bore out his hunch: The waters of the Edwards Aquifer were lower in sodium and higher in magnesium than Perrier's. With $25,000 borrowed from a Houston bank, he set up shop in an old Pic-A-Pop Bottling plant in San Antonio, just off the freeway. There, he dug a well and began pumping. Since Perrier then came in three different size bottles (6½-ounce, 11-ounce, and 23-ounce), Scoville put his in Texas-size containers (7-ounce, 23-ounce, and 32-ounce). More to the point, he set his prices strategically below the foreign import's. And in contrast to Perrier's understated green bottles, Scoville's new amber bottles featured a white and blue waterfall on the label, topped proudly with a Texas Lone Star. Say *au revoir,* Perrier; say howdy, Artesia.

At times, Scoville sounds nostalgic for the rough and tumble of those early days of 1980. Unable to find distributors, he sold his water himself from the back of his van, "a bit like an old-time medicine salesman." To convince bar owners to try his product, he would cart in samples of Perrier, Artesia, and plain club soda to run blind taste tests in such cities as Dallas and Houston. And in supermarkets, where grocery managers would line up ten rows (or "fronts," as they are called) of Perrier next to two of Artesia—in a very real sense dictating consumer preference—Scoville would quietly walk down the aisles and rearrange the lineup when the managers weren't looking.

That first year, Scoville lost money. With only $112,000 in sales, his volume was not enough to cover overhead and pay for a modest advertising campaign on billboards and radio. So he tried another marketing strategy. Rather than rearranging bottles on supermarket shelves, he began offering premiums to retailers who would give his product prominence: Build a large display and win a satin jacket; build a large display and win a pool umbrella. And instead of paid advertising, he began to test the potential of free advertising—public relations—by pitching himself to the Texas media as the patriotic underdog, the American David challenging the French Goliath. Why send dollars abroad, he would ask, when you can have "a star-spangled, sparkling mineral water from deep in the heart of the Texas hill country."

The media found him irresistible. And not just the local media, either. For remember, this was the era of Texas Chic, of John Travolta and Gilley's and all that. Furthermore, here was a family business worthy of the name: Scoville's sixty-four-year-old father, Bob, kept the production line clanking; his mother, Jeanne, also sixty-four, served as customer-service representative; and his sister-in-law Lenetta Scoville ran the office. *The Wall Street Journal, Texas Monthly, Beverage World,* and *Beverage Industry*—everybody wanted a piece of the story. And each time an article appeared, he'd make a copy and send it around to the next batch of potential interviewers.

By early 1985, Scoville had accumulated a media package as thick as the San Antonio white pages—and sales figures to match. Revenues were approaching $3 million and were expected to double the following year, with profits holding from 10 percent to 15 percent of sales. By now, his was the top-selling sparkling water in Texas, bigger even than Perrier, with distribution that spread to New Mexico, Florida, Oklahoma, Louisiana, and Georgia. *Inc.* listed Artesia as number 95 on its 1985 list of the 500 fastest-growing privately held companies in America.

To many in San Antonio, it now looked as if Rick Scoville had made it. There was a custom-modified Porsche, the gold gleaming from wrist and neck, the narrow pink tie set off against the pleated white shirt worn open over his chest. Unlike some entrepreneurs, Scoville never intended to grow old with his creation. His hope had always been to grow a company and sell out while he was still young enough to boogie through the night under Houston's bright lights. Now, as his fortieth birthday rolled around, the dream looked within his grasp.

But that was before Ron Bownds came along.

Rick Scoville admits he overreacted to the challenge—it's the redhead in him, he says. "I'm the James Dean of the bottled-water business. I live in the fast lane."

He was probably behind the wheel of his Porsche when he first heard the radio ads last summer for something called Utopia Sparkling Water, from "deep in the heart of the Texas hill country." And before long, billboards along the freeway were picturing the new product with a pretty blue waterfall right there on the label. The advertising appealed to Texas pride, and stressed purity and health: Tests showed that Utopia Sparkling Water had less sodium and more magnesium than any of its competitors.

To Rick Scoville, it was pretty clear that somebody was trying to do to him what he had spent six years doing to Perrier. It was a "me-too" copy, as far as he was concerned, and he was riled. But up in the tiny town of Utopia, population 350, Ron Bownds, the creator of Utopia Sparkling Water, was telling reporters that Scoville had it all wrong. "I didn't start the company with any kind of marketing strategy. I just thought people would enjoy a water from Utopia."

If Ron Bownds had not started out with a marketing strategy, he discovered one quickly enough. And his well-orchestrated campaign to out-Texas the original Texas water company became something of a press agent's dream. Bownds was a natural for the role, what with his muddy cowboy boots, silver belt buckle, and a wad of smokeless tobacco always wedged in his cheek. People in San Antonio would see him driving through town behind the wheel of a four-wheel-drive wagon, with a blue plastic spittoon mounted on the dash. A public relations agency was hired to stir up some attention, and journalists interested in the story would be invited to Utopia to eat chicken-fried steak in the local café. They'd hear Bownds recount the tales of his great-grandfather's covered-wagon trek to the Sabinal Canyon River Valley, or his own stint as deputy sheriff in nearby Bandera, the "cowboy capital of the world." On the way to see the spring, Bownds might point out a deer grazing in the oat fields. Then he'd show the reporters his source, bubbling up cool and clear, a constant sixty-eight degrees, spilling over into a perch-filled pool—"the old fishin' hole."

Bottling water from the family spring had not always been Bownds' ambition. At an early age he realized the family's 600 acres could no longer support a working ranch. And so, like countless Texans before him, he set out in search of oil—in his case, as the senior Gulf Coast petroleum geologist for a private independent driller. Then, in 1983, the company wanted to transfer Bownds from San Antonio back to Houston. Bownds had always hated Houston for lots of reasons, including the drinking water. And he was loathe to give up the family ranch. Backed by $150,000 in savings, Bownds decided to "switch natural resources" and went into water, bottling noncarbonated spring water from the family spread for homes and offices in San Antonio.

It was every bit as humble a beginning as Rick Scoville's: Bownds and two employees worked from a makeshift plant behind his mother's house. "God-made water" he called it, but even with the Deity behind his company, Hill Country Spring Water of Texas Inc., profits were limited by low margins and relatively high shipping costs. He needed something more lucrative. And, down in San Antonio, Rick Scoville was pointing the way.

Utopia Sparkling Water began appearing in the middle of the hot San Antonio summer of 1985, along with a strong advertising campaign. It wasn't long before the challenge to Scoville's Artesia spilled over into the columns of Texas newspapers. "Our water is from a place called Utopia. It's spring water. That has some mystique," Bownds boasted to *Austin American-Statesman,* in an article headlined "Water War Heats Up." Then, referring to the competition, Bownds said, "His water is well water. There's only so much you can say about a well. . . . I'm not knocking it, but it's not much different than San Antonio drinking water."

"Utopia is just a very weak copy of Artesia," Scoville snapped. "Our product has a real clean, crisp taste. I find that Utopia has a bitter aftertaste. Maybe that's because he hauls his water to a bottling place where they bottle all kinds of soft drinks."

The next day, Scoville had his lawyer send a letter to Utopia, accusing it of infringement of Artesia's copyright, and threatening legal action. It was a sound strategy, and one that, in hindsight, Scoville should have stuck with. But that was hardly his style. He had a few letters to write of his own. He wrote to people like Lenwood L. Scholtz, of the Texas Department of Health, and Jim Mattox, the state's attorney general, charging that Utopia had lied when it claimed to be "natural and pure sparkling"; as with every other sparkling water, carbon dioxide was added during bottling. To the largest nightclub owner in Texas Scoville wrote, "Mr. Bownds has misrepresented his product. . . . I feel your customers should not be duped, nor should you!" To restaurateurs and merchants he insisted that Utopia was worse than a copycat: It was a hazard to the consumer because of the possible pollutants on the surface of the spring. KTFM, a local radio station, and Rollins Outdoor Advertising Inc., the company responsible for Utopia's billboards, received letters putting them on notice that Scoville planned to seek "legal remedies" against Utopia; he demanded that they kill the spots and tear down the signs. "Please keep me posted," he wrote the state's food brokers, "so we can *bury* this product!" To many, Scoville seemed like a man possessed.

Utopia's sales had started strong: In the first week, H. E. B. Food Stores, a large food chain in Texas, sold ten times more than they had projected. But by the end of the month, Bownds was finding that he was not expanding as fast as he had planned. There was nothing he could put his finger on. It was just that food brokers now seemed hesitant to return his telephone calls; and restaurants that had initially agreed to carry his water suddenly backed out.

He discovered the problem soon enough, when the general manager called from KTFM. The radio station had just received the letter from Scoville. "I had expected competition," Bownds remembers. "I had expected the big boys to outspend me two hundred to one. But those letters were beyond what I expected.

"I just wanted to be left alone. But the best way to rile me up is to attack my livelihood. It's in my blood to be feisty. It's a Texas tradition."

His lawsuit was filed late in August in Texas District Court. In a sixteen-page complaint, Bownds outlined Scoville's activities, including the letters and comments to the press. Bownds charged that Scoville's comments "were false, were known . . . to be false, and were made with the malicious intent of destroying goodwill in [Utopia's] products, slandering [Utopia], and unfairly compromising [Utopia's] position in the marketplace." The letters, he said, were "a systematic program of interfering with the existing and prospective contractual or business relationships." Furthermore, by using the mails to interfere with interstate commerce, Bownds asserted, Scoville was violating the Racketeer Influenced and Corrupt Organizations Act. Bownds asked the court to enjoin Scoville from continuing with his campaign, and to assess actual and punitive damages.

Scoville met the challenge with bluster, telling the local papers he had his own plans for a countersuit. And yet, despite the failure of Utopia to gain more than a foothold in the local market, the situation seemed to be slipping from Scoville's control. His letters had left bad feelings within the business community. "I just hate to see that kind of conflict," complained George Farias, the bottled-water buyer for San Antonio's Sun Harvest Farms supermarket chain. "We're disgusted," was how J. R. McIntyre, the general manager of Rollins Outdoor Advertising, summed up the reaction. From Utopia, Bownds continued to charm the local press, which took a keen interest in the story, while Scoville stayed hunkered in his bunker. In conversations with several local reporters, Scoville seemed increasingly hostile and strident. "I was used to being the underdog," he explained. "We had played on the theme of the underdog versus number one heavily. Now we were number one ourselves." Being the overdog required a different strategy. And Scoville never discovered one.

Up in Greenwich, Connecticut, Ron Davis might have been excused if he'd allowed himself to gloat. For years, Rick Scoville had been taking potshots at Perrier. Now Artesia's water wizard was getting a taste of his own medicine. Scoville had written Davis, as president of the Perrier Group of America, looking for an ally in his latest crusade against Utopia. But as president of the International Bottled Water Association, the Perrier executive found it more diplomatic to take the high ground.

"It's ironic that two Texas people compete," he mused. "It's foolish. I think they would be a lot bigger a lot faster if they had a focus that was bigger."

To Davis, that bigger focus means such soft-drink giants as The Coca-Cola Company and PepsiCo, at whose expense he expects the bottled-water market to grow to a $4-billion-a-year industry by the year 2000. And to meet the challenge, Davis has increased Perrier's already sizable budget for promotion and advertising, and introduced three new flavors (orange, lemon, and lime). Perrier has also become a regional bottler in its own right, buying up such local brands as Poland Springs, in New England; Calistoga Mineral Water, in California; and Oasis Bottled Water, in Texas. The regionals would allow Perrier to expand its share of the water market by recapturing consumers who preferred to buy American. It would also allow the company to control an increasing number of the "fronts" on the all-important supermarket shelves.

It was just such pressure from Perrier, in fact, that finally forced

Rick Scoville and Ron Bownds to call a halt to their feud. The terms of the agreement, reached last November, are confidential, and both parties are pledged not to talk about each other or their dispute.

In a sense, they had no choice. By most estimates, the next two to five years will see a major consolidation in the water business, from which only a handful of players will survive. After that, according to Hank Forrest, director of sales and marketing for Utopia, the industry will be left to national companies with enough money to support national television advertising. Perrier will be one, of course. Anheuser-Busch Beverage Group Inc., which just bought New York–based Saratoga Springs Company's Sparkling Mineral Waters, may well be another. And the soft-drink companies might jump in, too—certainly it would be less risky than switching formulas for a sliver of the cutthroat cola market.

Ron Bownds hopes Utopia will be among the national brands that survive. Since he filed his suit last summer, sales have been growing by a third or more each month, and distribution has already spread to Arkansas, Oklahoma, Louisiana, and California. Within a few months, Utopia will introduce orange, lemon, lime, and cherry flavors and offer plastic containers for vending machines and airlines. A new half-million-dollar plant is under construction to bottle the expanded line. And to distribute it, Bownds looks to shift from food brokers, who bring everything from soup to nuts to stores once a week, to beer distributors, who make more frequent deliveries and specialize only in beverages. The Anheuser-Busch distributor in Yonkers, New York, has already taken on the Utopia line.

In fact, if things go according to plan, Ron Bownds expects to be shipping Utopia overseas before too long, perhaps starting with Perrier's home turf in France. "Wouldn't that be something," he marvels in his affecting Texas drawl, "to find Utopia on the Champs Elysées." You can tell this man is on a roll. Hardly a day goes by that Bownds doesn't get an offer to sell the company, or a few feelers or inquiries from investors. One promoter has even proposed turning Utopia into an upscale health spa.

Bownds says he doesn't worry much about Scoville anymore, although Utopia is still only about one-third the size of Artesia. He says he never wanted a feud in the first place, but once it started, he figured there was no way he could lose. Scoville had a good story to tell with his Artesia versus Perrier, but Bownds had a more powerful myth working in his favor. In Texas, there could be nothing so appealing as a country boy fighting to keep the family spread.

Down in San Antonio, Rick Scoville now understands the logic of all that. He sees more clearly his mistakes. It was bad enough that he had his white hat knocked off in public, that he allowed himself to get kicked around in the press. But he also knows that it could have been worse—much worse—if Bownds' suit had ever gone to trial.

Not that Scoville has any intention of letting Utopia walk away with the Texas water business. Like his competitor, he is charting a new course. After Bownds began new plant construction in Utopia, Scoville announced that he, too, would be building a new plant and introducing new flavors. And a new advertising campaign is in the works—something along the lines of "All waters are not created equal." The way Scoville figures it, his Artesia was the first local water, and that should count for something. And he's still the biggest, at least in Texas.

There is the impression, however, that Rick Scoville no longer has much zest for the battle. "It's getting to be a very dirty business, the water business," he complains. Scoville talks wistfully of selling out, as he had always planned. He's written to both Philip Morris Inc. and General Foods Corporation, but so far there has been no interest.

For now, the streets of San Antonio are calm. But it would not take much to rekindle the feud between Rick Scoville and Ron Bownds. "If the agreement is broken, we'll go back to open warfare," promises Scoville, somewhat ominously. Bownds' reaction is customarily sly. "What else can you expect from someone from Connecticut?" he asks, smiling. In Texas, that's a question that demands a response.

—CURTIS HARTMAN

CAT FIGHT

They gathered in the conference room, expecting an important meeting. After all, it wasn't often that Ed Lowe called together the seven family members who had much of the responsibility for running his company on a daily basis. He began talking, recalling how he had brought them into the company and had even given them shares. Those had been good years for Edward Lowe Industries Inc., which makes litter-box filler for cats. Now, however, in 1984, its position was under attack from Clorox Company, a *Fortune* 500 company. The family members might have been expecting Lowe to unveil a strategy they could follow in the future. That's exactly what he did, pointing to the folders on the table before each of them. "Inside each folder," Lowe said, "is your retirement package."

Ed Lowe was back.

And so was Clorox. Lowe could be excused for feeling a sense of déjà vu. Clorox, the consumer-products giant, had fought to take away Lowe's market a decade before. He was lucky he didn't lose the company then.

It was ironic that Lowe's Inc., as it was originally called, was most vulnerable on marketing. Here was the man who, in 1947, stuffed clay granules into bags and convinced millions of people that Kitty Litter Brand was the only civilized way to care for their cats. But he never took his litter much further than a dominant regional product. When Clorox first attacked in the early 1970s, it rolled out a *national* product priced about 250 percent higher than Lowe's. Much to his surprise, it practically displaced him as the leading seller of litter. Lesson: Add a few bells and whistles to a product, and people just might shell out more money for it.

Clorox had stumbled, however, and Lowe managed to recapture his dominant position. Now the $1-billion company was back for a second try at conquering the litter market. Lowe knew he was in for another marketing battle.

Markets divided among regional brands are often very inviting to such companies as Clorox, which can muscle their way to the top by taking advantage of their national distribution systems. And Clorox needed a boost. In 1979, profits had fallen for only the second time in the company's sixty-six-year history. Sales of bleach, its major product, were growing at under 2 percent a year, and efforts to diversify into faster-growing fields had foundered. There were also rumblings that Procter & Gamble Company would enter the bleach market. "Clorox was a company with a sword hanging over its head," says Edward Froelich, a securities analyst at Pershing, a division of Donaldson, Lufkin, & Jenrette.

Clorox looked enviously at the cat-litter business, a $200-million market that was growing at about 15 percent a year. It seemed like a perfect fit. The company could use its clout with food brokers and supermarket buyers to get shelf space nationwide. And it could take advantage of a strong national sales and distribution network already in place. Certainly Lowe was vulnerable on marketing, talking as he did about building sales by making cats more popular. After all, Lowe liked to say, "You can't make a cat take a crap more often to satisfy your sales volume."

Lowe had prospered over the years by doing things his own idiosyncratic way. In 1947, he launched the industry by scrawling the words *Kitty Litter* in grease pencil on a brown paper bag and making the rounds of pet stores and wholesalers. Lowe and his company initially met hostility in the supermarket aisles. One A&P buyer snubbed him by saying, "We'll never sell stuff for cats to shit in in *my* store."

When the supermarkets did start selling cat litter in the early 1960s, the only competitors were small regional companies. All of them treated cat litter as a commodity business of undifferentiated products—ten-pound bags of dirt selling for less than a buck. Lowe's was no different, selling its Kitty Litter Brand in pet stores and the cheaper Tidy Cat in supermarkets.

The company had a commanding 19 percent of the market by 1970 with its two products. But that only masked Lowe's deteriorating condition; increasing competition was cutting his usual 60 percent profit margins in half. "There was no real understanding of marketing," says a former employee. "There was nobody scratching the surface and looking at the what ifs." Adds Joe Miller, a son-in-law who served as chief operating officer, "Ed never realized the real potential of his business."

Sadly for Lowe, another company did. In 1971, Clorox plunged into the market with a brand called Litter Green and spent more than $2 million rolling it out nationally. Unlike most litters, it had a distinctive selling point that Clorox seized from market research: Litter Green, made of alfalfa instead of clay, promised to control odors. Consumers didn't seem to mind spending 250 percent more for an improvement they considered important. Clorox stole away about 20 percent of the market within a couple of years.

Lowe could easily have been crushed, but Clorox made one fatal mistake. It overlooked the fact that the ultimate consumers of cat litter are—of course—cats. And cats didn't like Litter Green. The bleach maker's litter business faded, but its influence was indelible. "What Clorox did taught a lesson to the people in this business," says Paul Bowles, president of Edward Lowe Industries.

The threat from Clorox forced Lowe to think about his company in a different way. "If we didn't do something to establish ourselves in the marketplace, somebody else could jump in there and do that," he says. He now had two major goals: hire experienced managers and roll out a national product with distinctive selling points. Lowe brought on son-in-law Miller, who had been a sales manager at Republic Steel Corporation, to build a management team that could create and market the product that Litter Green should have been.

Miller worked fast. He was able to get exclusive use for an odor-fighting chemical from Monsanto Corporation and added it to the higher-end Kitty Litter Brand. He also pushed the product out of pet stores, where sales were languishing, and into supermarkets. Then the company bought a small factory in California and began distributing Kitty Litter Brand all over the country.

To promote Tidy Cat, which was taking a licking from generics and private-label brands, Lowe's added a masking fragrance, blue flecks, and about 30¢ to the price tag. In 1981, Tidy Cat 3 was rolled out nationally, with ads featuring cats dancing to a snappy jingle.

They weren't dancing for long, though. Figuring there was more than one way to skin a cat owner, Clorox made its second move into the market. It began testing a new cat litter called Fresh Step. This time it came up with an ingenious gimmick to draw attention to its fragrance chips. Clorox's promotions promised that every time a cat pawed the special chips, a mint herbal fragrance would be released. Never had cat urine smelled so good. "It was good market positioning," says Thomas Kuczmarski, a Chicago consultant who works with Lowe. "None of the competing brands had that kind of theme."

As Clorox moved into test markets, Lowe's responded by flooding them with such promotions as consumer coupons and retailer discounts. "We tried to dissuade them from coming out of test market," says Thomas Ramey, who was director of marketing. Lowe's tried different combinations. In St. Louis, for example, a two-for-the-price-of-one coupon was supposed to take consumers out of the purchasing cycle. But litter buyers are fickle, and very willing to try a new brand. "We learned that there was no real way to stop the product trial," says David Tooker, who was senior vice-president of marketing and sales. "So we didn't panic during the trial phase."

Clorox wasn't rushing into anything, either. The company tinkered with different prices and sizes and added more test markets in 1982. The members of Lowe's team carefully monitored Clorox's actions, but they were confused about the company's intentions. Would Clorox actually roll out the new product? At what price? Or might it surprise them by competing with a different product, like a revamped Litter Green? "It wasn't a matter of us sitting and waiting until they rolled out," says Kuczmarski. "But you aren't going to spend millions of dollars to compete against a product that's not out there yet."

In April 1984, Clorox finally launched Fresh Step nationwide, boasting to the trade that it was going to spend $12 million to promote it. Some retailers received 20 percent discounts, plus catchy promotions, and more coupons than the industry had ever seen. Consumers were tuning in to a television campaign of unprecedented scope. This was the second major challenge to Lowe, and it boosted the price tag for defending his market. "Any money I spend comes out of my pocket; it doesn't come out of the shareholders," complained Lowe. "[Clorox] had this slush fund of twelve million dollars or so that they could pump into this with no loss to themselves, really. They weren't taking it out of the family jewel box." *His* jewel box, to be precise. Lowe had just kicked his seven family managers out of the company so he could resume managing it himself.

Lowe restructured management, this time with himself in the catbird seat. His plan called for each division to set up a committee to do long-term planning. Each group included outsiders. The Marketing Strategic Action Committee, comprised of two marketing consultants and six Lowe's managers, spent a day every month looking at how the company should defend itself.

Their first concern was that retailers, dazzled by Clorox's marketing campaign, would give it some of Lowe's precious shelf space. So Lowe's executives crisscrossed the country, demonstrating to food brokers how Lowe's intended to fight back. "We communicated very frankly and seriously to the brokers what the situation was," says Russell Fox, a retired Kellogg Company marketer who is on the committee. "If we lose our distribution, we've got one hell of a problem." The Lowe's team handed out NFL-style whistles to its sixty-five brokers, with tags that said, "Where's the 3 pounds?"—a reminder to them of the difference between a standard ten-pound bag of Kitty Litter Brand and a seven-pound bag of Fresh Step.

Lowe's wanted to find out as much as it could about the enemy's plans. Led by Tooker, the marketing department set up an "aggressive intelligence network" using suppliers, customers, and information about other product rollouts. It studied Clorox's costs, expenses, and promotions. "We developed a real war-room philosophy," says Tooker, who began calling Clorox "those Communists from Oakland."

Tooker started a role-playing game, too. One person would take the part of the Fresh Step brand manager; the others would pretend to be Clorox board members. They grilled the manager. How did she explain the weak test-market results when the product was eight pounds? Why, after only ninety days, did she decide that the seven-pound product was the right one? "It gave us a lot of what ifs and yeah, buts," says Tooker. "It enabled us to look at what we thought they were looking at in Oakland." Clorox's internal employee newsletter, picked up in the lobby of a mutual customer, became required reading. One issue, for instance, gave kudos to the research-and-development department for solving a production problem with Fresh Step. The special odor-fighter, which was supposed to be triggered by the cat, was instead firing off during shipping.

Once corrected, that problem didn't stop Clorox from stealing Lowe's share of branded products in the market, which was sliding from its high of 33 percent. The marketing committee strongly urged Lowe to acquire a few regional companies. It would make the company stronger, they argued, by giving Lowe's more shelf space and production capacity. But Lowe wouldn't hear of it; he didn't want to buy what he felt were inferior products that were probably losing market share faster than his own.

Lowe also refused to cut prices or to match Clorox's steep discounts to dealers. "You could say, 'Let's cut the price. Let's go right on down to the bare bottom,'" he says. But if the battle were defined by price cutting, Lowe felt there was no way he could win; Clorox certainly had the resources to outlast him. Fresh Step was priced at $1.99, 20¢ cheaper than Kitty Litter Brand and 30¢ more than Tidy Cat 3. He considered spending $5 million on consumer coupons but wasn't convinced that would lead anywhere in the long run, either. "You can hurt your competition," says Kuczmarski. "But after it's over, what long-term impetus is there for the consumer to buy?"

The only lasting consumer lure, as any good marketer knows, is a product that performs. And like Litter Green before it, Fresh Step's success highlighted the weaknesses of Lowe's products. But several committee members, especially Kuczmarski, felt strongly that Lowe's ought to move slowly on making improvements. The major risk, Kuczmarski argued, was that after making product changes, consumers would perceive the product as unchanged—or even worse. Lowe's couldn't afford to rush; it had to find out exactly what consumers wanted by doing an in-depth survey.

When Lowe heard about the survey idea, though, he "bit our heads off," says an ex-employee. He pointed out that he had been to more cat shows than anyone in the room. He was a specialist. He had lived with cat litter for nearly forty years. And now he was going to let some market researcher tell him how to make his product? "This'll cost me fifty thousand dollars, and what is it going to give us?" Lowe wanted to know. But after he had assuaged his pride, he was willing to negotiate. After all, Clorox was on to something better. "I know when something is good and when something is bad, and I knew that our product needed improvement," he admits.

Committee members argued that Lowe had to think even beyond the current Clorox threat. Ten percent annual growth in the litter market was sure to lure more big companies like a tabby to catnip. And the entry fee wouldn't strain the resources of a Quaker Oats Company or a Procter & Gamble. Now was the time to spend the money and raise the ante for potential competitors. The committee even dragged in the head of a local market-research firm to explain what the study could achieve. "He was not opposed to spending money, but it was a very painful exercise to convince him," says a former employee.

Lowe agreed to the strategy, which came to be called "the one-two punch." Ramey, a student of marketing warfare, was the lord of the ring. He reasoned that Tidy Cat 3 was most immediately threatened. It had the most shelf space to lose. Lowe agreed to dip into his "war chest" and match Clorox by spending $8 million promoting both brands. The strategy: As Clorox approached the end of its promotion budget, Lowe's would unveil an improved Kitty Litter Brand, reformulated based on results of the consumer survey.

It was no surprise when the survey showed that consumers wanted odor control. Lowe knew he could create a better odor-control additive that would match Clorox's Fresh Step; he even found a way to make it visual by adding green and blue flecks. But the survey also found a strong sentiment in favor of a product with far less dust than existing litters. Lowe mulled it over: Was this the value-added advantage that would catapult him past Clorox?

But dust control was difficult. And expensive. Lowe didn't want to make a costly product change if he could help it. So he built a contraption that utilized vacuum vents to shake the dust out of the litter before packaging. It didn't work; more dust was generated during shipping. Finally, Lowe made a commitment. He raised his R&D spending from $1 million to $4 million, putting the heat on employees at his "Cat Care Center," where cats answer nature's call in the name of commerce.

Lowe grew impatient as the months passed. The committee kept trying dust-free products and sending them back. Meanwhile, Clorox was gaining. Lowe had hoped to hold Clorox to a 14 percent dollar share of the market. If it was much more successful, it might spend another $8 million pouring concrete for a plant. And then the trouble would *really* begin. "Once you have the assets invested, you'll fight even harder," Tooker says.

By spring 1985, Clorox had captured 14 percent of the market. Lowe decided he couldn't wait any longer. With the dust-control additive still in development, the company introduced an improved, redesigned Kitty Litter Brand with "dual-odor control." Aah, but how to demonstrate the unique wonders of this new product? Lowe supplied his brokers with litter boxes and a vial of—you guessed it—cat urine. Never mind that it was an imitation; it smelled just as pungent. The brokers emptied the vial into the litter and invited retailers—who at the moment must have been questioning the price of success—to sniff it.

In January 1986, Lowe's threw its second punch: 99 percent dust-free versions of both Kitty Litter Brand and Tidy Cat 3. The two reformulated products seemed to hold Clorox at bay—its market share hasn't strayed in over a year. And Lowe's has shipped 22 percent more units of Kitty Litter Brand over last year, mostly at the expense of the regional brands. It has raised its total market share, including private labels, back to about 40 percent, just where it was when Clorox let the cat litter out of the bag.

To launch his dust-free products, Lowe made his debut in his company's ads last June, pouring out his litter alongside Fresh Step. Clorox filed a complaint, and Lowe sent Stanley Beals, vice-president of advertising, along with an attorney, to demonstrate that the product claims were true.

At one television network last July, Beals dumped a ten-pound bag of Kitty Litter Brand and a seven-pound sack of Fresh Step into the interoffice memo trays to demonstrate Lowe's claim. "The big guys come in here and they try to get us off the air by using the clout they have with all the advertising they do," says Lowe. "We had to run into New York and spend a lot of money to prove to the media that the complaint wasn't true. We have to defend ourselves."

That may be harder in coming years. Several of Lowe's key managers left last year, including Ramey and Tooker. Meanwhile, Clorox is showing persistence beyond its limited success: It has test-marketed another product, Litter Green 2, for yet a third assault on Lowe. "Ed has the myth that he is divine," says a longtime associate. Divine or not, he may need, like his favorite pets, nine lives to survive in the business.

—JOSHUA HYATT

KNOCK-OFF PUNCH

Noel and Adele Zeller were running their company, Zelco Industries Inc., pretty much as planned. They started out in 1976 with a foot-in-the-door strategy of importing cheap flashlights, figuring to plow the profits back into high-quality products that Noel designed. Revenues were increasing yearly and had reached a comfortable $2.5 million by 1981.

Then, in the fall of 1982, Zelco's "itty bitty book light" hit the stores. It was an instant success, the kind of breakthrough item every young company dreams about. It was so successful that the Zellers had to find money wherever they could to underwrite the costs of manufacturing—including a last resort loan from the kind of people who demand interest of 24 percent a month, people prepared to dispatch a doorway-filling collection agent whom a Zelco employee dubbed Bigfoot. By the end of the year, Zelco had sold 200,000 of the sleek, clip-on lights. In 1983, with an advertising campaign coaxing "take me to bed," the company shipped a million of the lights from its headquarters and warehouse in Mt. Vernon, New York. In 1984, another million. Revenues hit the $15-million mark.

Had the Zellers stopped to bask in their sudden good fortune, they might have been forgiven—but they might also have lost their company. You could say that the "itty bitty book light" was too successful. Unexpectedly, it had zoomed to 80 percent of Zelco's total sales in 1984, its peak year. The company had become, essentially, the book light. Though the light was patented, a hit-and-run horde of "me-too" pirates were ripping it off, selling their cheap imitations wherever they could. In 1985, with sales down, company revenues dropped by a third, to $10 million.

Still, the Zellers are far from discouraged. Sales may have dropped, but $10 million certainly beats the pre-book-light revenues of $2.5 million they were seeing in 1981. And they've learned a few things along the way. They'll tell you that they have, in fact, strengthened their company. How? With a strong defense and a strong offense: with lawyers, a Chinese detective agency, continuous new product development, even a technique borrowed from Noel's brief stint as a stock-car driver.

Noel, forty-nine, is president of Zelco; Adele, vice-president. Their duties overlap considerably, but he reigns in product development, she in sales and marketing. They've been married twenty-five years, have two teenage daughters, and are described as "nice people" by virtually everyone who knows them. One of the reasons they left comfortable corporate careers to start their own company was that they wanted to spend more time together. Both of them have an eye for modern art. Their three company cars are Mercedes-Benzes. They know and appreciate fine design.

Even before "European design" became widely fashionable in American housewares, the Zellers were attracting notice for the sleekly modern look of their products. Zelco's rechargeable fluorescent lantern, for example, is in the permanent design collection of New York City's Museum of Modern Art. That's the kind of standard the Zellers consider when introducing a new product, and it's one of the reasons they've been so aggressive in defending their patents on the "itty bitty book light." They are proud of the product that has taken them into millions of American bedrooms. Before that, the only choice people had were crazy, unwieldy contraptions with bulky, shadow-casting shades—none offered much of an improvement on the old flashlight-under-the-covers method of reading in bed. Zelco's tiny bulb is specially designed to burn cool and not cast eye-straining shadows. "In that tiny lamp there are three kinds of plastic," says Noel, who obviously gets his kicks from perfecting Zelco's products. "We practically invented a new switching system. It's a quality job all the way through."

What really gets Noel's dander up are the knock-offs. First of all, it riles him that somebody is getting away with stealing his patented idea. But, craftsman that he is, he just can't understand why anybody would *want* to manufacture junk or me-too products. He reacts with righteous indignation to the inferior imitations that cheat consumers with lousy bulbs, cumbersome design, and such foolish accessories as built-in radios. Mostly, he feels violated, creatively and financially. "A lot of people thought they could walk all over us. They get a Dun and Bradstreet on you, see you're a small company, and figure you're not going to bother suing them."

In the case of Zelco, a lot of people figured wrong. In the past two years, the Zellers have spent half a million dollars in legal defense of the "itty bitty book light." "Yes, they are probably more aggressive than the typical business their size," says Donald S. Dowden, Zelco's New York City lawyer, who agrees with the Zellers that it is possible to establish a litigious reputation and scare off some potential rip-offs.

Often, though, the trick is learning whom to sue, which is why the Zellers employ a Chinese detective agency. Most Zelco products are manufactured in Hong Kong. So are many of the me-too book lights and fluorescent lanterns that steal precious market shares. Both Noel and Adele and their Hong Kong staff of twelve are too well known locally to venture into rival manufacturing plants snooping for knock-offs. "They would never let us or our buyers in their doors," says Adele, explaining how they count on private investigators, posing as customers, truck drivers, or stevedores, to locate the knock-off shops and their customers. Even then, fighting back can be filled with complications. "Taiwan doesn't recognize international patents," Noel emphasizes. "Say a company there knocks off your item. It may be shipping to twenty or thirty importers in the United States. You've got to sue each importer. They're like cockroaches. You step on one of them, another one jumps up."

Patents. Pride. Detectives. Lawyers. All are helpful, but to stay ahead of the competition, Zelco relies much more heavily on its offense, devoting upward of 12 percent of revenues to advertising and as much as 5 percent to 8 percent to research and development. "Our best defense is being aggressive in the marketplace and coming up with new products," says Noel. As tempting as it is to look for another big kill, the Zellers say, "you can't hit a home run every time up." So they've decided to wing for singles—let the extra base hits come as they may—and run up the score slowly but steadily. Says Noel, "Eventually your line is big enough that people say, 'Give me six of this, and twelve of that.' And you end up with lots of four-hundred- to six-hundred-dollar orders." Already the Zelco line runs to abut two dozen products, and at any given moment there are probably five in some stage of development. Although there are thirty U.S.-based employees, Noel alone is the research-and-development department.

On the wall to the right of his desk are drawings of a likely new product, a specialty light, this time for picture frames. The drawings have been professionally rendered—as Adele will tell you, Noel can't draw a straight line. Maybe so, but he surely has a keen eye for opportunity—and for brainstorming a design to the brink of perfection.

Seeking proper illumination for his framed pipe collection, Noel saw at once the many shortcomings of the incandescent picture-frame lights currently available. Nobody had to tell him to start tinkering. The light he's developed will be fluorescent. Its bulb will be energy-efficient and will last up to ten times as long as incandescent versions. Moreover, his light will burn cool. There'll be none of the danger of an incandescent bulb's heat discoloring an important canvas. A special screen inside his fluorescent tube will make the lamp "color corrected," so pictures will appear more vivid. Noel even addressed the matter of attaching the light to the picture frame—by cleverly sidestepping it. "Anytime you put a screwdriver in a consumer's hand you've got a lot of problems," he says. Instead of screwing to the picture frame, his light will simply rest upon it. "If you can hang a picture, you can buy our light," he says, explaining that a telescoping rod carrying the light cord will be held to the wall with the same hook that supports the picture. Ah, but what about the bottom half of the cord dangling down the wall to the socket? For one thing, it's been made thinner. For another, the light will probably be packaged with a narrow length of plastic extrusion that can be painted the same color as the wall. When

Noel Zeller tries out a possible advertising slogan—"Zelco reinvents the picture frame light"—he isn't just blowing smoke.

"Noel is constantly talking about new ideas," says Donald Duke, a Canadian importer of the entire Zelco product line. "But he doesn't just talk. He'll take an idea and work on it and work on it." With the help of a freelance product designer and a mechanical engineer, Noel tries to leave no function unconsidered, no detail untended. He wants nothing less than an industry standard, a bulletproof product immune to legitimate competition.

Not all, of course, have worked out. An ill-conceived early effort, a window-washing gadget with telescoping handle, flopped miserably. More recently, Zelco shot through $100,000 and got as far as a working prototype of a high-tech "salt detective," a pocket-size probe for measuring sodium levels in food. A retail price tag of $80 to $100 pulled the plug on that one. The Zellers didn't think it could bring in the $1 million in annual sales they now expect of new products.

For the most part, though, the hits have kept coming. The "itty bitty" GroLite for houseplants, introduced last fall, sold well enough to account for 11 percent of 1985 sales. Another design marvel, Zelco's $60 Magnificent Magnifying Mirror (it lights, magnifies, mounts on the wall, can be hand-held or handle-turned to be self-supporting, plugs in or operates on batteries, folds for traveling, does everything but brush on shaving cream) chalked up 9 percent of total sales. With various flashlights accounting for 15 percent of revenues, and butane fire starters another 14 percent, the company is achieving its goal of putting more eggs in a larger basket. Last year, the book light tallied 42 percent of business, with revenues from other products totaling $5.8 million. Though the Zellers are considering a foray into the kitchen, with an as yet undisclosed twist on cookware, they try not to stray too far from their successes. At a recent trade show, this strategy was, in effect, on display in their booth. On a desk where orders were being taken stood what Noel now refers to as "our reading group." In their distinctive, booklike packages, neatly arranged between bookends, were grouped Zelco's four versions of the "itty bitty book light": the original $30 light with battery pack, AC adapter, and extra bulb; an abridged version, at $20, with no battery pack or extra bulb; a $40 international edition for travelers that converts to European voltage; and a $60 "Golden" with added features, including a telescopic arm adjustable to page size.

Continual innovation, yes, but also calculated. In stock-car racing, which Noel experienced firsthand as a teenager in Florida from inside a 1940 Ford, there is a technique known as "drafting." Close behind a speeding car lies a pull of wind, a partial free ride, that smart drivers take advantage of. In like manner, Zelco's latest editions of the book light are all drafting on the success of the original, riding on its reputation, its name, and its packaging. So, too, the bookends, which are also a Zelco product and, not surprisingly, ingeniously designed to crimp inward to hold a row of books steady when one is removed.

"Once we establish a category, we look high and low. We don't want to miss an opportunity," says Noel, hinting at more products in Zelco's reading group and probably several drafting on the "itty bitty" Gro Lite. He also speaks of another kind of fire starter, long in development, that could help anchor a third major product category.

Zelco's creativity, the competition should be warned, doesn't stop with new products or innovative packaging. Noel recently made a slight but telling change in the design of the wire racks that Zelco, like other companies, provides free to stores. These racks, often placed near checkout counters, hold products packaged on blister cards, and typically, after a few weeks, not just those of the company supplying the rack. It always bugged Noel to see someone else's product on his rack, trespassing on his turf, obviously dimming his sales of small flashlights. His solution: make his racks incompatible with standard, horizontally grooved blister cards. Next time you see a Zelco display rack, look closely. You'll see added evidence of Noel's inventiveness—an extra cut intersecting the vertical groove on the new Zelco blister cards. Yes, indeed, it runs horizontally.

—JOHN GROSSMAN

INDEX

C

D

E

F

G

H

I

J

K

L

Q

R

S

T

U

V

W

Y

Z